The Past Times Book of Diaries

THE PAST TIMES BOOK OF DIARIES

First published in Great Britain in 1998 by
PAST TIMES® Oxford, England

Typeset by Pitfold Design, Hindhead, Surrey
Printed and bound in Great Britain for Imago

Cover illustration: 'The Bookworm'
by Henry Stacy Marks (1829–98)
is reproduced by kind permission of
Chris Beetles Ltd., London/
Bridgeman Art Library, London/New York

Contents

INTRODUCTION

This collection of diary extracts leads the reader right through the year from January 1st to December 31st. In the course of this nearly one hundred diarists, spanning the last four centuries, reveal what was passing through minds on specific days – what was happening behind their own front doors and what was going on in the wider world.

On the public stage they provide eye-witness accounts of celebrated historic events: the Great Fire of London, the aftermath of Monmouth's Rebellion, Bonnie Prince Charlie's invasion of northern England. We also share the first news of Nelson's victory at the Battle of Trafalgar in 1805 and read what it was like to have fought at Waterloo ten years later.

Diaries and journals also allow the reader a private view of public events and public figures. So we read of Fanny Burney's alarm at being pursued by the deranged George III and Queen Victoria describes the day she inherited the throne as well as her happiness on the day of her marriage to Prince Albert.

In the same way diary entries reveal what was making the news at the time. Early in July 1733 the whole of Oxford is buzzing with excitement at the first performance in the city given by Handel. A century-and-a-half later Beatrix Potter writes in her diary of the concern in Manchester about a gang of muggers terrorizing the city's streets. In 1912, young John Knight notes the sinking of the *Titanic* before describing with rather greater interest playing with his Meccano.

Set against these fascinating historical accounts, are the equally intriguing private records that reveal so much about the individual diarist and the age in which he or she lived. We see Dorothy Wordsworth offering sustenance to weary travellers passing her door in the Lake District. John Wesley records the inseparable friendship between an elderly raven and a Newfoundland dog. The Revd F. E. Witts, travelling away from his Cotswold parish, makes his first rail journey to London on the Great Western line from Maidenhead to Paddington. In 1911 we read of two young friends cycling around Cambridge right through a balmy summer night until dawn. And Noël Coward reflects on a changing friendship after attending a party given by the Duke and Duchess of Windsor in 1959.

Whichever day of the year you turn to, this anthology provides a living link with our forebears and the world about them.

THE DIARIES

JANUARY

1st

As I am a wretched bad writer, many of my friends have advised me to practise more, to do which I have made many attempts but allways forgot or got tired so that it was never attended to. I am now about to write a sort of journal, to note down some of the chief things that come under my observation each day. This, I hope, will induce me to make use of my pen every day a little. My account of each subject will be very short – a sort of multo in parvo – as my book is very small and my time not very large . . . .

The first of January is ushered in with very cold frost and snow. This being Sunday, nothing has transpired of consequence. I got up at half past seven, cleaned the boys' clothes and knives [and] lamps, got the parlour breakfast, lit my pantry fire, cleared breakfast and washed it away, dressed myself, went to church, came back, got parlour lunch, had my own dinner, sit by the fire and red the Penny Magazine and opned the door when any visitors came. At 4 o'clock had my tea, took the lamps and candles up into the drawing room, shut the shutters, took glass, knives, plate and settera into the dining room, layed the cloth for dinner, took the dinner up at six o'clock, waited at dinner, brought the things down again at seven, washed them up, brought down the desert, got ready the tea, took it up at eight o'clock, brought it down at half past, washed up, had my supper at nine, took down the lamps and candles at half past ten and went to bed at eleven. All these things I have to do every day, therefore I have mentioned the whole that I mite not have to mention them every day.

WILLIAM TAYLER, 1837

2nd

Little round birds in the fire-tree at the side window, scouring the tree for food. I rumbled a piece of bread, but though the crumbs fell in the branches only two found them. There was a strange remoteness in the air, the scene, the winter cheeping. In the evening, for the first time for – I felt rested. I sat up in bed and discovered I was singing within. Even the sound of the wind is different. It is joyful, not ominous. And black dark looks in at the window and is only black dark. In the afternoon it came on to pour with rain, long glancing rain, falling aslant.

I have not done the work I should have done. I shirk the lunch party This is very bad. In fact I am disgusted with myself. There must be a change from now on. What I chiefly admire in Jane Austen is that what she promises, she performs, i.e. if Sir T. is to arrive, we have his arrival at length, and it's excellent and excels our expectations. This is rare; it is also my very weakest point.

KATHERINE MANSFIELD, 1922

3rd

Paid the following Bills whilst at Norwich. Qualification for killing Game, 2. 3. 0. Pension to College, 1. 12. 0. Incurations and Pascals for 2 Years, 0. 19. 3. Subscription to Clergymens Widows, 1. 1. 0. Mr Smith Mercer, 7. 16. 6. Mrs Garland, Taylor, 5. 14. 0. Mr Whistler, Painter, 6. 0. 0. Mr Lock, Coal Merchant, 12. 18. 6. Mr Forster, for College Land, 16. 0. 0. Mr Browne, Barber, 2. 2. 0. Mr Priest, Wine Merchant. 6. 12. 0. Mrs Brewster, for Tea, &c., 3. 10. 6. Ditto for Miss Woodforde, 3. 6. Mr Jagger, for a Picture Frame, 0. 15. 6. Mr Scott, Breeches Maker, 1. 17. 0. Mr Buckle, Ironmonger, 2. 12. 0. Mr Willmott, Hatter, 0. 19. 0. Mr Manning, Brazier, 1. 1. 0. Mr Rump, Grocer, 0. 18. 6. At the Kings Head, paid and gave, 1. 0. 0. At Mrs Brewster[s] Shop, gave 0. 3. 6. At Mr Lockes, Clerk gave 0. 1. 0. To my Barbers Boy, Tranch – gave 0. 2. 0. To Mr Studwell, China Man pd. 0. 5. 0.

JAMES WOODFORDE, 1787

4th

The roads are full of soldiers, on foot and in carriages, travelling towards Plymouth – Portugal and India supposed to be their destination. The villages on the road are in general not beautiful – the houses very poor indeed; the walls old and rough, but the windows generally whole and clean; no old hats or bundles of rags stuck in, as in America, where people build, but do not repair. Peeping in, as we pass along, the floors appear to be a pavement of round stones like the streets – a few seats, in the form of short benches — a table or two – a spinning-wheel – a few shelves – and just now (Christmas) greens hanging about. The people appear healthy, and not in rags, but not remarkably stout; the women, I think, are more so in proportion than the men. We meet very few beggars, and those old and infirm. Farm-houses, with their out buildings, look remarkably neat, and in great order; near them we see stacks of hay and straw, of prodigious size, covered with a slight thatching, and over that a sort of net of straw, to prevent the wind disturbing the thatch. Industry, method, and good order, are conspicuous everywhere. Most of the land is in meadow. Turnips are enormous; some as large as a man's head. The cattle do not look different from ours. We meet, however, with more *picturesque horses* than in America, with big shaggy legs, and heavy heads.

LOUIS SIMOND, 1810

5th

Then we took a tram to Kingston & had tea at Atkinsons, where one may have no more than a single bun. Everything is skimped now. Most of the butchers shops are shut; the only open shop was besieged. You can't buy chocolates, or toffee; flowers cost so much that I have to pick leaves, instead. We have cards for most foods. The only abundant shop windows are the drapers. Other shops parade tins, or cardboard boxes, doubtless empty. (This is an attempt at the concise, historic style.) Suddenly one has come to notice the war everywhere. I supppose there must be some undisturbed pockets of luxury somewhere still – up in Northumbrian or Cornish farm houses perhaps; but the general table is pretty bare. Papers, however, flourish, & by spending 6d we are supplied with enough to light a weeks fires. A man called Richardson works out a highly complex mathematical method of voting in the trenches.

VIRGINIA WOOLF, 1918

6th

Riviera Palace Hotel, Penzance

There is a constant drift of newcomers . . . . A dreary red-nosed dyspeptic clergyman at one table, at another a young man who smiles brilliantly to himself, at another a gloomy whiskered man, with brows drawn up and corrugated with care, who feeds himself carefully and compassionately and takes salt with his bananas – I like to watch all his little ways and manners; at another an elderly couple, a gross slow-moving old man, and a haughty female who has once been beautiful and now looks unutterably bored. A shifting pageant of human lives, like a big hotel, isn't a very encouraging affair. It doesn't give one the idea that life is very happy or satisfactory. At a place like this the people who come are mostly fortunate people – with more wealth than the run of men; but there seem few happy parties or happy faces – much that is tired and cross and bored and disillusioned. There is a cross man by the window with a waxed moustache, whose wife, a spectacled wretch, spends the end of every meal in shaking up for him a phial of purple medicine. It's no good

saying people *ought* to be more cheerful; it requires a good deal of character to be cheerful if you don't feel it. The wonder to me is why more of them are *not* cheerful, why life *should* be disappointing, what it is in experience which drains people of joy and hope, and whether they could help it.

A. C. BENSON, 1912

7th

Morning, read Hall; was at mill; rest of day at the auction, where in the evening had like to have been a dismal conclusion, but for the watchful providence of a merciful Saviour. The large chamber, being overcrowded with the press of people, in an instant sunk down about a foot at one end; the main beam breaking, gave so terrible a thunder-like crack, and the floor yielding below their feet, the people set up such a hideous noise, apprehending the fall of the whole house, at least the sinking of the room, (which, in all probability, had been the death of most present,) as was most doleful and astonishing, though I, sitting upon the long table by the books, was not at first apprehensive of the danger; but being informed by a friend of the imminent danger, I hasted out with what expedition I could, so as to take good Mr Wright (whose lameness and weakness prevented his haste in the crowd) with me; and perceiving how much it had sunk immediately below my seat, which had fallen the first part of the room, if the Almighty had not put under his omnipotent arm to sustain it, and how much of the plaster-work in the hall below was fallen down, my heart was overcharged with admiration, and I hope, I may truly say, thankfulness, for so signal a deliverance was above expression.

RALPH THORESBY, 1693

8th

The weather became so intensely severe, that the people of the house were busily employed in preparing puddings of the larks and other birds, which flocked into the house and sheds, and were

not only there, but even in the furze and on the shore, easily taken with the hand. I fired at 5 geese out of reach and shot a plover, which I lost (at night). Out sailing the whole day with a strong N. E. wind, and the severest cold I ever felt, and literally never saw a flock of wild fowl. Was all over Poole harbour, and very near Wareham, where, according to report of punters from that place, the same unheard-of scarcity prevailed. Such was the intensity of the cold that

I picked up pocketfuls of larks that had perished and fallen in the water, and on our return old Sturney and I had a hairbreadth escape of sharing the same fate, by getting driven on a mud bank 2 miles from land; luckily, however, by throwing our ballast overboard &c. we got afloat just in time to save the tide.

COLONEL PETER HAWKER, 1814

9th

I could not go sleep last night till past two, and was waked before three by a noise of people endeavouring to break open my window. For a while I would not stir, thinking it might be my imagination; but hearing the noise continued, I rose and went to the window, and then it ceased. I went to bed again, and heard it repeated more violently; then I rose and called up the house, and got a candle: the rogues had lifted up the sash a yard; there are great sheds before my windows, although my lodgings be a storey high; and if they get upon the sheds they are almost even with my window. We observed their track, and panes of glass fresh broken. The watchmen told us today they saw them, but could not catch them. They attacked others in the neighbourhood about the same time, and actually robbed a house in Suffolk Street, which is the next street but one to us. It is said they are seamen discharged from service. I went up to call my man, and found his bed empty; it seems he often lies abroad. I challenged him this morning as one of the robbers. He is a sad dog; and the minute I come to Ireland I will discard him. I have this day got double iron bars to every window in my dining-room and bed-chamber; and I hide my purse in my thread stocking between the bed's head and the wainscoat.

JONATHAN SWIFT, 1712

10th

Yesterday I was at Mr Hall's the bookseller, asking for a magical book, – 'Zouns,' says he 'Doct. you'l raise the divel,' at which I laughed. 'But hark you,' says he, 'I have a friend about 7 miles off who has lost a great many cattle by witchcraft, and he is now in the town at the Three Tuns, prathee go with me thither to him, and tell him what he shall do to save the rest?' to which I made answer that I was unwilling to go; and besides that I knew not how to help him. 'No matter for that,' says he, 'you shall then have some discourse with him and hear what he says, it shall cost you nought, I'll give you two or three pints of wine.' Then I went and we had a great deal of talk. He told me that he was once, about thirteen years ago, with several others set to keep a witch in a room, and sayd that before them all shee chang'd herself into a beetle or great clock, and flew out of the chimney, and so escaped. He told me also that a neighbour of his as he was once driving a loaded waggon out of the field, they came over against the place where a witch was shearing, and that then of a suddain (tho' there was no ill way or anything to throwgh a waggon over) the waggon was in a minnit thrown down, and the shaves became as so many piggs of lead, so that nobody could for two hours lift them upright.

ABRAHAM DE LA PRYME, 1692

11th

We arrived yesterday at Richmond. This morning I set out by myself for *town,* as London is called *par excellence*, in the stage-coach, crammed inside, and *herissé* outside with passengers, of all sexes, ages, and conditions. We stopped more than twenty times on the road – the debates about the fare of way-passengers – the settling themselves – the getting up, and the getting down, and damsels shewing their legs in the operation, and tearing and muddying their petticoats – complaining and swearing – took an immense time. I never saw any thing so ill managed. In about two hours we reached Hyde Park corner; I liked the appearance of it; but we were soon lost in a maze of busy, smoky, dirty streets, more and more so as we advanced. A sort of uniform dinginess seemed to pervade every thing, that is, the exterior; for through every door and window the interior of the house, the shops at least, which are most seen, presented, as we drove along, appearances and colours most opposite to this dinginess; everything there was clean, fresh, and brilliant. The elevated pavement on each side of the streets full of walkers, out of the reach of carriages, passing swiftly in two lines, without awkward interference, each taking to the left.

LOUIS SIMOND, 1810

12th

Su., at 1 in (the) morning at London (so news letter) a hideous tempestuous wind arose, the wind South West; [but did little or no harme here], much in London – very many houses shattered, chimneys blowne downe, some of the stone work of the Temple church blowne downe, the lead blowne up and shrivel'd, several of the elmes in S. James Park blowne up by the roots, and some in Moor fields. This wind began in Oxford about xi of the clock at night. It blew downe battlements at Wadham College, and painted windowes of the chapel there; mischief at Glocester Hall; a stack of chimneys at Magd. Coll. downe.

ANTHONY WOOD, 1690

13th

My poor wife rose by five o'clock in the morning, before day, and went to market and bought fowls and many other things for dinner, with which I was highly pleased, and the chine of beef was down also before six o'clock, and my own jack, of which I was doubtful, do carry it very well. Things being put in order and the cook come, I went to the office where we sat till noon and then broke up, and I home, whither by and by comes Dr Clerke and his lady, his sister, and a she-cousin, and Mr Pierce and his wife, which was all my guests. I had for them, after oysters, at first course, a hash of rabbits, a lamb, and a rare chine of beef. Next, a great dish of roasted fowl, cost me about 30s., and a tart, and then fruit and cheese. My dinner was noble and enough. I had my house mighty clean and neat; my room below with a good fire in it; my dining-room above, and my chamber being made a withdrawing-chamber; and my wife's a good fire, also. I find my new table very proper, and will hold nine or ten people well, but eight with great room. At supper, had a good sack posset and cold meat, and sent my guests away about ten o'clock at night, both them and myself highly pleased with our management of this day; and indeed their company was very fine, and Mrs Clerke a very witty, fine lady, though a little conceited and proud. I believe this day's feast will cost me near £5.

SAMUEL PEPYS, 1663

14th

I visited the condemned malefactors in Newgate, and was locked in by the turnkey, not with them, but in the yard. However, I stood upon a bench, and they climbed up to the windows of their cells; so that all could hear my exhortation and prayer.

CHARLES WESLEY, 1743

15th

There was a miniature edition of Plough Boys with their usual attendants of Fools with black faces and hump backs from this town the last two days, consisting for the most part of Boys from 10 to 12 years of age, dressed as fine as they could be made in Ribbons with most enormous paper Caps on their heads covered over with tinsel, which made them look as if they had extinguishers on their heads, then the little imps had swords in their hands not too bright; and sung and danced like their betters, if indeed they had any; the last night after paying the Fidler, they met to spend their money, while some of their mothers were obliged to fetch them home, this must be the march of folly.

ROBERT SHARP, 1829

16th

Lay down and tried to think of Hamlet. Acted the character pretty well; the effect of the influenza in the house obliged me to pitch my voice (for the sake of overmastering the coughs) in an unusually high key, which in some measure, I think, interfered with the nicety of many touches, but there was a good deal of earnestness in the performance. The play was disgracefully – *disgustingly* acted – Mrs W. West, Mr Thompson, Mr G. Bennett are really unfit persons to place in important characters on such a stage! This does not justify *my loss of temper*, which I have again to bewail and condemn; but, indeed, the conduct of the stage is most disgraceful. I was called for after the performance, and very warmly received.

WILLIAM MACREADY, 1837

17th

Between 6 and 7 o'clock this morning I rose and opened the window. It was frosty and cloudless, the moon was nearly full and shining brightly in the West, and the shadow of the great acacia lay still and black across the wide wet gravel reaching to the green terrace bank. A slow measured footfall was pacing down the gravel drive towards the white gate, the policeman Vincent on guard watching for the man who is supposed to be lurking about here. It was cock crow and the cocks were challenging and answering each other from farm to farm in the still early morning. Then the black gate clanged and the white gate clashed and the postman came up the drive at 7 o'clock meeting the policeman.

To-day the policeman went to the Superintendent, laid the case before him and received orders to be about this house a good deal at night for some time to come.

FRANCIS KILVERT, 1873

18th

My mother's funeral at Chipping Norton. A most gloomy wet morning after a stormy night was congenial to the depression of my spirits. It was half past ten before we could reach the church. The service was performed by the curate, a vulgar unfeeling man: his careless manner, his uncouth pronunciation and coarse appearance were all forbidding. Crowds of curious spectators flocked round the coffin and vault; but all was curiosity, no sympathy was visible; most trying is this appearance of indifference and equally so the suppressed voices of the assistants as they lowered the coffin through the narrow mouth of the vault, grating against the top of the arch and at length deposited beside the last inmate of the dark abode.

I cannot and ought not to lose sight of the blessings still reserved to me by a gracious Providence, an affectionate wife, a promising child, and ample provision of earthly comforts.

We returned to the mourning coach immediately after the funeral and reached Cheltenham at 7 p.m.

F. E. WITTS, 1825

19th

We have had an orgy of theatre-going and social junketing. The Windsors' party was very gay. She certainly is a most charming hostess and he was extremely amiable. The conversation was mostly general and largely devoted to the question of whether or not the Duchess should have her face lifted. The main consensus was no. Wallis brought this subject up herself with a sort of calculated defiance. I think, however, that she is a curiously honest woman and her sense of humour, particularly about herself, is either profound or brilliantly simulated. The evening finished with a blonde lady (French) pounding the piano and everyone getting a trifle 'high'. Princess Sixte de Bourbon was definitely shocked when the Duke and I danced a sailor's hornpipe and the Charleston, but there was no harm in it, perhaps a little sadness and nostalgia for him and for me a curious feeling of detached amusement, remembering how beastly he had been to me and about me in our earlier years when he was Prince of Wales and I was beginning. Had he danced the Charleston and hornpipe with me then it would have been an accolade to cherish. As it was, it looked only faintly ridiculous to see us skipping about with a will. The Princess needn't have been shocked, it was merely pleasantly ridiculous.

NOEL COWARD, 1959

20th

The weather has been fearfully cold and frosty all the week and it freezes just about it now. It is got in the ground a good depth and everything is frozen up and all ground work is topped and trade is fearfully dull now in everything. It has froze all the week and freezes now with a bitter cold wind and a little snow. The rivers are all frozen and flooded, and consequently there is an immense deal of skating going on and on Wednesday last there was a fearful accident on the Regent's Park water in London when all at once the ice broke and immersed 200 in the water. It was a fearful sight and one not to be forgotten for some time by those who saw it. 40 lives were lost and it is supposed there are some more in now. I have been shooting nearby all the week and storching [stonching?] about the fields till I am tired of it. There are a good many blackbirds and felps in our garden and I have shot a good many. I had a touch of lark shooting one day but I could not get at them they are so wild – wants more snow. An mmense number on the hills. Shredded trees and began tying up. The new choir has started last Thursday – a good man in it – and I heard them today for the first time. They sang very well. Nett did not come t the meet that night. Awful cold up here now. Haven't seen her all the week before. Sold all my onions to Murphy and all gone. New hymn books at Church. Joe Clarks party came back Monday. Mary Harper came back – married I think, rings on. Bought the last meal for my pigs.

JOSEPH TURRILL, 1869

21st

We had yesterday a very heavy fall of snow, accompanied with a very tempestuous wind which drifted the snow as it fell and so obstructed the roads. The fool-hardiest of travellers today was my neighbour Mr Dolphin who undertook to drive his coach and four from Lasborough, the seat of the Hon H. Moreton, five miles beyond Tetbury, a distance of 40 miles from Eyford. He had gone thither with his wife and her friend Miss Green on Tuesday with two female and three male domestics, to be ready to attend a ball given by Mr M. at Tetbury. He was entreated to stay, but my squire was a little wilful and started, with the addition of a couple of cart horses to force their way through the drifts in Lasborough Park. On the road through Tetbury, Cirencester, etc., he was more than once forced to put cart horses in requisition; no line of road can be more exposed. No carriage of any sort, cart or wagon had attempted to pass along. At times the drifts of snow were so deep, that the footboard in front of the box divided the snow like the prow of a vessel ploughing the waves; often the hind wheels were buried in the drifts, unable to revolve being entirely clogged with snow, so the machine was dragged on bodily, rolling and pitching from side to side. Much credit ought to be given to my neighbour for consummate skill in the art which he professes best to understand, the art of coachmanship. Between 6 and 7 o'clock the cavalcade had reached the purlieus of Upper Slaughter but here their progress was inevitably stopped. To force their way through the drifts extending to the Cheltenham road, up the hill through my fields was beyond even Dolphin's skill and daring, and in a few minutes the whole party, coach, horses, servants etc., came to an anchor in my stable yard. I was summoned from my fireside.

Not small was the confusion in the dark. Poor Mrs D. half dead with fright and cold, hysterical, fainting, fearing, and laughing, crying by turns; Miss Green more collected but sadly frightened. It was resolved that leaving the coach behind an attempt should be made to reach Eyford on foot. Wine and biscuits and the warmth of a good fire renovated the drooping strength and spirits of the ladies. The gala cloaks and muffs were left behind; my ladies equipped their friends in wraps of humbler pretensions but better calculated to face the inclemency of the night. We later learned with satisfaction the group had safely reached home.

F. E. WITTS, 1830

22nd

I privately named a child of the Widow Nobbes this morning at my house by name Elizabeth. To a poor old infirm man that came to my house this morning gave some victuals and, 0.0.6. Sent poor Harry Clarke who is still very bad, by his brother, some victual, and some money. My cook maid (Nanny Kaye) some few days ago gave my niece notice of leaving her service at Lady Day next, as she intends to enter into the marriage state. One Willm. Spraggs (son of the gardner whom I used to employ and who is now in Bridewell at Wyndham for stealing wood from Mr Brainthwaite at Tavernham) not more than 20 years of age, is the young man she is going to marry. I think she might do better. He also was with his father in the above affair and was very near being taken at the time.

JAMES WOODFORDE, 1791

23rd

Vita [the writer and gardener Vita Sackville-West] took me over the 4 acres building, which she loves: too little conscious beauty for my taste: smallish rooms looking on to buildings: no views: yet one or two things remain: Vita stalking in her Turkish dress, attended by small boys, down the gallery, wafting them on like some tall sailing ship – a sort of covey of noble English life: dogs walloping, children crowding, all very free & stately: & [a] cart bringing wood in to be sawn by the great circular saw. How do you see that? I asked Vita.

She said she saw it as something that had gone on for hundreds of years. They had brought wood in from the Park to replenish the great fires like this for centuries: & her ancestresses had walked so on the snow with their great dogs bounding beside them. All the centuries seemed lit up, the past expressive, articulate; not dumb & forgotten; but a crowd of people stood behind, not dead at all; not remarkable; fair faced, long limbed; affable; & so we reach the days of Elizabeth quite easily. After tea, looking for letters of Dryden's to show me, she tumbled out a love letter of Ld Dorsets (17th century) with a lock of his soft gold tinted hair which I held in my hand a moment. One had a sense of links fished up into the light which are usually submerged.

VIRGINIA WOOLF, 1927

24th

The frost continuing more and more severe, the Thames before London was still planted with boothes in formal streetes, all sorts of trades and shops furnish'd and full of commodities, even to a printing presse, where the people and ladyes took a fancy to have their names printed, and the day and yeare set down when printed on the Thames; this humour tooke so universally, that 'twas estimated the printer gain'd £5 a day, for printing a line onely, at sixpence a name, besides what he got by ballads, &c. Coaches plied from Westminster to the Temple, and from several other staires to and fro, as in the streetes, sleds, sliding with skeetes, a bull-baiting, horse and coach races, puppet plays and interludes, cookes, tipling, and other lewd places, so that it seem'd to be a bacchanalian triumph, or carnival on the water, whilst it was a severe judgment on the land, the trees not only splitting as if by lightning struck, but men and cattle perishing in divers places; and the very seas so lock'd up with ice, that no vessells could stir out or come in. The fowles, fish, and birds, and all our exotiq plants and greenes universally perishing. Many parkes of deer were destroied, and all sorts of fuell so deare that there were greate contributions to preserve the poore alive. Nor was this severe weather much less intense in most parts of Europe, even as far as Spaine and the most southern tracts. London, by reason of the

excessive coldnesse of the aire hindering the ascent of the smoke, was so fill'd with the fuliginous steame of the sea-coale, that hardly could one see crosse the streetes, and this filling the lungs with its grosse particles, exceedingly obstructed the breast, so as one could scarcely breathe. Here was no water to be had from the pipes and engines, nor could the brewers and divers other trademen worke, and every moment was full of disasterous accidents.

JOHN EVELYN, 1684

25th

In running this morning, at seven o'clock, along my dark passage, I nearly fell over a pail, carelessly left in the way by a housemaid, and broke my shin very painfully. Unable, therefore, to walk, yet so strongly enjoined to take the air, I could not escape accompanying Mrs Schwellenberg [the diarist's immediate superior at court] in a little tour round Brentford, which, that we might see a little of the world, was the postillion's drive. But the ill humour of my companion during this rural ride was of so affronting a cast, that I wished myself a thousand times hopping with my broken shin over the worst ploughed land in England, rather than so to be seated in a royal vehicle.

FANNY BURNEY, 1789

26th

Out all day. Had worked till I had not a guinea left. Called on Lord Grey. Found him happy, healthy-looking and in good spirits, thank God. We are pretty much on a level. Antwerp plagued him as pecuniary matters plague me, and Reform plagued the King. We all have our plagues.

'He agreed to let me dedicate the work to him, and I went away without his alluding to my affairs. I then went to Colonel Grey, and left with him a short note I had written at a bookseller's shop. I was in great agitation for fear of offending him. I drove into the city, and went to Fletcher, the chairman (a fine manly fellow), to tell him my wants, and to ask him for £5 to get through the night. As I had not paid him the £12, he said he ought not. I returned home in a state not to be described. When I came home the children had been all fighting, and no water had come to the cistern. Mary was scolding; and I went to my painting room, and d – d all large pictures, which always bring this evil on me.

The evening passed on, as it always does in a family where the father has no money. The children smoke it; the servants suspect it. There is either an over-kindness, an over-irritability or an affected unconcern, which opens at once their lynx eyes. Tea passed off. I went to my picture; apostrophised my art; complained of Lord Grey, and sat down with a pain in my lumbar vertebrae. As I had appointed a great many people for small sums, I marched off to my landlord, Newton. Knowing he would relieve me, and anticipating success, I knocked. I heard the light steps of a girl; down went the candlestick, and the door opened. 'Mr Newton at home?' said I, marching in, praying to God it might be so, but half fearing it might not, when I was suddenly stopped by, 'No sir; he is gone to the play.' D – n the play!' thought I; 'this is the way. What business had he to be giggling at some stuff in the pit, while I am in danger of having no money?' Away I marched again, tired, croaking, grumbling and muddy, and came home in a state of harass. 'Sir, the man won't send the wood without the money!' was the first salutation. 'Sir, there is no water in the cistern, and has not been all day!' 'Why,' thought I, 'the very lead pipes begin to perceive their masters won't be paid for their trouble.' I sat down in a rage, and pulling off my greatcoat sallied up to my dear. 'At least,' thought I, 'this is left me, and woe to any mortal who stops me here.'

'Mary, like an angel, consoled me in my affliction, and I came down in high glee, bidding defiance to all obstructions, and swearing I would again apply to my work on Monday at light.

'Just as I had made up my mind in came the servant with a letter from Lord Grey, marked 'Private.' My heart jumped. It contained a cheque! I read it, and vowed vengeance against all rascally tradesmen on earth. This was wrong. By degrees I recovered my good feelings, and went to bed thanking God, grateful to Lord Grey and at peace with my family and the world.

B. R. HAYDON, 1833

27th

A sudden and general thaw, with a strong wind and an incessant pour of heavy rain. Nothing could be more novel or beautiful than the appearance of the harbour, which was one solid region of ice, with pyramids formed by the drifted snow, and frozen like glass; and on the thaw setting in the whole harbour appeared like a huge floating island as it was carried off by the fall of a high spring tide; and to see this huge movable body in motion with 14 wild swans sitting upon it, as it receded, and looking as if formed by nature for the only inhabitants of such a wild region, gave one more the idea of a habitable country. Under an idea that every vagabond would eagerly seize the first day's shooting after the thaw, I, to be well to windward of the butterfly shooters, weathered the torrent of rain all day, and, by capital locks and good management, contrived to keep my gun dry for the five shots which I got. The geese were scattered in every direction, so that I could not bag more than 5 at a shot, and so drenching wet was the day that after the first half-hour not a dry stitch could be found to wipe out the pan of my gun, except the tail of my shirt, and while paddling to birds I had three inches of water under my stomach. I fairly brought home 17 geese. I took one very long shot at 8 swans, heard the shot strike them, and afterwards saw one leave the company and drop on the sea, where I dare not venture (about two miles to leeward), consequently had not the good fortune to bring one home. Wet all the evening, a west wind, and as mild as May.

COLONEL PETER HAWKER, 1823

28th

Burke the murderer hanged this morning. The mob, which was immense, demanded Knox and Hare, but though greedy for more victims, received with shouts the solitary wretch who found his way to the gallows out of five or six who seem not less guilty than he. But the story begins to be stale, although I believe a doggerel ballad upon it would be popular, how brutal soever the wit.

SIR WALTER SCOTT, 1829

29th

This is Sunday and I have *realy* been to Church. We have had a great deal of snow today. This day for dinner had a part of a round of beef with potatos, cabbage and carrots, scimmerlads and bread pudding. For supper roast beef, pickle cabbage &c. &c. Had a Lady to dinner here today. The Lady's maid is taken very sick today: I sopose she has been eating to much or something of the kind. But she is very subject to sickness. Last summer, when we were coming home from Canterbury, she actually spewed all the way, a distance of sixty miles and not less time than eight hours. The people stared as we passed through the towns and villages as she couldent stop even then. It amused me very much to see how the country people stood stareing with their mouthes half open and half shut to see her pumping over the side of the carriage and me sitting by, quite unconserned, gnawing a piece of cake or some sandwiches or something or other, as her sickness did not spoil my apatite. It was very bad for her but I couldent do her any good as it was the motion of the carriage that caused her illness. I gave her something to drink every time we changed horses but no sooner than it was down than it came up again, and so the road from Canterbury to London was pretty well perfumed with Brandy, Rum, Shrub, wine and such stuff. She very soon recovered after she got home and was all the better for it after. It's eleven o'clock. My fire is out and I am off to bed.

WILLIAM TAYLER, 1837

30th

After I had praied priuatly I dressed apoore boies legge that Came to me, and then brake my fast with Mr Hoby: after, I dressed the hand of one of our seruants that was verie sore Cutt, and after I wrett in my testement notes Vpon James: then I went about the doinge of some thinges in the house, paiynge of billes, and, after I had talked with Mr Hoby, I went to examenation and praier, after to supper, then to the lector: after that I dressed one of the mens handes that was hurt, lastly praied, and so to bed:

LADY MARGARET HOBY, 1599

31st

Business as usual. Jimmy much better though still confined to bed. Read Macaulay's 'England,' the account of the death of Charles 2nd – a superb piece of word painting far more telling to the mental eye than the great picture of Frith's which endeavoured to the physical sight to realise this great scene – thank God such things have passed away and we reign under a sovereign whose purity of character and lofty ideal of royal life has made the name of Victoria a synonym for true royalty. In the evening worked on the survey of 1 Wiltshire Regt. and so ends the month of January. Thank God for the peace, joy and happiness of God's mercy towards me. The weather this month has been wonderfully mild, more like a gentle spring than the usual dull, bitter cold of the season, while I write the sun is shining in at the window and the air so clear and fresh that it quite refreshes me.

CHARLES COMPTON, 1882

FEBRUARY

1st

I find that my worthless tenant, Lewis, is determined to do all he can, under the influence of Day, to annoy me.

I left my study after breakfast, with the intention of calling upon Hicks, the Overseer. In my way, within two hundred yards of my own house, I met Keel, my churchwarden, who immediately said, 'Hello! I was going to call upon you, Mr Skinner, for I insist upon knowing who told you what you told my wife yesterday, and frightened her out of her wits, namely, that I had said you had been at Camerton long enough, and that we would strip your gown from your shoulders?' I said I should not tell him who told me, but I firmly believed it was true since his subsequent conduct was so insolent. He replied, he would be d – d, but he would know! I said that his swearing to his clergyman did not give me a better opinion of his veracity, neither did the menacing attitude in which he put himself; if the farmers chose to insult me in the manner they did of late, that I could not stir from my house without experiencing some fresh aggravations, I could let the whole of my tythe and have nothing further to say to them. 'Aye,' said he, 'you may take mine to-morrow.' I said very well. I would after Lady Day; but in the discharge of my duty at Church and when I was called upon to visit the sick I would ever do my duty, so that there should be no fault to find with me. 'Aye,' said he, 'but we won't come to Church.'

JOHN SKINNER, 1827

2nd

I went to see Benjamin Hawkins. 'The times were much harder for poor folk when I was a lad, let people say what they will,' said Benjamin. Sometimes when an outstanding field rick was threshed or brought into the barn the shepherd or carter had the privilege of planting a few potatoes there and he was so overjoyed with his good fortune that he thought he had got a small farm. There was no such thing known then as planting potatoes in the field, and this made every foot of the garden ground so precious that people could not spare room for flowerbeds. Some of the old women would have a flower border and raise a few pinks and roses and a little thyme and lad's love, make up the flowers into knots and nosegays, and sell them at halfpenny apiece. The lads would buy them and stick them in their hats on Sundays. Nosegays were very much sought after. Benjamin thought the new law compelling boys to go to school till they are 12 years old a bad law, unjust and hard upon the parents.

FRANCIS KILVERT, 1875

3rd

Took another dose of physick a little stronger than the last. Agreed well with me and am much easier in my stomack. I find that the Bills of Mortality in London are higher this last week than they have been since the Plague, above 1586. Very stormy weather yesterday and today. Mr Harrison sent me a 2nd. Hand Gold Watch at 12 guineas, made by Burckham London as good as new, the size perfecly fashionable. I wrote to him that I desired to try it for 8 or 10 days.

THOMAS WILSON, 1733

4th

I was much troubled with the blacke providence of putting the King to death; my teares were not restrained at the passages about his death; the Lord in mercy lay it not as sinne to the charge of the kingdome, but in mercy doe us good by the same; the small poxe on some familyes of the towne but spreadeth not, to God be the glory therof: this weeke I could doe nothing neither in my Hebrew, nor in my reconciler.

The death of the king talked much of; very many men of the weaker sort of Christians in divers places passionate concerning it, but so ungroundedly, that it would make any to bleed to observe it; ye Lord hath some great thing to doe; feare & tremble att it, oh England.

Monday it was debated about Kings and Peeres; on Tuesday the house of Commons ordered to null the house of Lords as uselesse, & on the next day to lay aside the Govermt by Kings, & to sett up a councell of state.

RALPH JOSSELIN, 1648

5th

My poor Cow rather better this morning, but not able to get up as yet, she having a Disorder which I never heard of before or any of our Somersett Friends. It is called Tail-shot, that is, a separation of some of the Joints of the Tail about a foot from the tip of the Tail, or rather a slipping of one Joint from another. It also makes all her Teeth quite loose in her head. The Cure, is to open that part of the Tail so slipt lengthways and put in an Onion boiled and some Salt, and bind it up with some coarse Tape.

JAMES WOODFORDE, 1790

6th

I went to dine at Lord Masham's at three, and met all the company just coming out of court; a mighty crowd: they staid long for their coaches: I had an opportunity of seeing several lords and ladies of my acquaintance in their fineries. Lady Ashburnham looked the best in my eyes. They say the court was never fuller nor finer. Lord-Treasurer, his lady, and two daughters and Mrs Hill, dined with Lord and Lady Masham; the five ladies were monstrous fine. The Queen gave Prince Eugene the diamond sword to-day; but nobody was by when she gave it, except my Lord Chamberlain. There was an entertainment of opera songs at night, and the Queen was at all the entertainment, and is very well after it. I saw Lady Wharton, as ugly as the devil, coming out in the crowd all in an undress; she has been with the Marlborough daughters and Lady Bridgewater in St James's, looking out of the window all undressed to see the sight. I do not hear that one Whig lady was there, except those of the Bedchamber. Nothing has made so great a noise as one Kelson's chariot, that cost nine hundred and thirty pounds, the finest was ever seen. The rabble huzzaed him as much as they did Prince Eugene. This is birth-day chat.

JONATHAN SWIFT, 1712

7th

Father says that when there was a hanging at Dorchester in his boyhood it was carried out at one o'clock, it being the custom to wait till the mailcoach came in from London in case of a reprieve.

He says that at Puddletown Church, at the time of the old west-gallery violin, oboe, and clarinet players, Tom Sherren (one of them) used to copy tunes during the sermon. So did my grandfather at Stinsford church. Old Squibb the parish-clerk used also to stay up late at night helping my grandather in his 'prick-noting' (as he called it).

He says that William, son of Mr S – the Rector of W –, became a miller at O – Mill, and married a German woman whom he met at Puddletown Fair playing her tambourine. When her husband was gone to market she used to call in John Porter, who could play the fiddle, and lived near, and give him some gin, when she would beat the tambourine to his playing. She was a good-natured woman with blue eyes, brown hair, and a round face; rather slovenly. Her husband was a hot, hasty fellow, though you could hear by his speech that he was a better educated man than ordinary millers.

G. R. – (who is a humorist) showed me his fowl-house, which was built of old church-materials bought at Wellspring the builder's sale. R.'s chickens roost under the gilt-lettered Lord's Prayer and Creed, and the cock crows and flaps his wings against the Ten Commandments. It reminded me that I had seen these same Ten Commandments, Lord's Prayer, and Creed, before, forming the sides of the stone-mason's shed in that same builder's yard, and that he had remarked casually that they did not preent the workmen 'cussing and damning' the same as ever. It also reminded me of seeing the old font of – Church, Dorchester, in a garden, used as a flower-vase, the initials of ancient godparents and churchwardens still legible upon it. A comic business – church restoration.

A villager says of the parson, who has been asked to pray for a sick person: 'His prayers wouldn't save a mouse.'

THOMAS HARDY, 1878

8th

Was out all the morning with Mrs Wells, dined with Mr Bishop and went to the play at Drury Lane to see Hamlet and Blue Beard. We had an exceedingly bad Box up one pair of stairs, nothing but fine *Damsels* about us, which I found not a little annoying. Blue Beard is vastly pretty but it was interrupted in the most interesting part by a great noise and cry of fire. All the ladies fainted away and were greatly alarmed. I was not much frightened. It proved to be nothing but a boxing match. Our Beaux chose to leave us alone in one of the Lobby boxes whilst they went to look for the carriages. Two drunken young men came in and were exceedingly impudent taking us for other sort of women. I was very much alarmed but we got however rid of them.

BETSY FREMANTLE, 1798

9th

A splendid bit of Virgil – Evander's lament for his son – full of grammar, idiom, and sentiment. I tried the patience of the boys with wanton digressions till we were getting late for school.

In school the same Virgil: not a boy could construe the hard lines properly; they had wretched editions; if I had not been so hoarse I should have railed at them. In the midst of the exposition came the Head Master's servant to say that they were wanted at 11.30 to hear Speeches, so that the grand lesson was broken up, and this by men who profess to care for classics: may Virgil's ghost rebuke them!

Talked outside in the sun with my old comrade John Yonge about the lesson: we taught each other in a simple way. He told me what I had forgotten – that Lord Falkland turned out, as a *Sors,* the lines we had just been reading about 'dura rudimenta.' &c. . . Think that a thousand years hence they will quote Virgil.

11.40. Themes, or rather versions – lukewarm Latin, anyhow.

Miscellaneous business with some brats. Shute set down to verses by himself.

12.40. F. Wood and I went out, ride and tie, up the bank of the still, cold river, taking it by turns to give Myrtle a canter, in which the dogs shared . . .

At Surley corner was a regular picture, a barge laden with wood, with the slenderest, straightest thread of smoke at each end, one horse pulling it down stream, the poplars behind, Myrtle and her glowing young rider in the foreground . . .

Galloped back in time to release the captive, who had done nine verses on Cassandra – alone for forty minutes – finished Latin prose work; then came N. Lyttelton with a bit of Greek prose, done from Hooker, rather a good job. Then Hale for a gossip. Then I wrote a vicious letter to the Windsor paper about the unbearable filthiness of the College streets. 3.45. Small boys came for verses, &c., and I read sundry bits of Greek and Latin and choice bits of Motley's *Dutch Republic,* though wishing to sleep . . .

WILLIAM CORY, 1864

10th

The Ceremony was very imposing, and fine and simple, and I think *ought* to make an everlasting impression on every one who promises at the altar to *keep* what he or she promises. Dearest Albert repeated everything very distinctly. I felt so happy when the ring was put on, and by Albert. As soon as the Service was over, the procession returned as it came, with the exception that my beloved Albert led me out. The applause was very great, in the Colour Court as we came through: Lord Melbourne, good man was very much affected during the Ceremony and at the applause. We all returned to the Throne-room, where the Signing of the Register took place: it was first signed by the Archbishop, then by Albert and me, and all the Royal Family, and by: The Lord Chancellor, the Lord President, the Lord Privy Seal, the Duke of Norfolk (as Earl Marshal), the Archbishop of York, and Lord Melbourne. We then went into the Closet, and the Royal Family waited with me there till the ladies had got into their carriages. I gave all the Train-bearers as a brooch a small eagle of turquoise. I then returned to Buckingham Palace alone with Albert: they cheered us really most warmly and heartily; the crowd was immense; and the Hall at Buckingham Palace was full of

people; they cheered us again and again. The great Drawing-room and Throne-room were full of people of rank, and numbers of children were there. Lord Melbourne and Lord Clarendon, who had arrived, stood at the door of the Throne-room as we came in. I went and sat on the sofa in my dressing-room with Albert; and we talked together there from 10 m to 2 till 20 m. p. 2.

QUEEN VICTORIA, 1840

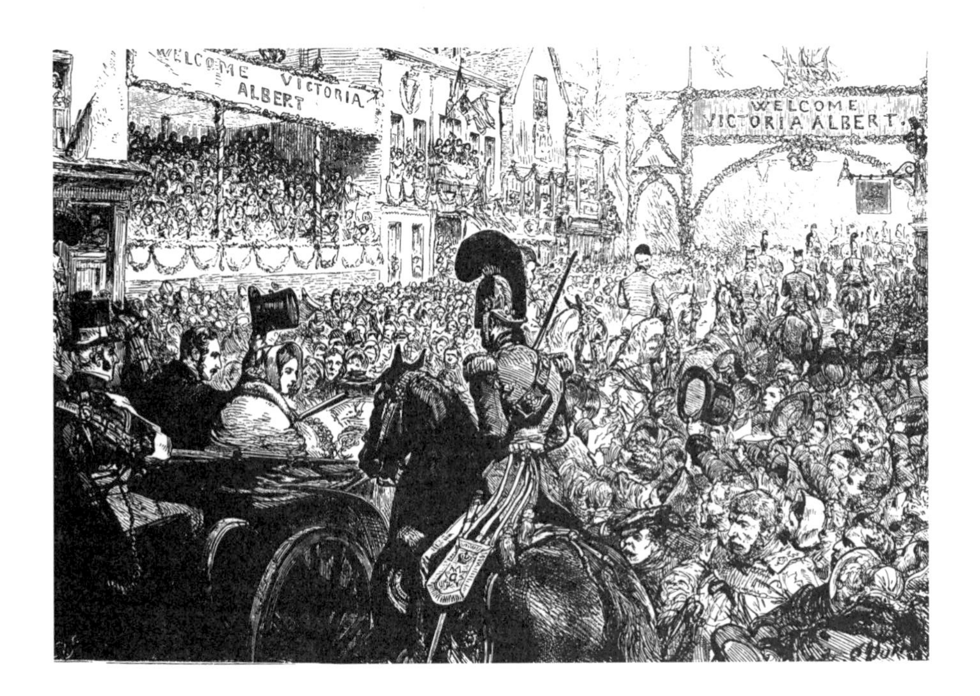

11th

The infirmities of age come on, particularly an almost perpetual catarrh.

DR JOHN RUTTY, 1770

12th

Already the 2nd day since our marriage; his love and gentleness is beyond everything, and to kiss that dear soft cheek, to press my lips to his, is heavenly bliss. I feel a purer more unearthly feel than I ever did. Oh! was ever woman so blessed as I am.

QUEEN VICTORIA, 1840

13th

There was seen in the air like the appearance of a fire-brand wrapped in a red cloak, and shining at both the ends, as John Harvy wrote (Francis Haies) from London, and that he the said Jo. Harvy and many other saw it. – Dictu Francisci Hayes.

About the same time was seen at Wellington the like sight; viz. the likeness of fire in bigness as big as a child of seven or eight years old, which fell out of the air, making a very great noise, and to the seeing of those who saw it fell on a house, but did no harm. It was seen by one Mr Prouse's man and divers other, being then going with the constable in a search about nine of the clock at night.

WALTER YONGE, 1617

14th

To Children being Valentines day under 14. Years of Age and able to say 'good Morrow Valentine', in Number 40. at 1d each, gave 3. 4. We dined and spent the Afternoon at Weston-House with Mr and Mrs Custance and Mr Du Quesne. Mr Custance sent his Coach after us and we were brought back in Mr Du Quesne's Chaise. After Tea, we got to Loo, neither won or lost. Nancy lost about 4. or five Shillings. We had for Dinner Cod and Oyster Sauce, a Fillet of Veal rosted, boiled Tongue, stewed Beef, Peas Soup and Mutton-Stakes. 2nd Course, a rost Chicken, Cheesecakes, Jelly-Custards &c.

JAMES WOODFORDE, 1791

15th

Tried to kiss her in a taxi-cab on the way home from the Savoy – the taxi-cab danger is very present with us – but she rejected me quietly, sombrely. I apologised on the steps of the Flats and said I feared I had greatly annoyed her. 'I'm not annoyed,' she said, 'only surprised' – in a thoughtful, chilly voice.

We had had supper in Soho, and I took some wine, and she looked so bewitching it sent me in a fever, thrumming my fingers on the seat of the cab while she sat beside me impassive. Her shoulders are exquisitely modelled and a beautiful head is carried poised on a tiny neck.

W. N. P. BARBELLION, 1913

16th

My morning was cut into as many portions as I had boxes, bags, notes, messages and hundreds of etceteras. I gave too *much* to the porter at the coach; this is a very *silly* fault, and a wrong to any poor creature that may need one's charity. There was nothing remarkable in the three passengers with whom I started; the woman was very vulgar, which was not her fault – her husband, an outside, was equally so and rather drunk, but redeemingly civil. I passed Edwardes Place, and marked the house where I left my dearest Catherine nine years ago; never shall I forget my feelings in quitting her. I looked with extreme interest too at the Inn at Hounslow where we breakfasted and changed our clothes on the morning of our marriage. Few have more cause to bless that important day than I.

WILLIAM MACREADY, 1833

17th

In the night it raind, the wind rose and was 18, violent beyond measure, ov'turning a windmill at Colchester, wherein a youth kild, divers barnes, stables, outhouses, trees, rending divers dwellings; few escapd, my losse much, but not like some others; God sanctifie all to us; throwing down stackes of chimneys, part of houses; the Lady Saltonstall kild in her bed, her house falling. Whitehall twice on fire that day, some orchards almost ruind. 27, Trees blown down within priory wall. Timber trees rent up in high standing woods; the winde was generall in England & Holland sea coast, but not in Scotland.

RALPH JOSSELIN, 1661

18th

Last night I was drunk – very drunk – and feel a little the better for it. The sherry and whisky I had ordered in Oxford came. Before dinner Gordon and I drank the sherry – which brought back a thousand sentimental associations. After dinner we took the whisky to Watson's room and I drank about half of it while Watson and Dean

drank a quarter each. The result was that I was sick. I have not yet met Amy and am rather unwilling to do so. I think she will not report it to the proprietor Banks. The debauch has caused something of a feud in the common-room – I must confess to finding Chaplin somewhat tiresome.

Today I have had a delightful afternoon and evening. I went to Rhyl for the the afternoon and got permission to stay out to dinner. I bought a lot of things which I do not particularly want and spent most of the time in the hands of a most interesting barber who talked of phallic symbolism and the Gnostics. A lovely dinner and good wines and brandy. On Saturday I went to the Naples of the North with one of the ushers called Gordon and had dinner at the Grand Hotel. It was not very grand but there was some of the burgundy which I last drank on the regrettable evening when I went to the home of Lady Plunket – Clos de Vougeot 1911. A kind man took us home in an automatic carriage. No letter from Olivia, no shoes from Oxford, no money from anywhere.

On Sunday I started on an awful thing called week's duty. It means that I have no time at all from dawn to dusk so much to read a postcard or visit a water-closet. Already – today is Tuesday, Shrove Tuesday – my nerves are distraught. Yesterday I beat a charming boy called Clegg and kicked a hideous boy called Cooper and sent Cooke to the proprietor. Yesterday afternoon I had my first riding lesson and enjoyed it greatly. It is not an easy sport or a cheap one but most agreeable. No letter from Olivia.

Yesterday in a history paper the boy Howarth wrote: 'In this year James II gave birth to a son but many people refused to believe it and said it had been brought to him in a hot water bottle.'

EVELYN WAUGH, 1925

19th

This hath been such a severe Winter that the like hath not been known since the Year 1683. In some respects it exceeded that. For tho' the Frost did not last so long as it did at yt time, yet there was a much greater & deeper Snow. Indeed, it was the biggest Snow yt ever I knew: as it was also ye severest Frost yt ever I have been sensible of. It began on Monday, Dec. 5th, & continued 'till Friday, Febr. 10th following, which is almost ten weeks, before there was an intire Thaw. Indeed, it began to thaw two or three times, but then the Frost soon began again with more violence, & there was withall a very sharp & cold & high Wind for some Days. When it first began to thaw & afterwards to Freeze again, it made the ways extreme slippery & dangerous, & divers bad accidents happen'd thereupon.

THOMAS HEARNE, 1716

20th

We breakfasted, dined, &c. again at home. Briton was out all Night last Night at Js. Peggs but not without my consent, Js. Pegg had a few Friends of his to spend the Evening. Dinner today, Knuckle of Veal, Bacon & Greens &c. Meat, by my Butchers Acount this Day, was at the following high Price – Beef at 7d pr. lb, Mutton at 7d1/2., Veal at 7d. per lb. Briton returned home early in the Morning.

JAMES WOODFORDE, 1801

21st

Pianoforte recital by F. M., at Frinton Hall last night in aid of Tendring Parish funds. Hall centrally heated, but draughty. Uncomfortable chairs. Rush-bottomed chair (cost about 3s.) for pianist. Old Broadwood baby grand. Pedal creaked. Rotten tone. Ladies of Frinton and of Tendring parishes in evening dress. Two parsons, who felt they must speechify afterwards. Pianist a man about 40, agreeable slightly curt smile. Ferocious look when he was playing often. Beethoven, Rameau, Chopin, Scarlatti, Debussy, Liszt, etc. Piano impossible. Intense, almost tragic sadness of provincial musical affairs, second-rate or tenth-rate under bad conditions.

ARNOLD BENNETT, 1914

22nd

About four p.m., I walked down to Whyly. We played at bragg the first part of the even. After ten we went to supper on four boiled chicken, four boiled ducks, minced veal, sausages, cold roast goose, chicken pasty, and ham. Our company, Mr and Mrs Porter, Mr and Mrs Coates, Mrs Atkins, Mrs Hicks, Mr Piper and wife, Joseph Fuller and wife, tho. Fuller and wife, Dame Durrant myself and wife, and Mr French's family. After supper our behaviour was far from that of serious, harmless mirth; it was down right obstreperious, mixed with a great deal of folly and stupidity. Our diversion was dancing or jumping about, without a violin or any musick, singing of foolish healths, and drinking all the time as fast as it could be well poured down; and the parson of the parish was one among the mixed multitude. If conscience dictates right from wrong, as doubtless it sometimes does, mine is one that I may say is soon offended; for, I must say, I am always very uneasy at such behaviour, thinking it not like the behaviour of the primitive Christians, which I imagine was most in conformity to our Saviour's gosple.

THOMAS TURNER, 1925

23rd

We found the roads abundantly worse than they had been the day before; not only because the snows were deeper, which made the causeways in many places unpassable, but likewise because the hard frost, succeeding the thaw, had made all the ground like glass. We were often obliged to walk, it being impossible to ride, and our horses several times fell down while we were leading them, but not once while we were riding them, during the whole journey. It was past eight before we got to Gateshead Fell, which appeared a great pathless waste of white. The snow filling up and covering all the roads, we were at a loss how to proceed; when an honest man of Newcastle overtook and guided us safe into the town.

Many a rough journey have I had before, but one like this I never had; between wind, and hail, and rain, and ice, and snow, and driving sleet, and piercing cold.

JOHN WESLEY, 1745

24th

Our maid told me that Mr Bunbury brought home the news last night that the lords were reprieved for forty days. I could not give much credit to that, knowing the Tories love to deceive themselves with agreeable news. I resolved therefore to go immediately into the city and know the truth of it. Went to brother's and there heard that there was no reprieve and the guards were gone to the Tower. So went to Tower Hill and got a convenient place to see the execution [resulting for the 1715 Jacobite rebellion].

The whole hill was full of people that I neer saw so large a collection of people in my life, and a vast circle was made by the horse guards round about the scaffolds and a great many foot guards in the middle. At length Lord Derwentwater and Kenmure came in two hackney coaches from the Tower to the transport office over against the scaffolds. I saw them both. Lord Derwentwater looked with a melancholy aspect, but Lord Kenmure looked very bold and unconcerned. Derwentwater was executed first. After he was brought upon the stage and was saluted by several officers and others that were there, he prayed and spoke to them and told them, as I am informed, that since he was to die he was sorry he pleaded guilty, for he was an innocent man, for he knew no king but King James III. He was a papist and therefore had no priest along with him. He seemed to behave himself very well and make his exit decently enough, though with but a melancholy and pious aspect. Sir John Fryer, one of the sheriffs of London, attended both of them upon the scaffold. The executioner struck off his head at one blow and then held it in his hand and showed it to the people and said 'Here is the head of the traitor. God bless King George!' His head and body were wrapped in a black cloth and put into the coach in which he came and carried back to the Tower.

About half-hour after that Kenmure came upon the scaffold and looked with all the courage and resolution of an old Roman. He walked about the stage with a great deal of unconcernedness. Two clergymen attended him upon the stage and prayed, he being a Protestant. When he was beheaded his body was put into a coffin. What he said I have not heard. There was no disturbance made at all, while the mob were as quiet as lambs, nor did there seem to be any face of sorrow among the multitude.

It is very moving and affecting to see a man that was but this moment in perfect health and strength sent the next into another world. Few that die in their bed have so easy an end of life.

DUDLEY RYDER, 1716

25th

Felt some ill effects of yesterday's indulgence. In the Birmingham coach was accosted by Graham Clarke, whom I remember a handsome, gay young man in Newcastle, and now see a portly white-haired "country gentleman." Another of "the *bench*" rode ten miles with us, and afforded me an amusing insight into the quality of mind peculiar to this species – county magistrates. Turnpike roads, covers, poachers, rents, county politics, and important county persons, never heard of beyond the boundaries of the shire, give unwearied exercise to their tongues. Such men are not without a certain interest to me

in my cogitations on mankind and his purpose here. Possessed of thousands per annum, this person G. C. gave a ready, and seemingly an *habitual,* refusal to a beggar's request, and a most imperious "good day to you" to the village inn-keeper on the road. Is this superiority of sense, good breeding, or charity?

WILLIAM MACREADY, 1833

26th

Took a walk to Wigan after dinner, and accidentally met with my nephew, William Stock, in Moyle's the tea-dealer's, shop. Some months ago I had had some conversation with him about purchasing an organ; the subject was again resumed, and he now walked down with me to Atherton's, in Queen Street, who is an organ-builder. I was pleased with what I saw and heard there, and am strongly tempted to order one; but although he says he can make a good one for 15 to 20£, yet it is a serious sum to me, and I must deliberate a little.

EILEEN WEETON, 1824

27th

With my wife to the King's House, to see 'The Virgin Martyr,' the first time it hath been acted a great while, and it is mighty pleasant: not that the play is worth much, but it is finely acted by Beck Marshall. But that which did please me beyond anything in the whole world was the wind-music when the angel comes down, which is so sweet that it ravished me, and indeed, in a word, did wrap up my soul so that it made me really sick (just as I have formerly been when in love with my wife), that neither then, nor all the evening going home, and at home, I was able to think of anything, but remained all night transported, so as I could not believe that ever any music hath that real command over the soul of a man as this did upon me: and makes me resolve to practise wind-music, and to make my wife do the like.

SAMUEL PEPYS, 1668

28th

What a boon is Sunday! I can get out of bed just when the spirit moves me, dress and bath leisurely, even with punctilio. How nice to dawdle in the bath with a cigarette, to hear the holiday sound of Church bells! Then comes that supreme moment when, shaven, clean, warm and hungry for breakfast and coffee, I stand a moment before the looking-glass and comb out my towzled hair with a parting as straight as a line in Euclid. That gives the finishing touch of self-satisfaction, and I go down to breakfast ready for the day's pleasure. I hate this week-day strain of having to be always each day at a set time in a certain place.

W. N. P. BARBELLION, 1919

29th

Strange that I have not begun my Papers. A Journal is certainly of use: at least it letls us see how little we do, and how difficult it is to carry good resolutions into effect. Every week, for some time past, I have intended to begin upon these Papers, yet have not.

W. J. TEMPLE, 1796

MARCH

1st

Rather heay snow. There has been a most singular nuisance going on since Christmas about Manchester. A gang of young men calling themselves *Spring-heeled Jacks* hve been going about in the dusk frightening people. They wore india-rubber dresses which would puff up at will to a great size, horns, a lantern and springs in their boots.

One jumped right over a cab in the Eccles Road, nearly frightening the gentleman inside out of his wits. One poor girl in Swinton Lane had a fit. They were cowardly bullies, also thieves, for they took money. Some say the are Medical Students from Owens College, and it is not impossible I am afraid.

They were bad to catch, but the authorities sent some detectives. One of these met a *Jack* who demanded his money or his life. The detective pretended to be frightened and get out money, but instead he produced some handcuffs and caught him. Another was captured on a Sunday evening by some young men who beat him soundly, and then discovered he was an acquaintance. One was in the next garden to *Hopefield* a fortnight since.

The maids durst not stir out a step in the evening, which, my Aunt remarked, was well.

BEATRIX POTTER, 1886

2nd

Davis, the cowman, caught and killed a fine badger. It was sleeping in a corner under the manger at the stalls. He was feeding the cows and first stuck his foot into its rump, and beat it on the head. They are getting rare. I do not remember one being caught here before though we have often found their holes in the wood. They are not in the least destructive of anything one wishes to preserve. We had it stuffed at a cost of 20/- and put into what the taxidermist called a menacing attitude.

DEARMAN BIRCHALL, 1886

3rd

OXFORD. The weather is delightfully mild and we walked all the morning with Mrs Fremantle and Mr Phillimore. Saw most of the colleges – some of the buildings are very fine. Called on Mrs Cleaver and met her walking with her three little girls; they are as hideous as herself. Col. Fremantle looked much better to-day, he was rather overcome at seeing us yesterday. I had a letter from my husband today. Portsmouth is all bustle and confusion, they are to sail today for the Downs. Lady Nelson is sueing for a separate maintenance. I have no patience with her husband, at his age and such a cripple to play the fool with Lady Hammilton.

BETSY FREMANTLE, 1801

4th

Writing Memoirs for Mr Calamy, till four: at church; the vicar preached the funeral sermon for old Mrs Pullain, mother of the late High Sheriff, who was born here, where his father, Mr Pullain, is yet living, and can read without spectacles (which he formerly used), though ninety-two years of age. *Poulain,* in French, signifies a colt. And his son, Thomas Pullain, Esq Stud-master to his Majesty, rose from a small beginning to a great estate by horses.

RALPH THORESBY, 1702

5th

A melancholy event indeed – my poor friend Henry B. destroyed himself this morning in his room at Limmer's Hotel, Conduit-street. Continued losses at play and other pecuniary embarrassments drove him to despair and he cut his own throat, after shaving and dressing himself completely, while the breakfast was preparing by his servant. It was an infatuation of long standing; his father had twice paid his debts to a large amount, and they were unfortunately not on speaking terms for some time past. His poor mother was burnt to death not two months ago, and he never saw her in her last moments. This sad event, and the recollection of his intimate friend –, who last year drowned himself in the Serpentine from the same dreadful cause, most probably accelerated this catastrophe. He left no letter to anyone – merely the following words, scribbled on the back of a kind note, which he had receved the preceding evening from his friend the Duke of Dorset, 'I cannot pray, and am determined to rush unbidden into the presence of my God!' What a sickening thought.

THOMAS RAIKES, 1832

6th

I forgot to mention an odd thing Arabella and I did this morning. A. got out of bed early, and woke me. I felt wonderfully tired and sleepy, but got up not very long after. Just as I had done dressing, I heard it strike four o'clock. I hastened downstairs, and found A. in

the dark, so I unfastened the shutters of our sitting-room. The sun, of course, had not risen; the moon was shining beautifully in the north-west, and several stars were visible; a very thick fog hung about the trees. It was not light enough to read or write, and nobody was up besides ourselves, so we sat a whole hour in the cold, talking together. Just as it struck six, Richard came down, and at the same time Frederick got up and struck a light, so that we obtained a candle and went to our employments.

EMILY SHORE (AGED 13), 1833

7th

We continued drinking like horses, as the vulgar phrase is, and singing till many of us were very drunk, and then we went to dancing and pulling wigs, caps, and hats; and thus we continued in this frantic manner, behaving more like mad people than they that profess the name of Christians. Whether this is consistent to the wise saying of Solomon, let any one judge: 'Wine is a mocker, strong drink is raging, and he that is deceived thereby is not wise.'

THOMAS TURNER, 1758

8th

Being Wensday, hora noctis 10, 11, the strange noyse in my chamber of knocking; and the voyce, ten tymes repeted, somewhat like the shrich of an owle, but more longly drawn, and more softly, as it were in my chamber.

JOHN DEE, 1581

9th

Went to the theatre and tried to act Macbeth; but, the witches first – ducking or burning could only have properly rewarded them; then Banquo, shutting his eyes, and making himself amiable and heroic in turns; then Duncan, an out-and-out-wretch; but it was all so bad – Banquo coming on as the ghost with his face painted exactly like the clown in a pantomime! It was so bad that I felt and said, "money could not pay for the sense of degredation endured in such a set of persons." Nor can it – it is impossible to preserve one's self-respect. I laboured – I thought of Goethe, I thought of using the occasion as a study – it would not do, *it was too bad.* I was "hewed like a carcase fit for hounds." Was called for, and well received.

WILLIAM MACREADY, 1840

10th

She acts Macbeth herself better than either Kemble or Kean. It is extraordinary the awe this wonderful woman inspires. After her first reading the men retired to tea. While we were all eating toast and tingling cups and saucers, she began again. It was like the effect of a mass bell at Madrid. All noise ceased; we slunk to our seats like boors, two or three of the most distinguished men of the day, with the very toast in their mouths, afraid to bite. It was curious to see Lawrence in this predicament, to hear him bite by degrees, and then stop for fear of making too much crackle, his eyes full of water from the constraint; and at the same time to hear Mrs Siddons' 'eye of newt and toe of frog!' and then to see Lawrence give a sly bite, and then look awed and pretend to be listening. I went away highly gratified, and as I stood on the landing-place to get cool I overheard my own servant in the hall say: 'What! is that the old lady making such a noise?' 'Yes.' 'Why she makes as much noise as ever!' 'Yes,' was the answer; 'she tunes her pipes as well as ever she did.'"

B. R. HAYDON, 1821

11th

Some Oxford Scholars had Wine for Br [breakfast]. Call'd at Marriott, the Wool Dealer but not at Home. Walk'd about the Church Yard [at Witney]. Knock'd twice at Mrs Cole's door & retir'd again as no one came to me. Should it be my Lott to marry her Daughter, I trust through the Blessing of God, to live very easy & comfortable & above all to spend my Days after a very holy & religious manner, & to encour[ag]e one another in the Progress of Virtue & Religion & to make that our chiefest Study & Delight.

Din'd at Ensome [Eynsham] Ferry on a Jack. Many Years ago Self & James Taylor was at this Place in my Way to Bath. I am alive, the other is Dead, & I am thankfull to Providence for the Prolongation of

my Life. My Business in that Expedition was to trye my Fortune with Miss Longman, but after I had waited on her Father, I found it would not do, & if she killd her Self with Drinking, what Pleasure could such a Wife have given Me, so that all things consider'd, may I ever conclude, that Providence always orders all my Affairs after the best manner for my spiritual Interest, & therefore may his Will & not mine always take. Spoke to Mr Patten. Got home in good Time.

JAMES NEWTON, 1760

12th

Finished Flora Macdonald. She does not remind me of her namesake whom I saw at 3 Hobart Place last January. Sunshine and cold N. wind. A graceful girl riding by fast on a roan, her long habit floating out far.

Luncheon at the Vicarage with Lord and Lady Hereford, two Miss Ravenscrofts and Miss Baskerville. Afterwards they went up to the Bron and Pen y Llan to see the view as the N. wind had cleared the air. I left them at the Post Office and went to Upper Cabalva where Mrs Dyke gave me a pocketful of golden pippins. Annie up at Llwyn Gwillim, but before she went she had gathered a glassfull of primroses from the rickyard hedge. On to Lower Cabalva. Women carrying home on their heads heavy burdens of wood from the dingle and fields where a fall of timber is going on. Mrs Collett with a new baby to be christened at Bettws Chapel tomorrow. Mary Collett proud to show me her Whitney School prizes and all her little treasures. She is a very good girl very fond of reading and going to school and devours books. I lent her Miss Edgeworth's *Parent's Assistant*. She has good eyes but she will never match her mother's beautiful noble face. Mrs Collet says they must have their turkey cock killed because he knocks the children down and stocks (pecks) them. Collett set one child to drive the turkey with a stick but the bird flew at her, knocked her down and stocked her too, so there were two children roaring at once and the turkey triumphant.

FRANCIS KILVERT, 1870

13th

The cocktail party at Alec's was quite fun although Elizabeth Ponsonby never came. I got drunk. Tony was there. Alec has fallen in love with a hideous and stupid woman who is married. We went to Sherry's and ate a good dinner. Hors d'oeuvres, chicken broth, grilled salmon, caneton à la presse (but all unlike the duck of the silver tower) and omelette surprise. Murdocke mistook the place of meeting. I drove home that night instead of waiting until morning and found it bitterly cold.

I have had three tea parties this week, the first on Tuesday consisting of Gleed, the two Miss Crawfords and Bill Holmes à Court who is not as frightful as everyone has led me to suppose; on Thursday Charles and Edmund; and today the prefects and Baxendale who ate prodigiously and I think enjoyed it. Tomorrow I purpose to go to communion if I can wake up early enough. I think it is just to record that Matthew sent me a letter of apology for his drunkenness – but no money for his dinner.

The children have begun to be a little naughty so I have started being strict with them, which is a bore.

Claud has broken Alastair's motor car against a lorry. Alastair has not returned yet – Mrs G. wired for me to come and see her on Thursday but I could not.

EVELYN WAUGH, 1926

14th

Dinner to day, odds and ends &c. Js Pegg called on me this Morning and left me an account of the new additional Taxes per annum exclusive of the old, which amount to my Share 25. 5. 6. Very heavy indeed are the new Taxes on the Clergy in short. How the new taxes will go down with the People in general I know not, I hope they will not create more new Taxes after these, tho' at present are talked of.

JAMES WOODFORDE, 1798

15th

During his absence a sailor who was travelling from Liverpool to Whitehaven called; he was faint and pale when he knocked at the door – a young man very well dressed. We sate by the kitchen fire talking with him for 2 hours. He told us interesting stories of his life. His name was Isaac Chapel. He had been at sea since he was 15 years old. He was by trade a sail-maker. His last voyage was to the coast of Guinea. He had been on board a slave ship, the captain's name Maxwell, where one man had been killed, a boy put to lodge with the pigs and was half eaten, one boy set to watch in the hot sun till he dropped down dead. He had been cast away in North America and had travelled thirty days among the Indians, where he had been well treated. He had twice swum from a King's ship in the night and escaped. He said he would rather be in hell than be pressed. He was now going to wait in England to appear against Captain Maxwell. 'O he's a Rascal, Sir, he ought to be put in the papers!' The poor man had not been in bed since Friday night. He left Liverpool at 2 o'clock on Saturday morning; he had called at a farm house to beg victuals and had been refused. The woman said she would give him nothing. 'Won't you? Then I can't help it.'

DOROTHY WORDSWORTH, 1802

16th

What will be blown up next? Last night an attempt was made to blow up the Government Offices in Parliament Street. Not so much damage was done to the building, owing to its great strength, but the streets for some distance round were strewn with glass.

One thing struck me as showing the extraordinary power of dynamite, a brick was hurled 100 feet and then through a brick wall into some stables. Some one said the noise was like the 80 ton gun. I believe it was heard here.

An attempt was also made, but failed, on *The Times* office, which seems to prove it was the work of Irishmen, that paper having had a leading article in its last number in which it was stated the Irish had got enough and more than enough, and need ask for no more.

Papa says it is Mr Gladstone's fault. He takes the side of these rogues and then, if they think he is slackening, they frighten him on a bit – really we shall be as bad as France soon.

BEATRIX POTTER (AGED 16), 1883

17th

Went to London to see the Pompe of Prince and Peeres goeing to Parliament in this Order. 1. Trumpeters. 2. Guard in scarlet. 3. Ye 4 masters of ye Chancery in blacke. 4. Barons. 5. Judges. 6. Byshops. 7. Vicounts. 8. Earles. 9. King [Charles I]. 10. Duke Buckingham. Earl of Holland. The King's speach signifying 3 causes of calling ye parliament. 1. for ye Kingdomes defence against 2 potent forraine Kings Spain & France. 2. his private wants noe way soe well releived as by this meanes. 3. redresse of greivances in the Land. Speaker in parliament Sir John Finch. Prolocutor Dr

Curle – preacher at Parliament Bishop Laud, endeavor to keepe Unity in the Bond of Peace.

THOMAS CROSFIELD, 1628

18th

Ran out to Penjerrick. On return found Don M. Moreno (Buenos Ayrean Minister to London) at office, just landed from *Seagull,* highly indignant at the unsubservient disposition of the Custom House officers in not allowing his baggage to pass unsearched in virtue of his office. On returning through the Moor heard of the 'Chartists' (deputies from 'the grand Convention' in the North) holding forth to the populace on the oppression of the poor, tyranny of government, slavery of governed, & they bitterly complained of the unnecessary tax of a war establishment after 23 years' peace, the injustice of every Englishman not being entitled to vote, the iniquity of new poor law &c. Called on all to come forward & sign their petition. 'We *demand* universal suffrage &c.' Said Christ was crucified between 2 thieves & so were the English people between the Whigs and Tories. Both speakers were eloquent, one especially so, very specious & plausible, adducing from the mass of statutes just those which bore out his position & produced an effect. Both were inflammatory, not to say seditious, shrewd designing scamps, *ignes fatui* misguiding honest men with a blaze of enthusiasm. Can't do much harm here, I think. People too well off to kick up a row. The hearty cheers seemed to indicate that a flame was lit, but I know enough of Falmouth zeal to feel pretty sure of its going out unless well fanned.

BARCLAY FOX, 1839

19th

The paths of our gardens have all been nicely sanded; and in lieu of a mound,which I cannot make nicely, I cut away the earth pretty deeply in one part, so as to leave a space standing in the

middle, down which the potentilla may climb. I then went with a spade and wheelbarrow to the bottom of the garden. Here we dug up two or three wild plants, two sorts of ranunculus, hyacinths, and strawberry. We then went into the lower part of the cow-pasture, a damp meadow separated from the garden by a paling and low hedge, over which we easily climbed. From thence I got other plants – some *Geranium Robertianum*, primroses, a cowslip, strawberries, and others which I do not know. All these I put in my garden, with the proper soil in which I found them; when blooming they will look very pretty.

EMILY SHORE (AGED 13), 1833

20th

I bounced out of bed very early and found it hard snowing and very deep with a drifting wind, the greatest fall I ever knew in one night. The barometer is so low the mark will not follow it. The wind so high and the snow so penetrating that it is driven under the new tiling into the upper Garret and from thence distills drop by drop through the ceiling into our bed chamber a thing I never knew before. Had it happened in the night we should have been in an awkward situation.

WILLIAM HOLLAND, 1812

21st

A gentleman named Feilding went into his barn and took an ear of corn into his mouth and by chance the beard of it stuck under his tongue so that he could not get it out. He did not trouble much about it, but after five or six hours it became troublesome, and after thirteen or fourteen hours the wound turned septic and he died. Cousin Isham said that the young man who came to the house saying his name was Isham was a scoundrel and fit for the gallows, and in fact had narrowly escaped hanging for having raised a mutiny in the fleet.

THOMAS ISHAM (AGED 16), 1672

22nd

I dined on some salt-fish, egg-sauce, parsnips, and potatoes. In the even read part of Homer's 'Odyssey,' translated by Pope, which I like very well; the language being vastly good, and the turn of thought and expression beautiful.

THOMAS TURNER, 1765

23rd

The daffodils were nodding in bright yellow clumps in the little garden plots before the almshouse doors. And there a great ecstacy of happiness fell upon me. It was evening when I met her and the sun was setting up the Brecon road. I was walking by the almshouses when there came down the steps a tall slight beautiful girl with a graceful figure and long flowing hair. Her lovely face was delicately pale, her features refined and aristocratic and her eyes a soft dark tender blue. She looked at me earnestly, longingly and lovingly, and dropped a pretty courtesy. Florence, Florence Hill, sweet Florence Hill, is it you? Once more. Thank God. Once more. My darling, my darling. As she stood and lifted those blue eyes, those soft and dark loving eyes shyly to mine, it seemed to me as if the doors and windows of heaven were suddenly opened. It was one of the supreme moments of life. As I stood by the roadside holding her hand, lost to all else and conscious only of her presence, I was in heaven already, or if still on earth in the body, the flights of golden stairs sloped to my feet and one of the angels had come down to me. Florence, Florence Hill, my darling, my darling. It was well nigh all I could say in my emotion. With one long lingering loving look and the clasp of the hand we parted and I saw her no more.

FRANCIS KILVERT, 1874

24th

I went to the Court of Requests, where I met the Archbishop of Tuam and Bishop of Killala, and was engaged by his grace to dine with him, but, meeting Sir St. John Brodrick and Sir George St. George, we were persuaded to dine all together, which we did at Hell, where I eat the worst dinner since I came to London for one shilling and six pence. After dinner we went all to the Castle in Palace-yard, where I spent six pence; then with the Archbishop I went to the Banqueting-house in Whitehall, and saw the King receive an address from the House of Commons, which he told them he received kindly, and that he doubted not but they would consider the things which he had recommended to them in his Speech, as he hoped that they did not doubt his readiness to hazard his life and all that was dear to him to serve them and the kingdom. Then we returned, and walked some time in the Park, where Captain Cross joined me, and we went home with the Archbishop, and sat awhile. Then, having been promised a horse for my man by Major Palmes, I sent my man to Watford to receive him, with a saddle, bridle, and pair of boots given me by Barry Love, and gave him a letter to the Major, and ten shillings to bear his charges. I also bought a horse for myself of Haws Cross for fifteen pounds, and pawned fifteen broad pieces and paid him. I also bought four coloured handkerchiefs or three shillings and six pence, and lent Denny Muschamp one shilling.

Roland Davies, 1690

25th

London. Here we are once more, after an absence of nine months. This second first sight made much the same impression as the first. London does not strike with admiration; it is regular, clean, convenient, (I am speaking of the best part) but the site is flat; the plan monotonous; the predominant colour of objects dingy and poor. It is altogether without great faults and without great beauties. Suppose yourself in one of the best streets, it extends *à perte de vue* before you, in an undeviating strait line; the side walks wide and smooth; every door with its stone steps, its iron railing, and its lamp;

one house differing from its neighbour in no one thing but the number on the door and the name of the occupant. Turn the next corner and you have another street as long, as wide, and as strait, and so on from street to street. At night you have eternal rows of lamps, making the straitness of the streets still more conspicuous and tiresome. this palpable immensity has something in it very heavy and stupifying. The best houses in Edinburgh are very inferior certainly to those of the same rank in London, yet the difference of the materials, a bright crystallized stone, instead of dingy bricks, gives them a look of superior consequence and cheerfulness; the variety of views also, and the proximity to the country, without the fag-end of suburbs, are invaluable advantages. There is no doubt, in London a greater choice of society, the best probably, and the pleasantest; but it is, in general, out of the reach of a stranger, and of no sort of consequence to him.

LOUIS SIMOND, 1811

26th

Today I have been entertaining Young – the lecher from Denbighshire. He came on a marvellous bicycle – a Sunbeam. We lunched at the Bell and went to see the children at football. He fell in love with R –. I fell down rather painfully trying to take the corner up to the speed-hill. I am very much tired tonight.

Yesterday I went to a point-to-point meeting at Kimble and lost £4 which I can very ill afford.

We had a party at the Bell. We got drunk. When we were all in bed David and Babe and Eliza arrived with a car full of Charleston records from London.

EVELYN WAUGH, 1926

27th

Mr C [the historian and essayist Thomas Carlyle] took Nero out with him to-night, and half an hour after he opened the door with his latch-key and called in, 'Is that vermin come back?' Having received my horrified 'No!' he hurried off again, and for twenty minutes I was in the agonies of one's dog lost, my heart beating up into my ears. At last I heard Mr C.'s feet in the street; and, oh joy! heard him gollaring at something, and one knew what the little bad something was. Ach! we could have better spared a better dog.

JANE WELSH CARLYLE, 1856

28th

In the afternoon rode over to Chiddingly, to pay my charmer, or intended wife or sweetheart or whatever other name may be more proper, a visit at her father's where I drank tea, in company with their family and Miss Ann Thatcher. I supped there on some rasures of bacon. It being an excessive wet and windy night I had the opportunity, sure I should say the pleasure, or perhaps some might say the unspeakable happiness, to sit up with Molly Hicks, or my charmer, all night. I came home at forty minutes past five in the morning – I must not say fatigued; no, no, that could not be; it could be only a little sleepy for want of a rest. Well to be sure, she is a most clever girl; but however, to be serious in the affair, I certainly esteem the girl, and think she appears worthy of my esteem.

THOMAS TURNER, 1765

29th

There are only two more days – a thing I find it very hard to believe. Today there was a dreadful concert at which all the boys played the pieces they had learned during the term and Mrs Banks said polite things about the women who had taught them. During the last ten days we have spent most evenings at the village pub where an aged eunuch has tried to teach us Welsh. I have learned very little, however, except Iechyd da i bob un and Llywddiant ir archos, which are toasts, because he gets too drunk to say anything else. On Saturday I felt so sad that I very nearly gave notice – proprietor Banks was rude to me unjustly and before a number of boys but the prospect of the holidays has buoyed me up a little. A man called Gregg whose father is an archbishop came the other evening and talked bawdy until I wanted to cry. We all do nothing but talk bawdy and lay absurd wagers – 6d in the pool for the man who can keep the ash on his cigar the longest, etc. Audrey gave a party a week ago which I think was unfriendly of her. Baldhead writes despondently that no one is giving any parties now.

EVELYN WAUGH, 1925

30th

A certain barbarous Sect of People arose lately in London who distinguish themselves by the Name of Mohocks. There are great Numbers of them, & their Custom is to make themselves drunk and in the Night-time go about the Streets in great Droves & to abuse after a most inhumane Manner all Persons they meet, by beating down their Noses, pricking the fleshy Parts of their Bodys with their swords, not sparing even the Women, whom they usually set upon their Heads & committ such Indecencies towards them as are not to be mention'd; nor indeed shall I descend to any other particulars about these Brutish People, against whom there is a Proclamation issu'd with the Tender of a considerable Reward for Discovery of any of them. Divers have been taken up, & strict Watches are kept every Night. They are found to be young, lewd, debauch'd Sparks, all of the Whiggish Gang, & the Whiggs are now so much ashamd of this great Scandal (provided Whiggs can be asham'd) that they publickly give out there have been no such People, nor no such Inhumanities committed, thereby indeavouring to perswade People out of their Senses. But this is only one Instance of their abominable Lying, &c.

THOMAS HEARNE, 1712

31st

A great fit of the stone in my left kydney: all day I could do but three or four drops of water, but I drunk a draught of white wyne and salet oyle, and after that, crabs' eys in powder with the bone in the carp's head, and abowt four of the clok I did eat tosted cake butered, and with suger and nutmeg on it, and drunk two great draughts of ale with it; and I voyded within an howr much water, and a stone as big as an Alexander seed. God be thanked! Five shillings to Robert Webb, part of his wagis.

JOHN DEE, 1594

APRIL

1st

Mr Custance sent after Nancy this morning to spend the Day with Mrs Custance and to have her Hair dressed by one Brown, the best Ladies-Frisseur in Norwich. About Noon the Weather turned out very wet and the Wind very high and so continued till 9 at Night. The Barometer sunk from this morning at 10 o'clock to 10 at Night 13 Degrees from No. 28-17 to 28-4. Nancy returned home about ½ past 9 o'clock this Even', with her head finely dressed of but very becoming her. Mrs Custance would not let Nancy pay the Barber, but she paid for her and it cost no less than half a guinea. Mrs Custance gave the Barber for dressing her Hair and Nancys the enormous sum of one guinea – He came on purpose from Norwich to dress them.

JAMES WOODFORDE, 1782

2nd

I went with Haws Cross, who came early to my lodging, to wait on the Earl of Cork, but he was gone abroad; wherefore we went to the Park, and then to the Court of Requests, where we met the Archbishop of Tuam, who took me with him to the city by water, and we dined wth Sir H. Bingham and his Lady at Mr Frederick's and were treated very sumptuously. After dinner we were some time diverted by viewing some very fine Indian screens of great value. Then we returned by water, and in the Park I met my brother and sister Matthew, with whom I conferred a while, and then went to the coffee-house; and then with my brother Aldworth, T. Gash, and Mr Brooks, I went to York-buildings, and spent the evening at the expense of three pence. The parliament voted to supply his Majesty with one million two hundred thousand pounds, but resolved not yet how to raise it. The Danes are almost all in Ireland, which so disheartened the Irish that King James issued a proclamation that no man should report that they were landed, on pain of death.

ROLAND DAVIES, 1690

3rd

We met a remarkable Bulldog to-day in the street, humbly following behind a tiny boy to whom it was attached by a piece of string. At the time we were following in the wake of three magnificent Serbian Officers, and I was particularly interesting myself in the curious cut of their top boots. But the Bulldog was the Red Herring in our path.

'Is that a Dog?' I asked the little boy.

He assured me that it was, and so it turned out to be, tho' Bull-frog would have been a better name for it, the forelegs being more bandied, the back broader and the mouth wider than in any Bulldog I have ever seen. It was a super-Bulldog.

We turned and walked on. 'There,' said R –, 'now we have lost our Serbian Officers.'

W. N. P. BARBELLION, 1916

4th

There stood before me a little, pale, rather don-like man, quite bald, with a huge head and dome-like forehead, a ragged red beard in odd whisks, a small aquiline red nose. He looked supremely shy, but received me with a distinguished courtesy, drumming in the ground with his foot, and uttering strange little whistling noises. He seemed very deaf. The room was crammed with books: bookcases all about – a great sofa entirely filled with stacked books – books on the table. He bowed me to a chair – 'Will you sit?' On the fender was a pair of brown socks. Watts-Dunton said to me, 'He has just come in from one of his long walks' – and took up the socks and put them behind the coal-scuttle. 'Stay!' said Swinburne, and took them out carefully, holding them in his hand: 'They are drying.' Watts-Dunton murmured something about his fearing they would get scorched, and we sate down. Swinburne sate down, concealing his feet behind a chair, and proceeded with strange motions to put the socks on out of sight. 'He seems to be changing them,' said Watts-Dunton. Swinburne said nothing, but continued to whistle and drum. Then he rose and bowed me down to lunch, throwing the window open.

A. C. BENSON, 1903

5th

Here I met with one of the most extraordinary phenomena that I ever saw, or heard of: – Mr Sellers has in his yard a large Newfoundland dog, and an old raven. These have fallen deeply in love with each other, and never desire to be apart. The bird has learned the bark of the dog, so that few can distinguish them. She is inconsolable when he goes out; and, if he stays out a day or two, she will get up all the bones and scraps she can, and hoard them up for him till he comes back.

JOHN WESLEY, 1790

6th

Charles in the garden putting down potatoes. I walked with Little William to Stowey, paid the malster for making the malt and grinding. Met two Miss Pooles at Mr Francis Pooles, bought some cakes and returned. The ladies walked out after dinner. While I was alone the servants uncommonly playful and gigling in the kitchen. I called to 'em and observed to Charles that he stayed within doors to play with the woman. Edith and he are like two elephants at gambols. Night drew on and we sat by a good fire, some to reading and others to writing and afterwards to bed.

WILLIAM HOLLAND, 1803

7th

Colonel Pearson gave us some of his Crimean reminiscences. Most of the English officers could speak French. Hardly one of the French officers could speak English. The Russian officers could speak both French and English fluently. Colonel Pearson was on Sir George Brown's staff. The old General was not much of a linguist and knew but little French. One night an Aide de Camp came from Marshal Canrobert with a message about an attack that was to be made or expected in the morning. The French officer was grinning, bowing, scraping, grimacing and gesticulating. Sir George could not understand a word. He used some strong language and turned to Colonel Pearson. 'What does he say, Master Dick? Give him a glass of sherry and tell him to go away.' *Tell him to go away!* As if he had been an organ-grinder! 'And,' said Colonel Pearson with an expressive shrug, 'perhaps next morning a hundred lives might depend upon that message.'

FRANCIS KILVERT, 1872

8th

Passing through the village of Sodbury, we came to the market town of Chipping Sodbury, an old, *triste* and deserted-looking place. Here the aspect of the country is uninteresting, pastured by ragged horses and donkeys and geese, and bordered by mean-looking cottages, half dilapidated and a general air of discomfort prevailed.

The country is indeed more populous than our Cotswold hills; but the people have a less rural cast, being chiefly colliers or engaged in the hat and other manufactories. One tract of common over which we passed is called Coalpitheath, a ragged-looking spot, people and their dwellings being all out at elbows. As we drew nearer to Bristol the country improved . . .

F. E. WITTS, 1833

9th

Across the wall and fields to Cwmbythog and the magnificent regal mistress of the miserable shanty came to the rickety door with a brilliant smile in her deep grey eyes shadowed with long black lashes and over her grand richly browned face. She was preparing the clean clothes for Sunday. Black haired Mary nursing the baby, and brown haired Elizabeth feeding the roaring oven fire. The draught through the old hovel enough to blow one's hair about. From Cwmbythog I crossed the dingle and the brook and the little meadow and so up the path by the quarries along the hillside to John Morgan's the old soldier's. He and Mary his wife were cosily at tea. And after the veteran had done and pocketed his clasp knife he covered his face with his hand and whispered his long grace audibly. Talking of the Peninsular War he said he well remembered being in a reserve line at Vittoria when a soldier sitting close to him on the edge of a bank had

his head carried off by a cannon ball which struck him in front on the throat. The head rolled along the ground, and when it ceased rolling John Morgan and the other soldiers saw it going and 'playing' on the ground with a twitching of the features for five minutes after. They thought it so extraordinary that the subject was often talked over round the camp fires as an unprecedented marvel. There was one Lieutenant Bowen an Irishman who joined the regiment between the battles of Vittoria and the Pyrenees. He was very vicious to the men and much hated. Just before the battle of the Pyrenees (which John Morgan calls the Battle of the Pioneers) this Lieutenant Bowen became very mild and humble to the men fearing he should be shot on purpose by his own soldiers in the battle from revenge. He was not shot.

FRANCIS KILVERT, 1870

10th

It is nearly two years since I wrote anything in the way of a diary. I now take up my pen to resume the task. It has been a very poor time for me all the time owing to the American war, which seems as far off being settled as ever. The mill I work in was stopped all last winter, during which time I had 3s. per week allowed by the relief committee, which barely kept me alive. When we started work again it was with Surat cotton, and a great number of weavers can only mind two looms. We can earn very little. I have not earned a shilling a day this last month, and there are many like me. My clothes and bedding is wearing out very fast and I have no means of getting any more, as what wages I get does hardly keep me, my daughter and son-in-law having gone to a house of their own during the time I was out of work. I went twice to Preston to see my brother Daniel, but him and his family were no better off than myself, having nothing better than Surat to work at, and it is the same all through Lancashire. There has been some terrible and bloody battles fought in America these last two years . . . The principal reason why I did not take any notes these last two years is because I was sad and weary. One half of the time I was out of work and the other I had to work as hard as ever I wrought in my life, and can hardly keep myself living. If things do not mend this summer I will try somewhere else or something else, for I can't go much further with what I am at.

JOHN WARD (O'NEIL), 1864

11th

To-day I called on 'my lady' come to town for the season. She was perfectly civil, for a wonder. To-day also I lighted upon an interesting man. It was in our baker's shop. While the baker was making out my bill he addressed some counsel to a dark little man with a wooden leg and a basket of small wares. That made me look at the man to watch its effect upon him. 'I'll tell you what to do,' said this Jesuit of a baker; 'Go and join some Methodists' chapel for six months; make yourself agreeable to them, and you'll soon have friends that will help you in your object.' The man of the wooden leg said not a word, but looked hard in the baker's face with a half-perplexed, half-amused, and wholly disagreeing expression. 'Nothing like religion,' went on the tempter, 'for gaining a man friends. Don't you think so, ma'am?' (catching my eye on him).

JANE WELSH CARLYLE, 1856

12th

We went off in a Post Chaise to Bridgwater where we stayed till Saturday the sixteenth. Great rejoicing on Wednesday evening. We got a position in a room on the Cornhill where we could see the Bonfire and Squibs and Rockets thrown. In a narrow passage we had a Squib thrown amongst us and Margaret's gown was burnt and when we got upstairs a Squib with a stone was thrown through the window and the broken glass flew to Mr John Symes face. Buonaparte at last finishes his Career of Wickedness like a Poor Cowardly Scoundrel in the Hand of Providence. On the sixteenth there was a meeting of the Mayor and Corporation to form an Address to the Prince Regent, I was present and among others appointed to the committee to draw up the address, which was done.

WILLIAM HOLLAND, 1814

13th

When I first got up this morning, I found the whole Village assembled in the Church yard, to see an old Gypsey woman who died suddenly last night in the lane, I walked to the Church where the Corpse of the wretched woman was laid, merely wrapped up in the blanket she slept in with her black hair all over her head and face, not at all disfigured, the women were just going to wash and dress out the corpse, in the church yd. the daughters and sons of the deceased formed a most interesting Groupe, really all in the most deep affliction. The poor woman had been telling fortunes till quite late last night, apparantly in perfect health, she was in her tent in the lane with her two daughters, complained of sickness in the night and died quite suddenly. After breakfast we all walked to the church, where the corpse was very tidily laid out, it must remain there until it is buried. The poor Gypseys continue in affliction and will not take food until their poor old mother is buried.

BETSY FREMANTLE, 1815

14th

Advance of age. I now sit down to brush my hair and put my collar and tie on. I also take a decided pleasure in foming habits, and re-forming old ones connected with the furniture from Fontainebleau, whose little peculiarities of locks and knobs etc. I recognize again with positive satisfaction. The pleasure of doing a thing in the same way at the same time every day, and savouring it, should be noted.

ARNOLD BENNET, 1913

15th

The execution of poor Edmund Jeffrey took place this forenoon. It proved impossible for the chaplain to extract anything from the miserable man as to the suspicion that he had an accomplice. He underwent the extreme penalty of the law with great firmness and decorum; he addressed the assembled crowds at some length, warning them against bad associations, sabbath breaking and frequenting beer houses.

F. E. WITTS, 1835

16th

The liner Titanic runs into an iceberg and after her passengers and crew are rescued sinks near the shore. I go out a little before breakfast and afterwards we go to the park and then go and pick flowers for Miss Grigg. After lunch Daddy and I paint a little and then go and discover a beautiful way to Hartland by which we are probably going tomorrow. There is an old right of way along a bridal path. After tea we again play with the Meccano and have some successful runs. I then write this diary.

John Knight (aged 12), 1912

17th

This being my Rotation Day Mr and Mrs Bodham with them Miss Kitty Johnson, Mr Du Quesne, Mr Smith and Mr and Mrs Jeanes, all dined, and spent the Afternoon with us – We had for Dinner, some Skaite and Oyster Sauce, Knuckle of Veal and a Tongue, a fine Fore Quarter of Lamb and plumb Pudding. 2nd. Course, Asparagus, Lobster, Rasberry Tartlets, black Caps set into Custard &c. We had also Cucumbers and Radishes. There were three Carriages, 5 Servants and 8 Horses Soon after Coffee and Tea, they all left us.

James Woodforde, 1787

18th

The Opera-house of London is, like all the theatres I have seen in England, in the shape of a horse-shoe. The side-boxes are ill turned to see, and the front ones too far to hear. The height of the ceiling is so great that the voice is lost. It seems strange that the semicircular shape should not have occurred, or should not have been adopted. Each spectator would have the actors precisely in front of him, and at a mean distance equal for all. Such a theatre would moreover contain more spectators. I would lower the ceiling one-third at least, dispensing with the two upper tiers of boxes. It would be a very small pecuniary sacrifice – this high region being always but thinly filled, and by spectators whose presence, or behaviour at least, is either a great scandal, or very inconvenient – that is to say, in the side-galleries, certain ladies, who carry on their business quite openly, selling and delivering the articles they trade in under the eye of the public, and with a degree of shamefulness for which the inhabitants of Otaheite alone can furnish any precedent. That part of the upper region which fronts the stage is occupied by a less indecent, but more noisy sort of people; sailors, footmen, low tradesmen and their wives and mistresses, who enjoy themselves, drinking, whistling, howling as much as they please. These gods, for so they are called from their elevated station, which is in France denominated the *paradis*, assume the high prerogative of hurling down their thunder on both actors and spectators, in the shape of nut-shells, cores of apples, and orange-peel. This innocent amusement has always been considered in England as a sort of exuberance of liberty, of which it is well to have a little too much, to be sure that you have enough. Going to the play is not a habit with anybody here; it is in fact unfashionable: but London is so large, and the theatres so few, that they are always full. Paris has twenty-three theatres; London four or five, and these shut up part of the year. The hour of dining is precisely that of the play, which is another considerable obstacle.

LOUIS SIMOND, 1810

19th

I heard the famous singer, Cifaccio, esteemed the best in Europe. Indeed, his holding out and delicateness in extending and loosing a note with incomparable softness and sweetness, was admirable; for the rest I found him a mere wanton, effeminate child, very coy, and proudly conceited, to my apprehension. He touched the harpsichord to his voice rarely well. This was before a select number of particular persons whom Mr Pepys invited to his house; and this was obtained by particular favour and much difficulty, the Signor much disdaining to show his talent to any but princes.

JOHN EVELYN, 1687

THE PANTOMIME
GALLERY
BOXES

20th

This morning I first became acquainted with Arise Evans, a Welsh prophet; and speaking of the Parliament, I asked him when it would end? He answered, the time was short, and it was even at the door; this very morning at eleven a'clock, the Mace was taken away from the Speaker, and the Parliament dissolved; and I conjecture it was much about the time that Arise Evans and I had this discourse.

ELIAS ASHMOLE, 1653

21st

Saw the papers, and went to the theatre, where I was startled at learning that there was only just enough cash to meet the day's demands; and this included the remainder of my Benefit. The prospect is fearful. I sent for Willmott, and immediately made arrangements to dismiss *Sindbad* from the bills, and reduce every expense. Went to the Garrick Club, where I saw White, Collier, etc. In the Committee I put in a white ball to Lord de Tabley, but did not ballot for the friends of Messrs Oyle, Evans, and Bacon. They were elected, and I requested Winston to take my name off the books, 'knowing nothing of the two latter persons, except that they were the intimate associates of the greatest scoundrel and blackguard I know (Mr Bunn), I did not choose to meet the society of their recommendation; that if hereafter the Club should undergo re-organization I should be very happy to return to it.' Stanfield motioned me to return; this was strange, as he was most resolute to leave the Club! – but men are very uncertain. On consideration I regret I did not leave the Club without any notice of these people. Walked home and in the evening learned second act of Thoas. Oh, what a life!

WILLIAM MACREADY, 1838

22nd

This Day Sennight between six and seven in the Evening, the pretended Princess of Wales was safely delivered of a Prince (as he is called), at Leicester-House, the news of which was immediately proclaimed by discharging the Park and Tower Guns; the People in several Parts of the Town express'd their Joy by Bonfires, Illuminations, and Ringing of Bells; and on this Occasion three or four Hogsheads of Wine were given away at the Gate of the said Leicester House. Monday, Humphrey Parsons, Esq, Alderman of Portsoaken-Ward, and William Billers, Esq, one of the Sheriffs for London and Middlesex, waited on his (pretended) Royal Highness with the City's Compliment of Congratulation on the account of the Birth of his Son. And, in the Evening, his (pretended) Majesty (K. George) visited her (pretended) Royal Highness and the (pretended) young Prince. The next day the House of Commons waited on the (pretended) King at St. James's with an humble Address, to congratulate his (pretended) Majesty on the Birth of his Grandson. As did also the Lord Mayor and Court of Aldermen. The House of Commons likewise sent a congratulatory Letter to their (pretended) Royal Highnesses on this Occasion.

THOMAS HEARNE, 1721

23rd

And the King [Charles II at his coronation] came in with his crown on, and his sceptre in his hand, under a canopy borne up by six silver staves, carried by Barons of the Cinque Ports, and little bells at every end. And after a long time, he got up to the farther end, and all set themselves down at their several tables; and that was also a brave sight: and the King's first course carried up by the Knights of the Bath. And many fine ceremonies there was of the Heralds leading up people before him, and bowing; and my Lord of Albemarle's going to the kitchen and eating a bit of the first dish that was to go to the King's table. But, above all, was these three Lords, Northumberland, and Suffolk, and the Duke of Ormond, coming before the courses on horseback, and staying so all dinnertime, and at last bringing up the King' Champion, all in armour on horseback, with his spear and target carried before him. And a Herald proclaims 'That if any dare deny Charles Stuart to be lawful King of England, here was a Champion that would fight with him'; and with these words the Champion flings down his gauntlet, and all this he do three times in his going up towards the King's table. At last, when he is come, the King drinks to him, and then sends him the cup which is of gold, and he drinks it off, and then rides back again with the cup in his hand. I went from table to table to see the Bishops and all others at their dinner, and was infinitely pleased with it. And at the Lords' table, I met with William Howe, and he spoke to my Lord for me, and he did give me four rabbits and a pullet, and so I got it, and Mr Creed and I got Mr Minshell to give us some bread, and so we at a stall eat it, as everybody else did what they could get. I took a great deal of pleasure to go up and down, and look upon the ladies, and to hear the music of all sorts, but above all, the 24 violins. About six at night they had dined, and I went up to my wife and thus met with a pretty lady, Mrs Frankleyn, and kissed them both. And strange it is to think that these two days have held up fair till now that all is done, and the King gone out of the Hall; and then it fall a-raining and thundering and lightening as I have not seen it do for some years: which people did take great notice of; God's blessing of the work of these two days, which is a foolery to take too much notice of such things. I observed little disorder in all this, only the King's footmen had got hold of the canopy, and would keep it from the Barons of the Cinque Ports, which they endeavoured to force from them again, but could not do it till my Lord Duke of Albemarle caused it to be put into Sir R. Pye's hand till to-morrow to be decided. At Mr Bowyer's; a great deal of company, some I knew, others I did not. Here we stayed upon the leads and below till it was late, expecting to see the fireworks, but they were not performed tonight: only the City had a light like a glory round about it, with bonfires. At last, I went to King Street, and there sent Crockford to my father's and my house, to tell them I could not come home tonight, because of the dirt, and a coach could not be had. And so I took my wife and Mrs Frankleyn (who I proffered the civility of lying with my wife at Mrs Hunt's to-night) to Axe Yard, in which, at the further end, there were three great bonfires, and a great many gallants, men and women; and they laid hold of us, and would have us drink the King's health upon our knees, kneeling upon a faggot, which we all did, they drinking to us one after another, which we thought a strange frolic; but these gallants continued there a great while, and I wondered to see how the ladies did tipple. At last I sent my wife and her bedfellow to bed, and Mr Hunt and I went in with Mr Thornbury (who did give the company all their wine, he being yeoman of the wine-cellar to the King); and there, with his wife and two of his sisters, and some gallant sparks that were there, we drank the King's health, and nothing else, till one of the gentlemen fell down stark drunk, and there lay; and I went to my Lord's pretty well. But no sooner abed with Mr Shepley but my head began to turn, and I to vomit, and if ever I was foxed it was now, which I cannot say yet, because I fell asleep, and slept till morning.

Samuel Pepys, 1661

24th

Helped to pack Jack's boots and things. Said goodbye to him, as he goes up to Town today; Annie Bell, Ann & I put on our swell bonnets & drove to the trysting place [on their way to Cheltenham Races], Smyth's Livery Stables; Colonel Coley was the only one there. Ann introduced us & he took us into the little room to wait for the rest, presently Mr Conway came & last Miss Podmore & her cousin Miss M (?). Mr Croker sat on the box blowing his horn all the way down the promenade which sounded very cheery, Annie Bell Colonel Coley and I sat behind then the Sitwells when we picked them up & the servants were put inside. In Pittville it began to rain & tho not heavy never stopped till we arrived at the race

course at Beckford, we were very early & thought we had mistaken the day. We had a very good luncheon. Colonel Coley helped everyone & scarcely had anything himself; the races were poor, I won a pair of gloves from Colonel Coley as I bet on 'Blue Bonnet' which Holmann was riding; there were only three races all day: jokes & puns & laughter & noise never ceased on our drag; just as we started to come home it began to rain again but nothing could damp spirits which rose higher and higher as the day proceeded The country round Beckford is quite lovely, so hilly & yet so beautifully cultivated like a garden. I saw a little piece of May out. Everything went off so beautifully except that Major Sitwell asked to drive and was not allowed; coming home we sat in the same order which could not have been improved except that Miss Podmore sat on the box. We got home at half past seven after the most delightful day I have spent this year, it was better than ten Balls.

A 'YOUNG LADY', 1868

25th

Maxpopple dined and slept here with four of his family, much amused with what they heard and saw. By good fortune a ventriloquist and partial juggler came in, and we had him in the library after dinner. He was a half-starved wretched-looking creature, who seemed to have ate more fire than bread. So I caused him to be well stuffed, and gave him a guinea, rather to his poverty than to his skill.

SIR WALTER SCOTT, 1829

26th

I went with Mr Brown to Greenwich, where I visited Mr Flamsteed, saw his two famous clocks of a year run, which varied at that time 2 and 30; also his thermometer, called a perpetual motion, because moved by itself, as the mercury rises and falls with the weather. From the top of his house I had a very fair prospect of the river, city, and country. Then I returned by boat to London through a vast number of ships of all sorts; and after my landing went to the top or flame of the pyramid or Monument of the fire of London, being two hundred and two feet high, and was carried up by three hundred and forty-five stone steps and twenty-seven steps of iron, under which there are seventeen more leading into the cellar, in all making three hundred and eighty nine; and then I returned to Camberwell.

ROLAND DAVIES, 1689

27th

I was surprised to see women carrying heath from Quantock almost half naked, they generally put all the rags they have on on the occasion as they find the Heath to tear their peticoats. One woman seemed to have nothing but a flannel peticoat on. I could not see what was the matter but while I passed by she sat down and two others put a large bundle of heather on her to cover. I took no notice but went on yet thought they should have been further removed from the side of the road. The day not quite so cold on the Hill as the time before.

WILLIAM HOLLAND, 1812

28th

Bought 6 pigs last Wednesday 4 at 24/0 and 2 at 26/0 each. I got 2 at 24/0 and 2 at 26/- so that I owe Baker for [my] pigs £5-0-0. The least are the best pigs. I had them bring directly and done styes up and put them in and with the exception of the two over the way who cough, they are going on allright. Very clear.

Went round money hunting again last night and got some more tickets today. The weather has been very warm this last day or two and now it rains well and looks like it. I have sowed some convolvulus, aster and stock seed today and stuck nearly all my peas in Q.G. and some down the Common. Poll Townsend's baby died yesterday. Saw Netta Thursday night, it was a beautiful night, warm, moon light and dry. The nightingales singing lovely. We stopped and talked latish Frank Nailsman here. A good deal of excitement and interest just now about the Reform Bill. It is expected it be settled now. Jack Thomson married last Tuesday at Chiselhampton. Sent 17 dozen of lettuce to market and 2 dozen cabbages. Went to Great Milton sale last Monday and had a good hard days work of it but I didn't mind it much. The trees are coming out in leaf and the plum and early fruit trees are out well now but there is not much blossom this year. Onions are up in Q.G. and Common and G. well and potatoes are up but rather straggling – growing well. Wheat looks yellow. E. Clinkard and Liz and I sat down the garden last night and they sang and played. Beautiful night. Mrs Harper Sen. is much against our courting now, for what reason I don't know. Heard from Ted Watson, he is got over there all right but can say nothing else yet. Bought broccoli. Snows Early White, Winter and dwarf chrysanthemums, Turnip and carrot seed today. Planted row of peas and finished potatoes down common yesterday.

JOSEPH TURRILL, 1866

29th

Last night – to relieve myself for a moment from correcting that silly book Flush, – oh, what a waste of time – I will record Bruno Walter. He is a swarthy, fattish, man; not at all smart. Not at all the "great conductor". He is a little Slav, a little semitic. He is very nearly mad; that is, he cant get 'the poison' as he called it of Hitler out of him. "You must not think of the Jews" he kept on saying "You must think of this awful reign of intolerance. You must think of the whole state of the world. It is terrible – terrible. That this meanness, that this pettiness, should be possible! Our Germany – which I loved – with our tradition – our culture – We are now a disgrace." Then he told us how you cant talk above a whisper. There are spies everywhere. He had to sit in the window of his hotel in Leipzig? a whole day, telephoning. All the time soldiers were marching. They never stop marching. And on the wireless, between the turns, they play military music. Horrible horrible! He hopes for the monarchy as the only hope. He will never go back there. His orchestra had been in existence for 150 years: but it is the spirit of the whole that is awful. We must band together. We must refuse to meet any German. We must say that they are uncivilised. We will not trade with them or play with them – we must make them feel themselves outcasts – not by fighting them; by ignoring them. Then he swept off to music. He has the intensity – genius? – which makes him live every thing he feels. Described conducting: must know every player.

VIRGINIA WOOLF, 1933

30th

Mr Greene came and said that Dr Owtram, Archdeacon of Leicester, has castigated the clergy, saying that not one in a hundred is sober, but they all love the bottle, and that he has heard this from a most illustrious nobleman. We hear that Mistress Mary and Mistress Sibyl, the daughters of Sir Edward Nicholls, have met at Old and have been very ill. We had a litter of ferrets. Last night the servants of four farmers, with Mr Baxter's man and Henry Lichfield, went to Draughton to bring home the first drawing of beer, which they bought from Palmer. On the way back sixteen or seventeen Draughton men met them with stakes and began to lay about them; but being few and unarmed against a greater number of armed men, they were easily beaten, and Mr Baxter's man has had his skull laid bare in several places and almost fractured.

THOMAS ISHAM, 1673

MAY

1st

Up betimes: called by my tailor, and there first put on a summer suit this year; but it was not my fine one of flowered tabby vest, and coloured camelott tunic, because it was too fine with the gold lace at the bands, that I was afraid to be seen in it; but put on the stuff suit I made the last year, which is now repaired; and so did go to the office in it, and sat all the morning, the day looking as if it would be foul. At noon home to dinner, and there find my wife extraordinary fine, with her flowered tabby gown that she made two years ago, now laced exceeding pretty; and, indeed, was fine all over; and mighty earnest to go, though the day was very lowering; and she would have me put on my fine suit, which I did. And so anon we went alone through the town with our new liveries of serge, and the horses' manes and tails tied with red ribbons, and the standards gilt with varnish, and all clean, and green reins, that people did mightily look upon us; and, the truth is, I did not see any coach more pretty, though more gay, than ours, all the day.

SAMUEL PEPYS, 1669

2nd

I saw also this day many milkmaids dancing in the streets, with their pails upon their heads dressed with garlands, and hung with plate of great value.

ROLAND DAVIES, 1689

3rd

Dined at home; and though I ate only some minced veal, some spinach, and eggs, in moderate quantity, felt myself greatly oppressed, so as to afford a strong instance in confirmation of the opinion, that a solitary dinner, for whatever reason, does not so soon pass away as one ate in company. The reason first occurring would be, that for a dinner ate in company some time was taken; but the fact does not seem to correspond; or I have made, if I am not mistaken, as many intervals in dining alone, and have yet found that digestion does not take place so quickly. Besides the effect that company may have on the mind, much, I apprehend, is to be ascribed to the action given to the lungs and stomach by talking.

WILLIAM WINDHAM, 1787

4th

I had no companion inside the coach. We stopped for luncheon at Oxford, and reached the station house on the Great Western Railway at or near Maidenhead a little before 5 o'clock. The station is at the twenty fifth milestone from London. The railroad is carried on a very high embankment across the meadows between Maidenhead and Bray. I believe it will soon be completed as far as Twyford. The coach drove into the station yard where the passengers alighted, leaving their luggage with the coach which proceeds a little onwards and reaches the level of the railway by a road constructed for the purpose. There the carriages are placed each on a railway truck, ready to be hooked on to the train when it comes to that point. Meantime the passengers receive a railway ticket to London which purports to be worth 5s 6d. We arrived ten minutes before the hour of starting. There is much less bustle than at the Birmingham – Manchester railroad stations and no appearance of the transit of merchandize as yet. The railway is also on a different construction from those on which I have hitherto travelled, the width between the rails being 7 ft. and consequently the coaches are as wide, each

holding eight persons, or four in two breadths. The distance to Paddington 22 miles is traversed in 50 mins. including stoppages. The coach in which I travelled held only myself and Mr Palmer, M.P. for Berkshire, a very pleasant gentlemanly person. At the Paddington station the coach is met by a pair of horses, the passengers resume their seats, and the journey is continued by the Edgeware Road to Oxford Street, and I took a coach at the Green Man and proceeded to Ibbetson's Hotel, Vere Street, a quiet orderly place with good quiet sleeping rooms. Dinner and tea and to bed.

F. E. WITTS, 1839

5th

After sitting on the wall around the fountain in the middle of Trafalgar Square, eating my sandwiches and feeding the Pigeons with the crumbs, I listened for a moment to the roar of the traffic around three sides of the Square as I stood in the centre quite alone, what time one fat old pigeon, all unconcerned, was treading another. It was an extraordinary experience: motor horns tooted incessantly and it seemed purposelessly, so that one had the fancy that all London was out for a joy-ride – it was a great British Victory perhaps, or Peace Day.

Then walked down Whitehall to Westminster Bridge in time to see the 2 o'clock boat start upstream for Kew. I loitered by the old fellow with the telescope who keeps his pitch by Boadicea: I saw a piper of the Scots Guards standing near gazing across the river but at nothing in particular – just idling as I was. I saw another man sitting on the stone steps and reading a dirty fragment of newspaper. I saw the genial, red-faced sea-faring man in charge of the landing stage strolling up and down his small domain, – chatting, jesting, spitting, and making fast a rope or so. Everything was *alive* to the finger tips, vividly shining, pulsating.

W. N. P. BARBELLION, 1916

6th

A sweet morning. We have put the finishing stroke to our bower, and here we are sitting in the orchard. It is one o'clock. We are sitting upon a seat under the wall, which I found my brother building up, when I came to him with his apple. He had intended that it should have been done before I came. It is a nice, cool, shady spot. The small birds are singing, lambs bleating, cuckow calling, the thrush sings by fits, Thomas Ashburner's axe is going quietly (without passion) in the orchard, hens are cackling, flies humming, the women talking together at their doors, plumb and pear trees are in blossom – apple trees greenish – the opposite woods green, the crows are cawing. We have heard ravens. The ash trees are in blossom, birds flying all about us. The stitchwort is coming out, there is one budding lychnis, the primroses are passing their prime, celandine, violets, and wood sorrel for ever more, little geraniums and pansies on the wall.

DOROTHY WORDSWORTH, 1802

7th

I play with my trains before breakfast. After breakfast I go with Pat, Mother and Miss Greer to Peter Robinson's and Libertys to get some things. Then Miss Greer and I return to Victoria Gate to wait for my horse after waiting three quarters of an hour we go round to the other gate and find that the horse had been there all the time and had just left. So I arrange to ride in the afternoon. Then Ian Crossley comes and we have lunch. After lunch I show Ian Miss Greer and Pat my trains etc. Then I have the most glorious ride of my life for we galloped our horses as hard as they would go. After tea I had a lovely game with Pat and Miss Greer. And then I took up my trains (for good) and stayed with Miss Grigg.

JOHN KNIGHT (AGED 12), 1912

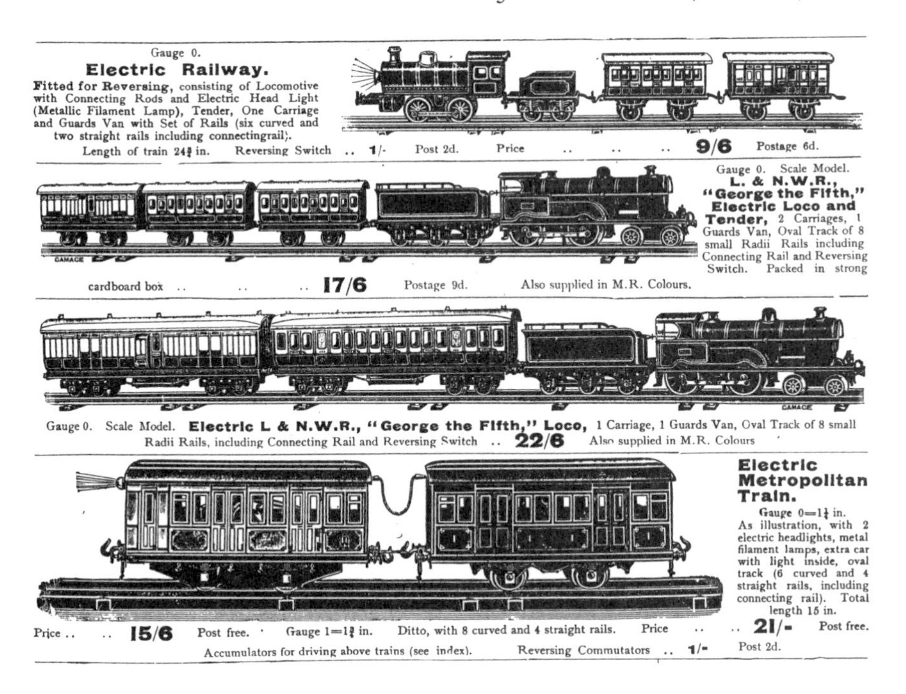

8th

Read the papers. Went to the theatre, where I was first in the house (alas! for duty paid for). Superintended and directed the new farce of the *Veiled Portrait*; afterwards read Kenney's farce of *Love Extempore*, which went off rather heavily. Dickens called with his wife and Forster, and asked me to dine *en famille,* to which I agreed. Dined with Dickens. Forster after dinner accompanied me to the Haymarket, where I saw an act and a half of a most wretchedly acted play, *The Wife*; it was *offensive.* Passed on to Madame Vestris's theatre, where I saw a stupid piece well done.

WILLIAM MACREADY, 1838

9th

This turned out a very good day. I went into the Sunday School, heard the children say and explain their Catechism. Grace Chidgey the Mistress to my great surprize brought a son of hers and placed him in the Upper Class who were saying to me, a short squat shrimpy cub with a large white face, rough with the marks of small pox, and without a neck at all. It seemed like a large block fastened between two shoulders. He was very like the Old Clerk his Grandfather. I was very surprised she pushed him there without my calling for him but there he stood rolling his large eyes like a large owl and grinning at everyone. The boy was not a fool but I did not perceive that he could say anything better than other children but Mammy was wondrous proud of the Cub. From the Sunday School I came to the house and read the Morning Service to my Family.

WILLIAM HOLLAND, 1813

10th

Mr Wadley called promptly at 1 p.m., complete with taxi, to transport me to Park Royal. Here I was able to choose from large array of cycles – but there seems every style of bike except *my* style – nothing in small enough frame.

The manager, like some Aladdin on a magic carpet, goes off and in next-to-no-time returns with a suitable size bicycle in the back of a car.

This is knocked up together and seems O.K. I then get photographed riding this "gift horse" up and down side roads and then we all adjourn to nearby tea hut and take in tea and cakes after this rather exhausting ordeal.

Now all is finished and I ride home 15 miles on this new mount – having got a bell for same at convenient shop near at hand.

Have to be very careful on a new and somewhat different type of bike. One gets so used to one bike, especially when it's seemed a part of oneself for over 14 years – so much so, that the least difference on another bike is apt to flummux one. Just a bit.

Find the 3-speed operates in reverse order to my old one and so I am letting in "high" instead of "low" when at my lasp gasp, which brings me to a standstill in awkward places.

Must get this order of working into my mind if possible. It is such a purely automatic thing, that it is rather a bore to have to *think* which way it goes.

But, on the whole, except for a certain engine-like clanking room the gear case, it is going all right and is rather a majestic-looking bike, and *such* a lot of it. (Determine either to scrap a lot of it or change it at first opportunity.)

Get home O.K., and having got a similar cyclometer at "Curry's" on way home, put this on so as to lose no further mileage recording (begrudged the 15 miles that will not count in my records). Went out then and got up 9 miles on cyclometer – testing it for accuracy over a given route measured many times over by old one. It tallies O.K., so I am satisfied.

'JOHN SOWERBY', 1938

11th

I know not whether to have faith in presentiments or not; but once or twice in my life 'coming events' have 'cast their shadows before,' in a manner almost supernatural. To-day, I experienced the most gloomy melancholy I ever felt, without at *the time* having a cause for so doing; but, late in the evening, as I was sitting with the Princess of Wales, she received a letter; I observed her change colour while perusing its contents, and, covering her face with her hands, she exclaimed, 'Oh! something dreadful has happened; I cannot read it aloud'; but she pushed the letter towards me, and signed to me to do so. The letter was from Madame de Haeckle, giving an account of Mr Perceval's [the Prime Minister] assassination, by a man of the name of Bellingham, as he was going into the House of Commons. – Revenge of private injuries was stated as the cause which led to the commission of this crime – that is to say, *conceived* injuries. Madame de Haeckle added, 'God grant this may not be the signal for many coming woes!' – The panic struck us all, but no one more than the Princess. I never saw her so deeply affected before, or since.

LADY CHARLOTTE BURY, 1812

12th

To London. Lord Sunderland being Lord President and Secretary of State, was made Knight of the Garter and prime favourite. –

This day there was such a storm of wind as had seldom happened, being a sort of hurricane. It kept the flood out of the Thames, so that people went on foot over several places above bridge. Also an earthquake in several places in England about the time of the storm.

JOHN EVELYN, 1687

13th

Myself, Mr Dodson, and servant at church in the morn. During the time we was at church, Mr Richardson and my brother came to see me. We dined on a calf's heart pudding, a piece of beef, greens, and green sallet. Mr Joseph Hartley came to bring me a new wigg. Paid him in full for a new wigg, £1. 15s., and new mounting an old one, 4s.

THOMAS TURNER, 1764

14th

Wm. and John set off into Yorkshire after dinner at ½ past 2 o'clock, cold pork in their pockets. I left them at the turning of the Lowwood bay under the trees. My heart was so full that I could hardly speak to W. when I gave him a farewell kiss. I sate a long time upon a stone at the margin of the lake, and after a flood of tears my heart was easier. The lake looked to me, I knew not why, dull and melancholy, and the weltering on the shores seemed a heavy sound. I walked as long as I could amongst the stones of the shore. The wood rich in flowers; a beautiful yellow, palish yellow, flower, that looked thick, round, and double, and smelt very sweet – I supposed it was a ranunculus. Crowfoot, the grassy-legged rabbit-toothed white flower, strawberries, geranium, scentless violets, anemones two kinds, orchises, primroses. The heckberry very beautiful, the crab coming out as a low shrub. Met a blind man, driving a very large beautiful Bull, and a cow – he walked with two sticks. Came home by Clappersgate The valley very green; many sweet views up to Rydale head, when I could juggle away the fine houses; but they disturbed me, even more than when I have been happier; one beautiful view of the Bridge, without Sir Michael's. Sate down very often, though it was cold. I resolved to write a journal of the time till W. and J. return, and I set about keeping my resolve, because I will not quarrel with myself, and because I shall give Wm. pleasure by it when he comes home again.

DOROTHY WORDSWORTH, 1800

15th

My walk to town to-day was after ten, and prodigiously hot: I dined with Lord Shelburn, and have desired Mrs Pratt, who lodges there, to carry over Mrs Wall's tea; I hope she will do it, and they talk of going in a fortnight; My way is this: I leave my best gown and periwig at Mrs Vanhomrigh's, then walk up the Pall Mall, through the Park, out at Buckingham House, and so to Chelsea a little beyond the church: I set out about sunset, and get here in something less than an hour: it is two good miles, and just five thousand seven hundred and forty-eight steps; so there is four miles a day walking, without reckoning what I walk while I staying town. When I pass the Mall in the evening it is prodigious to see the number of ladies walking there; and I always cry shame at the ladies of Ireland, who never walk at all, as if their legs were of no use, but to be laid aside.

JONATHAN SWIFT, 1711

16th

I did wake at the proper time, or was woke by the children; and at five o'clock Louisa and I took an exquisite walk through the wood (Whitewood). We went very slowly, and at almost every step Louisa called out, and with justice, "Oh wonders!" The nightingales were singing in great numbers; we saw two of them perched in the middle of a tall oak. There was also a blackcap hopping among some low bushes . . . I went a good way across the earth, with a trowel, to the bogs to get flowers. What grows here chiefly is a cotton grass, which has a stalk about four inches high, tipped with a waving substance which envelops the seeds. It looks just like the cotton which is put into ink-glasses; when it is in great abundance, the place seems to be covered with snow. I took up several plants of the *Drosera Rotundifolia,* or sundew; it is not yet in flower; the leaves are small and red, and covered with glutinous hairs, which catch flies in great numbers. I took up besides what I think is the *Pedicularis sylvatica*, a pretty pink flower; and, with some others, a most extraordinary plant, which looks like the Creeping cistus. It runs along the ground in singular joints, which twist and creep in a singular manner, and are all covered with either very minute leaves or prickles. I brought these home, with Louisa's help, planted them in my gardens, and came in at half-past seven.

Mamma takes a walk in the wood every morning, to hear the

nightingales and gather lilies of the valley, which are now extremely abundant, and when gathered scent almost half the house; besides which, they are very beautiful. I particularly admire the curl outwards of the blossom.

EMILY SHORE (AGED 13), 1833

17th

Morning, rode by Puckeridge to Ware, where we baited, and had some showers, which raised the washes upon the road to that height that passengers from London that were upon the road swam, and a poor higgler was drowned, which prevented our travelling for many hours, yet towards evening adventured with some country people, who conducted us (after we had passed Hogsden, which has a fountain in the midst of the town and several very good houses) over the meadows, whereby we missed the deepest of the Wash at Cheshunt, though we rode to the saddle-skirts for a considerable way, but got safe to Waltham Cross, where we lodged.

RALPH THORESBY, 1695

18th

This is a very buisy day as we are going to have a party this evening something larger than usual. We had four to dinner and about fifty or sixty in the evening. The plan of manageing these parties are thus : – there are two men besides myself, one opened the door and let the Company in, I shewed them into a parlour where there was three maidservants to make tea and give it to them and take off their cloaks and bonnets, and the other man shewed them up into the drawingroom and gave in their names as lowd as he can bawl in the drawingroom. There is very good singing and music in their way. After they have been here some time, we carrey them up some refreshments on trays and hand about amongst them. This is all kinds of sweet cakes and biscuits, lemonade, ashet, negos, orangade and many other pleasent drinks but the best is the different kind of ices. This is stuf made of ice pounded, mixed with cream, and juce of strawberrey, some of apricot and oranges – in short, there are many different kinds. It's quite as cold as eating ice alone. It's eat out of glass sawsers with a spoon. It's from ten to sixteen shillings a quart, it depends on what fruit it's made of. The company comes jeneraly about ten or eleven o'clock and stays until one or two in the morning. Sweet hearting matches are very often made up at these parties.

William Tayler, 1837

19th

The flowers of the lillys of the alley, which grow in vast quantitys in these Broughton woods, are now ripe and open. Here is come some men from Coronel Bierly's, that is above fifty miles of, to begg lieve to gather some. Others are come, some twenty, some thirty, some forty miles. There are at least gather'd in these woods yearly as many as is worth 60*L* or 100*L*.; for when they are dry'd they are commonly sold for seventeen, eighteen, and nineteen shillings a pound [for their medicinal value].

ABRAHAM DE LA PRYME, 1697

20th

I set out for Brighton this morning in a light coach, which performed the distance in six hours – otherwise the journey was uncomfortable. Three women, the very specimens of womankind, – I mean trumpery, – a child who was sick, but afterwards looked and smiled, and was the only thing like company. The road is pleasant enough till it gets into the Wealds of Sussex, a huge succession of green downs which sweep along the sea-coast for many miles. Brighton seems grown twice as large since 1815. It is a city of loiterers and invalids – a Vanity Fair for pipers, dancing of bears, and for the feats of Mr Punch.

SIR WALTER SCOTT, 1828

21st

Walked in the morning to Aber and back; bought a penny loaf at a little shop in Aber, and ate it in the Church yard under the shade of a yew tree. A young foal and its mother (I should suppose, belonging to the parson) were my only visiters. They came and looked at me; 'ye know ye need not fear me,' said I, 'for I would not so much as frighten any living creature intentionally.' For the first time I saw the manner of decking a Welsh grave; many of these were trimmed with – what had been green and pretty, but were all now withered, like those interred underneath. I sat a long time at my dinner, on a nice smooth grave-stone of blue slate, refreshed by the coolness of the shade, and a fine view of Beaumaris bay and town before me. Father! thou never ceasest to be kind to me.

Everything was new to me. As I suppose I am not so wise as Solomon, I can take delight in these varied scenes. I go along, speaking to no one, visiting no gentleman's domain, or attempting to see anything that is not open to every one; for I am of too retiring a disposition to intrude myself upon any one's notice: the open road and the mountain path suffice me.

I was much tired out when I got home to a late repast of tea. Mr Pritchard sent his daughter up at 6 o'clock to my bed room, to say he was going to Pentir, and wished to know if I would go with him. Tired as I was, I went; we could not talk, but I noticed that whoever he met, he had always something pleasant to say to them, for they all looked pleased and good-humoured. At last we got near to a public house at Pentir, where Mr Pritchard seemed to be going. I took leave of him here, and returned leisurely home alone, pleased although tired. My morning's walk had been 11 miles, and this, 7m. – 18.

ELLEN WEETON, 1825

22nd

Dr Owtram returned from Leicester. They say that Mr Hanbury won £100 at Boston by his cocks' winning. Dr Owtram returned from Leicester [sic.] Mother went to Faxton with sister

Mary. A sweep came here who could climb chimneys without instruments and clean them instantly. Benjamin Williams came from Northampton and said he had heard we had sunk and taken thirty Dutch ships. Mr Eyre came to see Dr Owtram.

THOMAS ISHAM, 1672

23rd

Lent my Maid, Winfred, to buy a Gown, 1. 1. 0. Gave to Dalliday of France-Green losing a Horse 5. 0. Recd for Butter this Evening at 10d. per Pint, 5. 0. To a travelling Man and Woman who sold all kinds of trifling Books &c – Robinson Crusoe – 2s/6d – The Life of Bampfield More Carew 2s/0d – Complete Fortune Teller – 9d – Laugh and grow fat 6d, in all 5. 9. Nancy bought a smelling Bottle of them. Nancy also bought a very handsome coloured Callico Gown of a travelling People by name Burdon from London, this Afternoon for which she paid 2. 10. 0.

JAMES WOODFORDE, 1792

24th

Rose at 6. We sat out for Bristol with Mr Powell. The journey there was but very indifferent, the weather being very bad and raining, but it was agreeable to me as it gave me the company now and then of Mrs Marshall. The road is full of stones and the worst I ever went. When we came there to our inn and had dined we walked to see the College Church.

I began now to be extremely uneasy, finding myself incapable of entertaining Mrs Marshall as I would do and Mr Powell so much more diverting and, as I judged, agreeable to her. Mr Powell is a strange, merry, rattling young fellow in the company of ladies. His conversation consists very much in joining together the most odd contradictory ideas in order to create a laugh. It is my misfortune that I cannot talk to the ladies with that indifference that is necessary to make me agreeable to them. This is the reason why they are always upon their guard towards me, and though Mrs Marshall will take a thousand freedoms and play abundance of little tricks with Mr

Powell she never said a familiar thing to me once or did a familiar action. I don't know how it is but there is I believe in me something of a forbidding reserved air in me that makes the ladies especially afraid to be familiar with me. And yet I remember I have sometimes been able in ladies' company to talk very freely. Mrs Marshall is of a pretty gay temper and loves nothing better than to laugh and be merry. They were continually complaining that we were dull and desired Mr Powell to make them laugh.

It rained so much that we were fain to stay at home from 5 o'clock all night. Bristol is but an indifferent city. The generality of the houses are not good and the streets very narrow, but there is one square which is extremely handsome and pleasant and is equal to most of our best squares in London.

DUDLEY RYDER, 1716

25th

In London all people go about three o'clock to make their morning calls; the consequence is that everybody is out at the same time, and it rarely happens that anybody is found at home, which the visitor knows very well. If by any rare chance they are at home, and wish not to be disturbed by visitors, they very cooly desire the servant to say, "Not at home" – a detestable practice; for, though its meaning is well understood by the visitor, it is not so by the servant, who is thus taught to lie. Besides, why not say they are engaged? which would be just as useful, and more honest.

I think much better of London now than when we first came, which was in very gloomy weather; and I admire many parts exceedingly. But still I am horrified at the mischief done by the smoke. Almost all the houses are blackened, the yards and back premises are covered with soot, the trunks of all the trees are black, all plants become dingy, clothes get tarnished by the smoke, the hands can hardly be kept clean, and in some winds great puffs of smoke enter the open windows. The extreme blackness and dinginess of the sparrows (which are numerous) is also worthy of note. I see jackdaws sometimes; they cannot be made blacker, but doubtless lose all their gloss, and I suppose their grey polls are darkened.

EMILY SHORE (AGED 15), 1835

26th

The bells ringing for the Ascension. Went to church with my Father through the sunny golden fields variegated with clover and daisies and ground ivy. The Church bell tolling for service through the elms. A small congregation, but many bees buzzing about the Church windows as if a swarm were flying. My Father says this has happened on several Ascension days and once the Churchwarden John Bryant came after a swarm of his to the Church on Ascension day, clinking a frying pan and shovel. My Father told him that the bees showed the people the way to Church.

Every morning Summerflower brings splendid watercresses from Kellaways Mill. Last Tuesday morning I was out early before breakfast, walking along the common on Maud Heath between the may hedges. Just as I heard the breakfast bell ring across the Common from the Rectory and turned in at the black gate a man crossed the stile carrying a basket. He said his name was Summerflower, that he had fasted since yesterday morning and that he could buy no breakfast before he had got watercresses to sell.

FRANCIS KILVERT, 1870

27th

To business. In the afternoon Priestly and his wife drove over to fetch us back to tea. It was a most delicious day, the wind pleasant and refreshing and tempering the heat and the country looks most lovely, especially when we turned out of Lewisham and drove round by Brockley. We had a very pleasant evening, a little music etc. and returned home thankful, refreshed and strengthened.

CHARLES COMPTON, 1882

28th

The 28th day of May Thomas Stafford was beheaded on Tower hill, by nine of the clock, master Wode being his gostly father [officiating priest]; and after there were three more drawn from the Tower, and through London unto Tyburn, and there they were hanged and quartered; and the morrow after was master Stafford quartered, and hanged on a cart, and so to Newgate to boil.

The same morning was burned beyond Saint George's parish three men for heresy, at this side Newington.

HENRY MACHYN, 1557

29th

By 3 in the morning we are under sail again with a small gale; and at anchor in Harwich Road about 3 in the afternoon. But about 12 a-clock all our ships, remembering the festival day, fired so many guns that they were buried in their own smoke; and at dinner we are fain to make shift with an excellent salad and eggs, a fillet of veal roasted, a grand dish of mackerel, and a large lobster – so hard is our fare at sea: and all washed down with good Margate ale, March beer, and, last of all, a good bowl of punch.

HENRY TEONGUE, 1678

30th

A very tempestuous night. At last Thomas came. He said he was at his Uncle Samuel Sully's and seems stubborn and hardly thinks he has done amiss. I spoke to Thomas sternly and remonstrated for his conduct. He had nothing to say in his defence but still did not seem sorrowful or ask pardon so I gave him Notice to Quit this place in a month's time. This is an inconvenient thing for me but what can one do. If servants are to do as they please there is no end to all subordination, indeed the tribe are come to a sad pass at this time of day. They have little sense of Honour or Morality and act the Masters rather than the Servants, they scarce ever do the Service they engage to do and if you speak to them they are highly affronted and make a Practice of Hiring themselves to this or that place and go from one to another by way of variety and Amusement. Nay they engage at many places at a time and pick and chuse where they will go and this without Scruple or Notice to the persons who are disappointed. There needs some effectual regulation among these Profligate and Unprincipled set of Beings. My wife and Margaret have been reading the History of Sir Walter Raleigh.

WILIAM HOLLAND, 1807

31st

At 3 o'clock I left Grantham, mount the hill to Gunnerby village, where appear'd something like a feast, which I love to see, or to hear the squeak of a fiddle; and allways look about for a cricket-match, or Fives playing: for little recreation have the poor, and but a short summer.

JOHN BYNG, 1792

JUNE

1st

In the even, Mr Banister and myself smoked a pipe or two with Tho. Durrant, purely to keep Mr Banister from quarrelling; his wife, big with child, lame of one hand, and very much in liquor, being out in the middle of the street, amongst a parcil of girls, boys, etc., Oh, an odoius sight, and that more so to an husband.

THOMAS TURNER, 1764

2nd

In the morning we observed that the scarlet beans were drooping in the leaves in great numbers, owing, we guess, to an insect. We sate awhile in the orchard – then we went to the old carpenter's about the hurdles. Yesterday an old man called, a grey-headed man, above 70 years of age. He said he had been a soldier, that his wife and children had died in Jamaica. He had a beggar's wallet over his shoulders; a coat of shreds and patches, altogether of a drab colour; he was tall, and though his body was bent, he had the look of one used to have been upright. I talked a while, and then gave him a piece of cold bacon and a penny. Said he, 'You're a fine woman!" I could not help smiling; I suppose he meant, 'You're a kind woman'. Afterwards a woman called, travelling to Glasgow. After dinner we went into Frank's field, crawled up the little glen, and planned a seat, then went to Mr Olliff's Hollins and sate there – found a beautiful shell-like purple fungus in Frank's field. After tea we walked to Butterlip How, and backwards and forwards there. All the young oak tree leaves are dry as powder. A cold south wind portending rain.

DOROTHY WORDSWORTH, 1802

3rd

We hoist sale; and, with Essex on the left hand, and Kent on the right, we come to the Buoy in the Oaze – a thing as strange to me as was the rest of their dialect. Hither many of our seamen's wives follow their husbands, and several other young women accompany their sweethearts, and sing *Loth to depart* in punch and brandy; so that our ship was that night well furnished, but ill manned, few of them being well able to keep watch had there been occasion.

HENRY TEONGUE, 1675

4th

Kingston this morning for various things. Job to do shopping, everywhere jammed up with things – extra traffic coming through for Whitsun making it still more congested. Went home and had some refreshment – then off down the by-pass and Portsmouth road to Ripley (picked up a sixpence on the way). At Ripley turned left (where it says 3½ to Horsley). Went this way, mostly gradual, some steep uphill, to East Horsley, then on to Leatherhead. Very high up here, fine views and well worth climbing for.

I think the new bike which I rode this journey is getting "run in" now – it goes much better than when I first had it. Dallied about a bit in Leatherhead, then came home the Ashtead and Epsom way, 30½ miles round.

After tea at home went to the Portsmouth road, had a "Wallsey" ice and came home through Ditton. 41 miles for the day; nothing like I used to do, but better than of late – warmer to-day – could ride without overcoat although still in June. Perhaps after all we shall have a less severe summer than seemed likely.

'JOHN SOWERBY', 1938

5th

This morning did give my wife £4, to lay out upon lace and other things for herself. Sir W. Pen and I went out with Sir R. Slingsby to bowls in his alley, and there had good sport. I took my flageolet, and played upon the leads in the garden, where Sir W. Pen came out in his shirt into his leads, and there we stayed talking and singing and drinking great draughts of claret, and eating botargo and bread and butter will twelve at night, it being moonshine; and so to bed, very near fuddled.

SAMUEL PEPYS, 1661

6th

To the Carlyles', where we were received with great cordiality in the library, which looks well suited to the work performed there. Wax medallions of Edward Sterling and his son hang over the chimney-piece. Thomas Carlyle came in in his blouse, and we presently got, I know not how, to Swedenborgianism. Swedenborg was a thoroughly practical, mechanical man, and was in England learning shipbuilding. He went into a little inn in Bishopsgate Street, and was eating his dinner very fast, when he thought he saw in the corner of the room a vision of Jesus Christ, who said to him, 'Eat slower.' This was the beginning of all his visions and mysterious communications, of which he had enough in his day.

CAROLINE FOX, 1842

7th

Set out for Harpenden. Manor of Shires 5 miles off. A beautiful common. Kept Court at the Red Lyon and dined at the Bull on the Common. Treated by Whitearminger Esq., who lives at Rothampstead and ought to renew near 9 years gone. Warm hot weather. Set out at 3 and went thro' Woburn to Newport Pagnell

(fine road) except a mile of Sands which we avoided by going thro' the woods the 2nd. turning after you set out from Woburn on the right hand. Got to Newport at 9. They had put up a New Ring of Bells and all the people drunk and noisy. In great pain with the cholick. Took Turpentine which eased me for a few hours.

THOMAS WILSON, 1750

8th

Rose at 7 though called at 6. Dined at my brother's. Bought 5 yards of cloth to make a suit of clothes at 18s. per yard. Met with Cousin Watkins. Saw his house and shop he is fitting up. Will cost him a great deal of money to finish it. I wish it may turn to account. Bespoke a wig of Colebuck.

After 7 o'clock brother called me to go to park with sister. Saw great deal of company at least there but little good. Never was walking there before with a lady. A little perplexed how to behave with respect to the giving her the right or left hand when we turned back. At first changed sides with her to keep her of my right hand but at last observing that ceremony not much regarded by others, I kept my own side in going backwards or forwards.

DUDLEY RYDER, 1715

9th

Turning to the right, a lane of a mile brought me to the banks of the Trent, which I cross'd at Twiford Ferry; Pony was very quiet in the boat, but Blacky was much alarm'd: another six miles of good road, in the second crossing the Mersey navigation, (having one shower of rain by the way) we enter'd Derby. – Here every house was adorn'd with oaken boughs in honor of the old 29th May; and the boys preparing and begging for their bonfires. The Derby militia are assembled here; and disturbing (as at Northampton) the sick, and quiet, by their uproar. – I put up at the Bell Inn; unluckily for me the players are just gone. After a good dinner on rost fowl, and asparagus, I meant for a ride; but the evening became so thundery, and gloomy, that I cou'd scarcely see to write.

Afterwards I toured around the town, and long attended to the building of the new bridge over the Derwent; then return'd to see the roll-calling of the militia (no remark necessary) and hear their noisy, useless music, and drummings.

JOHN BYNG, 1790

10th

'Up before 7, brkft. Did a little work, then into the kitchen, made a custard and tarts, was very notable. Footman came to summon me to the Castle, slipped on a gown and went, discussed a knotty point, staid till past 1, found Mr, Mrs and Miss Pain when I came back. Dressed in brown Neg. and produced myself in parlor by 2, after having made a fricasse and set the codlin barr in order; were mighty agreeable, dined at 3, in due time went into ye garden, chatted, sang, drank T, at 6 they went. We to the Bentons, found a Mrs Brown and her screaming boy there, another Miss Something, also Mrs Booth and 2 Misses with her. Drank tea in a scream, after which went in the garden 5 or 6 of us.'

ELIZABETH RAPER, 1757

11th

A very fine morning. Mr Amen busy about the staddle, the haymakers in the field. All up and breakfast over. We shall have plenty of haymakers to offer by and by but these are more eaters than workers. Got the hay in most excellent order and began to carry between eleven and twelve. They continued till almost nine in the evening. Wm Frost mounted the rick and made a handsome round cock of the best hay that ever was put together and the largest crop that the two Paddocks were ever known to give – above five tons from three acres and a half. The great horse performed gloriously this day in bringing in the hay but Robert was as crabbed and surly as an old sow. Mr Woodhouse directed everything but Robert swilled the beer handsomely. My wife, Margaret and Betty gathered and bottled of many gooseberries before night. The haymakers had a good hot supper with plenty of beer and so all ended well and joyfully. Old man Bishop got his quantum and marched off home before night.

WILLIAM HOLLAND, 1800

12th

I was drawn out of doors for half an hour this evening and enjoyed it much; I came in stronger and better . . . . This morning the grand scarlet poppy blew . . . . Our roses are most splendid; the west side of the house is covered with them in the richest profusion, and one of the drawing-room windows is half hidden by them. The red roses [China] are also splendid, and reach as high up the house wall. Both species can be gathered from, and look in at, the second story.

I rose to-day an hour earlier than usual, i.e. at eleven o'clock. I am not strong enough yet to be up all day. This is the sixth Sunday on which I have not been able to go to church, that is, not since May 1. Indeed, if I could have gone, I should have seen, at least in the evening, what it is no loss to have missed seeing – a most shameful quarrel between two women for places, which delayed the service for full five minutes. A similar scene, I am told, took place last Sunday, when two girls actually fought and struck each other while the congregation were on their knees, and made a great hubbub till the clerk, with some difficulty, turned them out. Such conduct is really unexampled.

EMILY SHORE (AGED 16), 1836

13th

From Nunney we proceeded in front of Mr Shore's house at Whatley, and traversing the Frome Road, turned off to the left, and entered Vallis near the Farm House formerly occupied by the celebrated Mrs Rowe. My guidance was here most severely reprobated, as I afterwards understood, by those of the party who had fourwheeled carriages and two horses, on account of the difficulty of quartering: the ruts being very deep; Colonel [Capt.] Scobel's gig also, in endeavouring to cross out of one of the deep ravines, had a wheel broken, and was obliged to be conveyed to Vallis Farm, the Colonel [Capt.] and his son being received by other conveyances in the rear. I had before mentioned the bad state of the road, but added, that a great deal of the most interesting scenery would be lost if the Party went round by Mells, instead of pursuing this road. I am happy to say on arriving at the beautiful little Cottage at Elm, all these difficulties were forgotten; and having obtained Mr Blakeney's permission, the whole party shortly after sat down to an excellent repast provided by the different families who composed it: cold meats, fowls, tarts, tongues, salads, etc., abound in profusion: also every kind of liquor calculated to relieve the burning thirst, so many hours exposure to a hot sun had occasioned: we afterwards retired from the Cottage to the Cavern above the brook leaving the servants to finish the repast, and heard some excellent songs from the ladies, Captain Scobel, etc., whilst the wine was passing round.

John Skinner, 1822

14th

This afternoon Mrs Rich gave a very pleasant picnic in Berry's Hill Mead down by the river. The company, some 26, met at our house and then we moved down to the riverside through the meadows in picturesque groups and parties, the girls' pretty summer dresses lighting up the scene charmingly. There were the Riches, West Awdrys, Rookes, Strongs, Frederick Awdrys, Falwasser. Sweet Florence Rooke was there in her pony carriage looking fragile and lovely. She drove the picnic baskets down to our camping ground, but she did not stay long as the air blew fresh and chill by the river and the clouds were rising in the west. From under the oaks by the river we startled two lovers lying on the grass, and they went off laughing and blushing, in crimson confusion, routed by the army of horse and foot and chariots which bore down upon them from the steep brow of Berry's Hill, the chariots being two pony carriages and a donkey chair with Nettie Rich riding postilion on the donkey. Teddy built a fireplace cleverly with two upright sticks crossed by an iron crowbar, from which the kettle was slung over a roaring fire of wood and coal, and we soon had boiling water and a merry gipsy tea party.

After tea we walked along the riverside through the meadows to the Peckingell lane and crossed on the hand-railed plank bridge the deep dark broad ditch where the ferns grow cool by the waterside and the overhanging drooping fronds make a delicately fringed vista in the cool green gloom As we walked the children made excursions into the mowing grass to gather oxeye daisies and tall red sorrel and clover and wag wantons.

FRANCIS KILVERT, 1877

15th

We afterwards went to the Opera and to our sorrow had again La Clemenza. Paul and Virginia pleased me as much as last time. We only had the Second Act of Ossian and when the Green curtain fell down, being only 20 minutes past eleven a scene of riot took

place which perfectly astonished me. The *Beaux* in the pit clapped for some time that the entertainment might continue, but upon nobody making their appearance they jumped upon the stage tore down the curtain and scenes, broke every instrument, threw chairs at the chandeliers, in fine the whole house in a few minutes was left in total darkness. We remained quietly in the box attended by Mr Salisbury and Tom Smith, and got away very well a long time before this scene of vulgarity ended. Kemble was collared and obliged to make an appology and the name of Goold resounded from every quarter, but he was in the country and could not make his appearance We left the *Monsieurs* busily employed in tearing up benches and only four Lustres escaped their fury. The damages cannot amount to less of 5000 Pounds.

HARRIET WYNNE, 1805

16th

Here I saw two strange sights to me. One was Deal Beach, reaching from the South Foreland almost to the North Foreland; and is nothing else but as it were a very great bank of stones and flints and shells of fishes: higher than the smooth sands by many fathoms and very broad, being daily augmented by the sea: and is so clear and void of sand or dust that the inhabitants (slighting the green grass which is close by it) do spread their linen on those stones to dry and whiten: which also lie so loose that you tread up to the ankles every step you go: yet on this bank stands the town of Deal. The other thing which was strange to me was that, in all places else wherever I yet was, the chiefest care of the neat housewife was to keep their rooms clean from all manner of dust, by sweeping, washing, and rubbing them. But here clean contrary; for, having first swept them clean, they then strew them all over with sand – yea their very best chambers. Here we dined. And here Mrs Walton, our landlady, gave me a little jugful of ink; which did me a great pleasure. Towards evening we were all carried from shore to our pinnace at least one hundred paces: the water being up to the middles of the seamen; the women for fear of falling, and especially the Lieutenant's wife, huggling the water-men about the necks till they had almost choked them; which caused much laughter, though our feet and garments wept.

HENRY TEONGUE, 1675

17th

I pursued my road to Tideswell, and was soon overtaken by Thomas Bush whose horse coughs sadly, not, I hope from the distemper, which is prevalent to Buxton. At Tideswell I turn'd to the right, and came to the village of Litton, and thence by a barrow stony road to above Monsal Dale, into which we descended.

The scenery of this spot is exceedingly beautiful; the miller's house lies in ruins, as if a judgment upon it. I here dismounted and gazed about for some time, but was more pleased when, having pass'd thro' the dale and mounted the steep hill, I could command the double sweep of the alley, which is a rich and truly romantic view well finish'd by the Hoff, an opposite farm. On this hilltop I came into the high road, and in a mile to Ashford [in the Water], a large and flourishing village, where are two bridges over the Wye; two miles more, and to Bakewell, a small market town.

A loin of mutton was nearly dress'd; so upon that, a cold veal pie and gooseberry tart I fared very well; and tho' the inn, the town and the day were gloomy, yet I joy'd to have escaped from Buxton. I am now only skimming about, to await the arrival of Col. Bertie, who will get from town as soon as possible; then we shall proceed away together: by that time I may be tired of my own company.

In the evening I took a walk to Mr Arkwright's great cotton mill at a small distance from the town; and would have enter'd it but entrance was denied; for this (no doubt right) reason, however odd, 'that I should disturb the girls'! It is work'd from a noble pool of water; Mr Arkwright's house adjoins it, placed under a steep hill, with a pleasant view.

I then skirted the town and, above the bridge, seeing some high artificial ground, I said to a countryman, as I often do upon trial, 'Is that the castle hill?' 'Yes, sir.' (Thus I often find out where many an old castle stood.) Within the top of the keep, where is a hollow, there lay a very proper piece of castle furniture, viz., a large iron cannon; this, at my return, the landlord told me, was fired at the King's restoration of health [on George III's recovery from madness] last year; and this was all he seem'd to know of the town or neighbourhood. Haddon Hall Park is the great feature of this neighbourhood, and stands well in the vale.

Cold ham and cold veal pie for supper. I had no one to speak to, my writing was quickly exhausted, and so I strove to think; but I (*now*) hate thinking – I left London to avoid thinking.

JOHN BYNG, 1790

18th

Went to Oxford about my son, who had suffered great privations, and lived on bread and water for breakfast, when not invited out. This astonished the opulent warden and proctors. Perhaps there never before was a scholar who did this. All my boys are brought up to think knowledge, virtue and fame can only be got by privations. I called on the warden, who gave him the highest character. The very porter at the gate looked mild when he spoke of him, and while I was talking, in he walked, looking good, pure and intellectual.

'Hyman will be distinguished, I am convinced. College life, properly taken advantage of, is a delightful life. Wadham is the most scholastic-looking place of all the colleges.

'The warden looked horror-struck when he said, 'I fear he does not always eat meat,' as if not eating meat was the *ne plus ultra* of college privations. I never saw a place that has so much the air of opulence and ease as Oxford.

B. R. HAYDON, 1831

19th

My wife and I having fixed to go to Hartfield, my wife endeavoured to borrow a horse of Jos. Fuller, Tho. Fuller, Will. Piper, and Jos. Burgess, to no purpose, they having no reason for not doing it, but want of good nature and a little gratitude; tho' I make no doubt but they will, some or other of them, be so good natured as soon to come and say, 'Come, do write this land-tax or window-tax book for us'; then I always find good nature enough to do it, and at the same time to find them in beer, gin, pipes, and tobacco; and then poor ignorant wretches, they sneak away, and omit to pay for their paper; but, God bless them, I'll think it proceeds more from ignorance than ill nature.

THOMAS TURNER, 1756

20th

I was awoke at 6 o'clock by Mamma, who told me that the Archbishop of Canterbury and Lord Conyngham were here, and wished to see me. I got out of bed and went into my sitting-room (only in my dressing-gown), and alone, and saw them. Lord Conyngham (the Lord Chamberlain) then acquainted me that my poor Uncle, the King, was no more, and had expired at 12 minutes p. 2 this morning, and consequently that I am Queen. Lord Conyngham knelt down and kissed my hand, at the same time delivering to me the official announcement of the poor King's demise. The Archbishop then told me that the Queen was desirous that he should come and tell me the details of the last moments of my poor, good Uncle; he said that he had directed his mind to religion, and had died in a perfectly happy, quiet state of mind and was quite prepared for his death. He added that the King's sufferings at the last were not very great but that there was a good deal of uneasiness. Lord Conyngham, whom I charged to express my feelings of condolence and sorrow to the poor Queen, returned directly to Windsor. I then went to my room and dressed.

Since it has pleased Providence to place me in this station, I shall do my utmost to fulfil my duty towards my country; I am very young and perhaps in many, though not in all things, inexperienced, but I am sure, that very few have more real good will and more real desire to do what is fit and right than I have.

QUEEN VICTORIA, 1839

21st

I lunched with Olivia at the Ritz and she came to see me off to Sezincote, where I spent a delightful weekend. Travelled down with John Betjeman and Frank Pakenham. Sezincote is quite lovely. Regency Indian style like Brighton Pavilion only everything in Cotswold stone instead of plaster. Fountains all playing and ferocious swans. A family pew which was like a box at the theatre with padded red balustrade above the heads of the congregation.

Colonel Dugdale said, 'The twenty-fourth of May is my day for haymaking.' 'Isn't that very early?' 'Yes, in fact the extraordinary thing is that I have never begun that day. Twenty-ninth this year. Thirtieth last year. Always well after twenty-fourth. Still I always keep twenty-fourth as my haymakin' day.'

Slept very badly all the weekend. There is a monument at Sezincote with huge plaques commemorating the Peninsular War, but it is also the chimney of the furnace which heats the orangery. The most lovely view in England.

EVELYN WAUGH, 1930

22nd

Very fine. Train to Lyndhurst Road and walk into Forest – beeches cut down – warm – pretty country towards Dibden and Southampton. Tents, with folk like gypsies (but they say *no*), peeling rushes for rushlights: you leave a strip of green on the pith for backbone. Beaulieu, the Duke's park, old church and ruins. Village, tide in. Cottage hung with roses, man in front garden tells me he has lived there fifty-three years. I praise the beauty and quiet, but he often thinks he 'ought to a'pushed out into the world – gone to London or some large place.' Boys fishing for bass. The miller's, a piano going inside ('it is the miller's daughter,' no doubt). Rasher and ale at the inn. The young lady at the bar with short curls and towny air finds it 'very dull here.' I walk away at 20 to 9, sunset light over heath and forest, long road. The night-jar whirring.

WILLIAM ALLINGHAM, 1866

23rd

Mr Pounsett and my Sister, Nancy and self took a Walk after Dinner to Pitcomb Church and there heard Mr Rich'd Goldsborough read Prayers and Preached but rather affected. As we came back from Church we stopped by a very fine Spring in Pitcomb Street in which I threw in a Shilling for the Boys there to scramble for 0. 1. 0. We also called in at Taylor Wilmots and drank some of his Ale – I gave his comical Maid Nan 0. 1. 0.

JAMES WOODFORDE, 1782

24th

Went to church at St Michael's. Annie and I went to Benedict's Concert at 2 o'clock & it was not over till seven, enjoyed it immensely. Madamoiselle Nillson sang some Swedish airs most beautifully, she is the new singer at Her Majesty's. She has a clear powerful voice & and is good looking: blue eyes, fair hair. Coming out on the stairs I met my charming partner of the Dyce Nicoll's dance, but was not quite sure of him; so did not like to bow & then he walked away without stopping & I saw him no more; I wish I had bowed, it must have been him, but then he said he was going to Glasgow; of course he will never speak to me now, as I did not bow, and my heart is broken. I don't even know his name – I am the unlucky(est) woman on earth.

A 'YOUNG LADY', 1867

25th

I left London on Friday morning, June 25th 1784 and in a post chaise overtook my horse at Uxbridge, that was sent forward under the care of Thomas Bush; who having formerly serv'd me as groom, still continues a retainer in my family, and being accustomed to my methods, becomes more useful, and agreeable to me, than any other servant would be. Having a most particular dislike to the company of a servant on the road, I detach'd him forward to prepare for me, & my horses, proper accommodations at night. This is the true use of servants on the road, tho but selldom what their masters require of them; trusting to the waiter, and chambermaid for dirty glasses, and ill made beds, and confiding the care of their horses to drunken, roguish, hostlers; & whilst their own genteel followers are regaling themselves in a genteel parlour, the horses are neither clean'd, nor fed As for my sheets I allways take them with me, knowing that next to a certainty, 5 sheets must be dirty, and 3 damp, out of a number ten: these with a very few other necessaries, travell behind my servant; as for my night cap, great coat, and such other etceteras, they travell behind my own person, in & upon, a small cloakbag.

JOHN BYNG, 1784

26th

Blanchard told me that at the theatre on Friday night Mr C. Kean, with two companions, by his indecent behaviour – sneering and observing upon the performance of the *Lady of Lyons* – attracted the attention and frequent notice of those around him; that no language of his could convey at all an adequate idea of the insolent and offensive conduct of this vulgar-minded and conceited young man.

There is no genius in such a nature. He asked my autograph for a young friend. Forster called, as also Cattermole. I did not feel much inclined to go to see the Coronation, though if I could have done so without much trouble I would . . . . Acted Claude Melnotte – indifferently, so wearied that I dropped asleep under my hairdresser; was called for, and went forward with Miss Faucit.

WILLIAM MACREADY, 1838

27th

Returned to Edinburgh late last night, and had a most sweltering night of it. This day also cruel hot. However, I made a task or nearly so, and read a good deal about the Egyptian Expedition. Had comfortable accounts of Anne, and through her of Sophia. Dr Shaw doubts if anything is actually the matter with poor Johnnie's back. I hope the dear child will escape deformity, and the infirmities attending that helpless state. I have myself been able to fight up very well, notwithstanding my lameness, but it has cost great efforts, and I am besides very strong. Dined with Colin Mackenzie; a fine family all growing up about him, turning men and women, and treading fast on our heels Some thunder and showers which I fear will be but partial. Hot – hot – hot.

SIR WALTER SCOTT, 1826

28th

We [the diarist was a Jacobite soldier at the Battle of the Boyne] marched again about five miles and encamped within three of Drogheda, near a small village, along cornfields, gardens, and meadows, the river Boyne in the rear. This night no word was given, but about midnight in great hurry ammunition delivered out, then orders to take down all tents and send away the baggage. This done the whole army drew out without beat of drum and stood at their arms the whole night, expecting the approach of the enemy.

JOHN STEVENS, 1690

29th

The three Eldest Master Custances made us a long morning Visit, eat some Gooseberry Fool &c. My Hay Stack thatched this Day – No Rain on it. Dinner to Day Beans and Bacon, and a green Goose rosted. There was a Tempest this Evening about 9 o'clock – we had not much of it thank God. About Reepham and Dalling it must have been very bad, as it mostly went that way, lasted till near 12 o'clock – that is, it lightened till that time. We did not go to bed till after 12 o'clock. The News of to day, is, that the French King and Queen &c. are retaken and carried back to Paris. I hope that it is not true, tho' on Lloyds Paper.

JAMES WOODFORDE, 1791

30th

The weather being fine, we took a drive to call on Lady Elcho at Stanway, who has been arrived from London some days, but unfortunately her Ladyship was gone to Cheltenham. On our return in the afternoon we called for half an hour at Mr Bowens' parsonage at Temple Guiting, who shewed us his handsome church, and took us a little circuit in Mr Talbot's grounds which are very pleasantly and tastefully laid out, the ground being undulating, the meadows rich and now all alive with haymakers, the distant plantations covering the horizon, the groves under which we strolled cool and umbrageous, the lawns pleasantly broken with single trees and bordered with thickets, the walks neatly kept, the grotto cool and dark, all bespeaking good taste and opulence. The family is in town: so it is that fashionable people desert their country seats, their rich parks and lovely gardens in the finest season and live there only in the gloomiest months of the year; for when the London season is over, fashion dictates a second edition on an inferior scale at some sea-bathing or watering place or some rambling tour in search of ever-eluding pleasure.

F. E. WITTS, 1827

JULY

1st

On going to the Glebe I found nine haymakers, including Moses Heal, White, and George, in the four-acre field which was cut, part of it on Saturday, and five mowers in the twelve-acre field. There ought to have been the whole of that ground down, as it is only about ten acres, although computed at twelve, and nearly three-quarters of an acres is in barley. I spoke to the haymakers about being idle; they said they only stopped to take a lunch at eleven, and had not been idle. White, who was the spokesman and had brought a clan of his relations into the field, said that they had been working very hard. I said I could not perceive it by what had been done in the field.

I went up into the Glebe field after tea. The haymakers had complained of the beer which was brewed by Feare, and some of which I drank at dinner and thought it very good. The mowers said they thought it excellent. I told them if they were dissatisfied I would not employ them. I went to White, who is a sly fellow and the secret instigator of this mutiny, and paid him off.

A little after all the women went, and were paid by my daughter at the Parsonage. As it seemed to threaten rain, and the grass was left about in the four-acre field, I desired the mowers to put it up in great cock. Moses Heal was inclined to be insolent when I spoke to him about permitting the haymakers to leave the field till the hay was put in cock, and said, instead of the beer being bad, it is actually to strong to be drunk in great quantities.

On my return home I spoke to Betty and her fellow servant, whom I had seen standing before the door to gape at everyone passing by, saying it was a discredit to any modest woman to do so. Betty then said that the month's warning I had given them was more than up, and that she and Goold wished to leave me to-morrow. I told them they certainly should do so.

JOHN SKINNER, 1828

2nd

Mr Saunders came and Mr Tyrrell invited himself as his companion, being confident that they would catch some fish with a hook. He waited a little while, but could not take any carp with the hook; so we ordered the net to be brought. Two or three boys waded naked into the pond to drive the fish out of the reeds, and one of them, feeling fish on the bottom, took them with his hands and by this manoeuvre he landed six. At length we hauled out the net with a great many carp; we threw the fish into a small pool filled with water and returned indoors, where we found Gilbert Clerk. He told us that on his way here he had come across a hare, and as it crossed his path he had lifted his stick, knocked it down and killed it; afterwards he was sorry he had done it, for in attacking the hare he had struck his little finger. Jackson came from Norwich.

THOMAS ISHAM (AGED 16), 1672

3rd

On leaving Welshpool, I was surprised at the goodness, & breadth of the road; and no less at the beauty of the country, diversified by the happiest scenes of wood, cultivation, and population; whereas I was expecting a view of naked wilds: tho that perhaps will soon arrive. The view from the hill over Llanvair, and the stream beyond it, meandring betwixt woods, aided by a glittering setting sun, was truly enlivening; as well as the sound of the church bells, and the buz of the people: but, too soon, I discover'd the little town to be throng'd with market folk, and uproar. T. B. came forth to say, that at the Goat ale-house (to which we had a recommendation) there were no horse-lodgings; and so, he had try'd the Cross-Foxes (the arms of Sr W. W. Wynn) where, at last, the horses were shelter'd in something like a stable; as for the house, it was fill'd by dancers, and drinkers, celebrating a wedding. I return'd to meet Mr P. and then we retir'd to a seat in the church yard; under an immense yew tree; (of which there are several of astonishing bulk;) whence we often arose to see the dancing, and observe the drunkenness. Heav'ns! What potations of ale, and clangor of unintelligible language! For here the English tongue is little understood. At length, we got tea in our bed room; and had you but seen it, such a broken window! such dirty walls! Few of the very worst English farm-houses cou'd equal it, in badness. The company now began to pair off; one or two of each couple very drunk: Mr P. smoked; & I wrote by the light of two farthing candles.

JOHN BYNG, 1784

4th

This Day I saw Commodore Anson's Treasure pass thro' the City, there were 32 Waggons loaded with Silver and Gold. Attended Lecture at Mr Smelleys. Lord, Prosper our Arms, and may Things go well with this our Land and Nation.

RICHARD KAY, 1744

5th

One Handel, a forreigner (who, they say, was born at Hanover) being desired to come to Oxford, to perform in Musick this Act, in which he hath great skill, is come down, the Vice-Chancellour (Dr Holmes) having requested him to do so, and as an encouragement, to allow him the Benefit of the Theater both before the Act begins and after it. Accordingly he hath published Papers for a performance today at 5s. a Ticket. This performance began a little after 5 o'clock in the evening. This is an innovation. The Players might be as well permitted to come and act. The Vice-Chancellour is much blamed for it. In this, however, he is to be commended for reviving our Acts, which ought to be annual, which might easily be brought about, provided the Statutes were strictly followed, and all such innovations (which exhaust Gentlemen's pockets and are incentives to Lewdness) were hindered.

THOMAS HEARNE, 1733

6th

An Account of the Prisoners [captured after the Battle of Sedgemore, which ended Monmouth's Rebellion] that were brought along by the Right Wing of his Honor Colon Windhams Regimt to Weston Church as they were tyed together: Adam Wheeler writeing them downe on his Drumhead as they passed by.

The first Number was Fifty and five, most of them tyed together.

The Second Number was thirty and two tyed in like manner.

The Third was Two wounded in theire Legs, crawling uppon the

Ground on theire Hands and Knees to Weston Church.

The Fowerth was Thirty seven in number, many of them tyed and pinnackled together.

The Fifth was One alone being naked, onely his Drawers on.

The Sixth was One Single one more.

The Seventh was One more running, being forced along by Two Horse Men with Blowes, and rideing close after him.

The Eighth Number was Fowerteene most of them being tyed together.

The Nineth was Forty Seven most of them tyed as the former, such of Them as had a good Coate or any thinge worth the Pilling, were very fairely stript of it.

The Seventeenth was One more, Hee was very remarkeable and to be admired, for being shot thorow the shoulder and wounded in the Belly; Hee lay on his Backe in the Sun stript naked, for the space of Tenne or Eleven Howers, in that scorching hot day to the Admiration of all the Spectatours; And as he lay, a greate Crowde of Souldiers came about him, and reproached him, calling him, *Thou Monmouth Dog* How long have you beene with youre Kinge *Monmouth*? His answer was, that if he had Breath, he would tell them: Afterwards he was pittyed, and they opened round about him, and gave him more Liberty of Aire, and there was One Souldier that gave him a paire of Drawers to cover his Nakednesse: Afterwards haveing a long Stick in his hand he walked feably to Weston Church, where he died that Night, and two wounded men more.

The Number of Prisoners that were led by the Right Wing of his Honors Regiment did amount to 228.

The Country men that gathered up the Dead slayne in this Battell gave an Account of the Minister and Church Wardens of Weston of the Number of One Thousand Three hundred Eighty and Fower; Besides many more they did beleeve lay dead unfound in the Corne.

ADAM WHEELER, 1685

7th

This town of Dundalke hath been a town of strength, and is still a walled town, and a company of fifty soldiers are here in garrison under the command of Sir Faithfull Fortescue. This town is governed by two bailiffs, sheriffs, an aldermen; the greatest part of he inhabitants of the town are popishly affected, and although my Lord Deputy, at the last election of burgesses for the Parliament, commended unto them Sir Faithfull Fortescue and Sir Arthur Teringham, yet they rejected both, and elected a couple of recusants. One of the present bailiffs is popish. Abundance of Irish, both gentlemen and others, dwell in this town, wherein they dare to take the boldness to go to mass openly. This town seated upon the sea so as barks may come within a convenient distance with the flood; much low, level, flat land hereabouts, which is often overflowed in the winter, and here is abundance of fowl, and a convenient seat. Here we lodged at one Mris Veasie's house, a most mighty fat woman; she saith she is a Cheshire woman, near related in blood to the Breretons; desired much to see me; so fat she is, as she is so unwieldy, she can scarce stand or go without crutches. This reported one of the best inns in north of Ireland; ordinary 8d. and 6d., only the knave tapster over-reckoned us in drink.

SIR WILLIAM BRERETON, 1634

8th

The army began to march early, but the rear stirred not till noon, and we moved but a mile from the place, encamping on a plainer, pleasanter ground than the last. This day was very remarkable, first for the violent scorching heat of the sun, which I then thought so excessive as to exceed what I had felt in three years I lived in Portugal; but the reason might (be) because in that country I was never much exposed to it whereas here I marched afoot without any better place to refresh in after all than a small soldier's tent; next for the prodigious thunder, which during three hours it continued at a great distance all men took for hot firing of cannon till coming near it lasted about an hour longer in monstrous claps so great as are seldom heard, and all ended in such a violent shower of rain as ran through the tents as if there had been none. Here our artillery encamped in the front of the first line.

John Stevens, 1691

9th

In the morning began my hed to ake and be hevy more then of late, and had some wambling in my stomach. I had broken my fast with sugar sopps, &c. I gave Letice my servant 5s. part of her wagis: with part whereof she was to buy a smok and neckercher.

John Dee, 1594

10th

There are two Fairs a Year at Wantage in Berks., the 1st on July 7, being the Translation of St Thomas à Becket, and the second on ye 6th of October, being St Faith's day. But this Year, the 7th of July being a Sunday, the Fair was kept last Monday, and 'twas a very great one, and Yesterday it held too, when there was a very great Match of Backsword or Cudgell playing between the Hill Country and the Vale Country, Barkshire Men being famous for this Sport or Exercise. And 'tis remarkable that at Childrey, by Wantage, lives one old Vicars, a Farmer, who hath been very excellent at it, and hath now five Sons that are so expert in it that 'tis supposed they are a Match for any five in England. They always come off Victors, & carry off the Hat, the Reward of the Conquest, so that they have not bought any Hats since they have been celebrated for this Exercise.

THOMAS HEARNE, 1723

11th

Delightful weather. After breakfast, and after transacting business as a Magistrate, left Upper Slaughter with Edward in the open carriage for Cheltenham. All the smart farmers and tradesmen's families on the road to a gipsy *fête champètre* at Casey Compton. Edward left me at Sandywell to botanize in an adjacent woods, and return in the open carriage. At the Plough a colloquy with Sir John Guise, while I was taking luncheon. Proceeded to Gloucester by a Bristol coach. Called on Mrs and Miss Davies in Wellington Parade. Pursued my journey by coach to Newnham, a very lingering conveyance: about 10 miles. Preparations for Gloucester races in the meadows. By Over Bridge, having Highnam on the right, now occupied by one Baker, a merchant at Gloucester, passed through a rich country, full of orchards: a great show of apples. At Minsterworth the road passes close by the Severn: then the river makes a long detour, and is not seen from the road till near Westbury, where the remains of an old mansion of the Colchesters, with formal gardens, canals, yew hedges, statue of Neptune etc.

F. E. WITTS, 1836

12th

The cholera is here, and diffuses a certain degree of alarm. Some servants of people well known have died, and that frightens all other servants out of their wits, and they frighten their masters; the death of any one person they are acquainted with terrifies people much more than twenty of whom they knew nothing. As long as they read daily returns of a parcel of deaths here and there of A, B, and C, they do not mind, but when they hear that Lady Such-a-one's nurse or Sir Somebody's footman is dead, they fancy they see the disease actually at their own door.

CHARLES GREVILLE, 1832

13th

We had for Dinner some Pyke and fryed Soals a nice Piece of boiled Beef, Ham and a Couple of Fowls, Peas and Beans, a green Goose rosted, Gooseberry Pies, Currant Tarts, the Charter, hung Beef scraped &c. For Supper fryed Soals, a Couple of Chicken rosted, cold Ham &c. Artichokes, Tarts &c., &c. Fruit after Dinner and Supper – Strawberries, Cherries, Almonds – Raisins &c., &c. Miss Pinchings Brother came to us from Norwich about 10 o'clock this Evening just as we were going to sit down to Supper and he supped &c. with us. Just as the ladies and Gentlemen were going to drink Coffee and Tea in the Garden, I was sent for to go to Weston House to name a Child of Mrs Custances who was brought to bed this Afternoon about 2 o'clock – I therefore walked up directly to Weston House and named the Child by name Mary Anne, the smallest Infant I think I ever had in my Arms – The Child came 10 Weeks before its Time, therefore afraid that it would not live. I soon returned to my Company but lost my Coffee and Tea. After Tea the Ladies and Gentlemen got to dancing and danced and sang till Supper Time – About 12 o'clock this night we all got to dancing again – We had many droll Songs from Mr Walker who sings with great good humour and very well – He is a mighty lively and agreeable young man indeed – They all stayed with us till 3 o'clock in the Morning and then they all returned to Mattishall but Betsy Davy who was left here to spend a few Days with us. – Upon the whole we spent a very agreeable, merry and cheerful Day, and every thing conducted and done extremely well by our Servants.

JAMES WOODFORDE, 1785

14th

We found a shepherd and his little boy reading, far from any houses or sight of people, the Bible to him; so I made the boy read it me, which he did, with the forced tone that children do usually read, that was mighty pretty, and then I did give him something, and went to the father, and talked with him; and I find he had been a servant in my cousin Pepys's house, and told me what was become of their old servants. He did content himself mightily in my liking his boy's reading, and did bless God for him, the most like one of the old patriarchs that ever I saw in my life, and it brought those thoughts of the old age of the world in my mind for two or three days after. We took notice of his woollen knit stockings of two colours mixed, and of his shoes shod with iron, both at the toe and heels, and with great nails in the soles of his feet, which was mighty pretty: and, taking notice of them, 'Why,' says the poor man, 'the downs, you see, are full of stones, and we are fain to shoe ourselves thus; and these,' says he, 'will make the stones fly till they ring before me.' I did give the poor man something, for which he was mighty thankful, and I tried to cast stones with his horn crook. He values his dog mightily, that would turn a sheep any way which he would have him, when he goes to fold them: told me that there was about eighteen score sheep in his flock, and that he hath four shillings a week the year round for keeping of them. And Mrs Turner, in the common fields here, did gather one of the prettiest nosegays that ever I saw in my life. So to our coach, and through Mrs Minnes's wood, and looked upon Mr Evelyn's house; and so over the common, and through Epsom town to our inn, in the way stopping a poor woman with her milk-pail, and in one of my gilt tumblers, did drink our bellyfuls of milk, better than any cream; and so to our inn, and there had a dish of cream, but it was sour, and so had no pleasure in it; and so paid our reckoning, and took coach, it being about seven at night, and passed and saw the people walking with their wives and children to take the air, and we set out for home, the sun by and by going down, and we in the cool of the evening all the way with much pleasure home, talking and pleasing ourselves with the pleasures of this day's work. Mrs Turner mightily pleased with my resolution, which, I tell her, is never to keep a country house, but to keep a coach, and with my wife on the Saturday to go sometimes for a day to this place, and then quit to another place: and there is more variety and as little charge, and no trouble, as there is in a country house. Anon it grew dark, and we had the pleasure to see several glow-worms, which was mighty pretty, but my foot begins more and more to pain me, which Mrs Turner, by keeping her warm hand upon it, did much ease; but so that when we come home, which was just at eleven at night, I was not able to walk from the lane's end to my house without being helped. So to bed, and there had a cerecloth laid to my foot, but in great pain all night long.

SAMUEL PEPYS, 1667

15th

Breakfast at Crown 9.30. A. T.[the poet Alfred Tennyson], Mrs T., Hallam and Lionel. A. T. and I out at 12 Swan Green, forest path, Haliday's Hall, we *swim* through tall bracken. T pauses midway, turns to me, and says solemnly, 'I believe *this* place is quite full of vipers!' After going a little further, he stopped again and said, 'I am told that a viper-bite may make a woman silly for life, or deprive a man of his virility.'

We entered Mark Ash, a wood of huge solemn Beech trees, the floor thick-matted with dead leaves; a few trees were broken or fallen; some towered to a great height before branching. We sat on the roots of a mighty Beech. T. smoked. We shared in sandwiches and brandy. Then he produced a little pocket *As You Like It*, and read some parts aloud.

WILIAM ALLINGHAM, 1866

16th

About two in the morning a terrible fit of the crampe above the ancle and about the lower end of the calf of my left legg, occasion'd by either throwing that leg out of the bed being hot weather or by over-retching my self. I was then in a sweat.

ANTHONY WOOD, 1689

17th

High time to be employ'd in some active pursuit, or to return. An inn is not the place for idleness or sickness. Mr Keteriche, the Minister of Water Newton, call'd upon me, and forced upon Frederick a quantity of Roman coins found in the Roman camp near to his village.

At our dinner-time Mr Osborn stept in for a minute; he was in his way to Ld Westmorland's to see a great cricket match.

Colman went to his rabbit-shooting, but with no great success, neither had I any luck at my last fishery. Should I ever return to this place to make a stay, I must find out some intelligent fisher to guide and instruct me. The evening was very gloomy and sultry; with sun, it had been intolerable. In the Stamford newspaper was an advertisement of the dog (Sancho) who follow'd us from Boston; so I wrote in answer, desiring that he might be sent for; heartily repenting my ever suffering him to come after us, as he has been an incessant plague. Just below this inn is a paper mill, of some benefit to the poor: but I wonder not to find the cotton mill erected in this country, whose advantages are now so manifest.

JOHN BYNG, 1790

18th

I sat to Mr Kneller for my picture. Received £20.3s for tithe, till Lamas 1686, of Mr Sheffield. Dined at home. Went with my wife to the goldsmith's. Bought two horses, one for eleven guineas, and the other £5. 1s. Supped at home with Sir Edmund and Sir Richard Wiseman, Dr Johnson, Dr Evans, and William Fanshaw.

THOMAS CARTWRIGHT, 1687

19th

I only got my ticket [for the coronation of George IV] on Wednesday at two, and dearest Mary and I drove about to get all that was wanted. Sir George Beaumont lent me ruffles and frill, another friend a blue velvet coat, a third a sword; I bought buckles, and the rest I had. I went to bed at ten and arose at twelve, not having slept a wink. I dressed, breakfasted, and was at the Hall-door at half-past one. Three ladies were before me. The doors opened about four, and I got a front place in the Chamberlain's box, between the door and the throne, and saw the whole room distinctly. Many of the doorkeepers were tipsy; quarrels took place The sun began to light up the old Gothic windows, the peers to stroll in, and other company of all descriptions to crowd to their places. Some took seats they had not any right to occupy, and were obliged to leave them after sturdy disputes. Others lost their tickets. The Hall occasionally echoed with the hollow roar of voices at the great door, till at last the galleries were filled; the Hall began to get crowded below. Every movement, as the time approached for the King's appearance, was pregnant with interest. The appearance of a monarch has something in it like the rising of the sun. There are indications which announce the luminary's approach; a streak of light – the tipping of a cloud – the singing of the lark – the brilliance of the sky, till the cloud edges get brighter and brighter, and he rises majestically into the heavens. So with a king's advance. A whisper of mystery turns all eyes to the throne. Suddenly two or three rise; others fall back; some talk, direct, hurry, stand still, or disappear. Then three or four of high rank appear from behind the throne; an interval is left; the crowds scarce breathe. Something rustles, and a being buried in satin, feathers, and diamonds rolls gracefully into his seat. The room rises with a sort of feathered, silken thunder. Plumes wave, eyes sparkle, glasses are out, mouths smile, and one man becomes the prime object of attraction to thousands. The way in which the King bowed was really royal. As he looked towards the peeresses and foreign ambassadors he showed like some gorgeous bird of the East.

B. R. HAYDON, 1821

20th

The village of Madeley, comprehending hundreds of detach'd houses, with the river, woods, rocks, shipping, &c, &c, reminded me of the drawings of a Chinese town, as the same indiscriminate jumble of beauties. But of the iron bridge over the Severn, which we cross'd, and where we stop'd for half an hour, what shall I say? That it must be the admiration, as it is one of the wonders, of the world. It was cast in the year 1778; the arch is 100 feet wide, and 55 feet from the top of the water, and the whole length is 100 yards: the country agreed with the founder to finish it for 6000 £; and have meanly, made him suffer for his noble undertaking. After this survey; we enter'd Mr Banks's iron furnace, (on the hillside) and were most civilly, shew'd by him all the astonishing progress of such (hellish hot) manufactories: he employs about 700 workmen, & said there were 7 other neighbouring furnaces of the same size; judge then of the flourishing state of this branch of trade, and how it must enrich this vicinage and the kingdom! Every cart belonging to this trade is made of iron, and even the ruts of the road are shod with iron!

JOHN BYNG, 1784

21st

This city [Waterford, Ireland] is governed by a mayor, bailiffs, and twelve aldermen. Herein are seven churches; there have been many more. One of these, Christ Church, a cathedral; St Patrick's, Holy Ghost, St Stephen's, St John, – but none of these are in good repair, not the cathedral, nor indeed are there any churches almost to be found in good repair. Most of the inhabitants Irish, not above forty English, and not one of these Irish goes to church. This town trades much with England, Fraunce and Spaine, and that which gives much encouragement hereunto is the goodness of the haven. This town double-walled, and the walls maintained in good repair. Here we saw women in a most impudent manner treading cloathes with their feet; these were naked to the middle almost, for so high were their clothes tucked up about them. Here the women of better rank and quality wear long, high, laced caps, turned up round about; these are mighty high; of this sort I gave William Dale money to buy me one. Here is a good, handsome market-place, and a most convenient prison that I ever saw for the women apart, and this is a great distance from the men's prison. Herein dwells a judicious apothecary, who hath been bred at Antwerpe, and is a traveller; is name is (as I take it) Mr Jarvis Billiard, by whose directions and good advice I found much good, and through God's mercy recovered from my sickness.

SIR WILLIAM BRERETON, 1634

22nd

We arrived at Sonning at one o'clock; always in company there; that is the life of the country! A garden full of raspberries and currants, but I dare not eat from a bowel complaint. Saying this is like my predecessor in diary Mr Ashmole; but all diaries, let them be ever so bad, will be read with avidity hereafter.

Nay, I am even vain enough to think this of my Tours, should they exist a hundred years, as descriptive of the manners of our travelling, the rates of our provisions, and of castles, churches and houses that may then be levell'd with the ground.

All diaries are greedily sought for, let them be ever so ill and foolishly written, as coming warm from the heart; for instance, that of the second Ld Clarendon, and those dirty, idle memorials of Lilly [the astrologer William Lilly], and Ashmole [Elias Ashmole], who tells us of every shocking ailment that assailed him and how often he sweated and purged.

Most modern Tours are written (in my mind) too much in the style of pompous history; not dwelling sufficiently upon the prices of provisions, recommendation of inns, statement of roads, etc., so that the following travellers reap little benefit from them.

I have often thought that maps merely for tourists might be made. And have wish'd that some intelligent traveller (for instance, Mr Grose) [Francis Grose, author of *The Antiquities of England and Wales*] would mark on such touring maps all the castles, Roman stations, views, canals, parks, etc., etc., which, accompanied by other common maps, would lead the researching Tourist to every proper point and object; and not subject him (as at present) to ask questions of ignorant innkeepers or to hunt in books for what is not to be found; for till lately we had no inqusitive travellers and but few views of remarkable places.

JOHN BYNG, 1787

23rd

At 2 a.m. began the great lightning storm. It was a beautiful glorious sight as I sat at my open window watching it. For an entire hour the lightning and thunder scarcely ceased playing and rolling in a circle round the house. There seemed to be a battle between several storms and the peals of artillery were incessant. The constant flaring of the broad brilliant lightning lighted up the country like the brightest sunshine. The Common, the fences, every tree and hedge stood out with the most vivid and terrible distinctness. Then the lightning rushed upwards as if from the earth in dazzling shoots of rose-coloured flame and fierce showers of brilliant sparks. The lightning showed all colours by turns, green, rose colour, white, red, yellow and violet.

Once there came a fierce and terrible glare so blinding that for some seconds afterwards everything seemed pitch black and I feared I had lost my sight.

There were lights in the houses all over the village and the cottage doors and windows were opened wide to let the lightning out easily if it should come in. The storm passed away to the eastward quietly in a quarter of an hour's heavy rain, without doing us any harm, thank God.

FRANCIS KILVERT, 1873

24th

After some fine pike, beef steaks, peas, Westmoreland ham and apple pye we left Grasmere, Anne being much recovered and never in my life did my eyes take in such a draught of pleasure from viewing scene of nature as in my ride to Keswick where we arrived at 9, the road barring the hilliness the best that can be travelled; it would have been unpardonable to have hurried over it. The forms of the mountains are the most grotesque and at time the most sublime that can be imagined. We had no sooner lost sight of the lovely Grasmere than Leathes water stretched itself before us and passing nearly three miles down to it and two miles along it its loss was fully compensated by the mountain scenery that surrounded us, till we got sight of Keswick, Derwent and Bassenthwaite Waters and walking down the steep descent to the turnpike arrived at nightfall at the Royal Oak at Keswick, where not being able to obtain a sitting room in the house we proceeded to the Queen's Head where we had been recommended by the landlord at Lowood; a boy knowing us for lakers put handbills in our hands to tell us of all the wonders to be seen at Keswick and its neighbourhood.

BENJAMIN NEWTON, 1818

25th

Went to dine to Barrie's with Thomas Hardy and wife. Barrie has an ugly little manservant, and the finest view of London I ever saw. Mrs Hardy a very nice woman, with a vibrating attractive voice. Hardy was very lively; talked like anything. Apropos of Tchekoff he started a theory that some of Tchekoff's tales were not justifiable because they told nothing unusual. He said a tale must be unusual and the people interesting. Of course he soon got involved in the meshes of applications and instances; but he kept his head and showed elasticity and common sense, and came out on the whole well. He has all his faculties, unimpaired. Quite modest and without the slightest pose. They both had very good and accurate appraisements of such different people as Shorter and Phillpotts.

Later in the evening Barrie brought along both Shaw and the Wellses by phone. Barrie was consistently very quiet, but told a few A1 stories. At dusk we viewed the view and the searchlights. Hardy, standing outside one of the windows, had to put a handkerchief on his head. I sneezed. Soon after Shaw and the Wellses came Hardy seemed to curl up. He had travelled to town that day and was evidently fatigued. He became quite silent. I then departed and told Barrie that Hardy ought to go to bed. He agreed. The spectacle of Wells and G.B.S. talking firmly and strongly about the war, in their comparative youth, in front of this aged, fatigued and silent man – incomparably their superior as a creative artist – was very striking.

ARNOLD BENNETT, 1917

26th

I went to church in the morning, having waited on the Judge to shew him all the parts and beauties of it but was so tormented by the piles that I could not kneel in the seat, nor hardly walk home, but as soon as I got into my chamber I applied cerous and honey as a liniment to them, and so lay until the evening, having never in my life had so severe a fit before.

ROLAND DAVIES, 1689

27th

Percy and I decided to bicycle. We started about 11.0: went slowly to Barton, and so to Haslingfield: then between Haslingfield and Harston we lay long on the grass, near ricks, listening to owls and the snorting of some beast that drew nigh, to far-off dogs barking, and cocks crowing. The stars were like the points of pendants in the irregular roof of a cave – not an even carpet or set in a concave. We went on about 1.0, and then made a long halt near the G. N. R. bridge on the way to Newton; but no trains passed, so we went on

abut 1.45 to Shelford; and this was very sweet, so fragrant and shadowed by dark trees, while Algol and Aldebaran and other great shining stars slowly wheeled above us.

We got to the G. E. R. bridge at Shelford – I was anxious to see trains – and half-a-dozen great luggers jangled through with a cloud of steam and coloured lights. There was one that halted, and the guard walked about with a lantern; a melancholy policeman was here, in the shadow. The owls again hooted and screamed and cocks roared hoarsely.

Suddenly we became aware it was the dawn! The sky was whitening, there was a green tinge to east, with rusty stains of cloud, and the stars went out. We went on about 2.30 to Grantchester, where the mill with lighted windows was rumbling, and the water ran oily-smooth into the inky pool among the trees. Then it was day; and by the time we rode into Cambridge, getting in at 3.30, it was the white morning light – while all the places so mysteriously different at night had become the places one knew. We found some bread-and-butter, and smoked till 4.0, when we went out round the garden, the day now brightening up: after which I went to bed, but P. walked till 5.0. The mystery, the coolness, the scent, the quiet of it all were wonderful, and the thought that this strange transformation passes over the world thus night by night seemed very amazing.

A. C. BENSON, 1911

28th

Plague grows hott; persons fall down in London streets, 1843 of plague, total 2785: Lord spare thy people.

RALPH JOSSELIN, 1664

29th

The President of St. John's told me some Memories of *Mr Nash's* Life who has been so famous at Bath for many years and which he had from good hands Viz:

That he was a Welchman, entered Servitor of Jesus in Oxon. but beat the Proctor Mr Wynne (now Bishop of Bath and Wells) and was expelled for it upon which he merrily said that they had hindered him from being a Bishop as well as Wynne. He afterwards went to sea before the Mast and was cast away upon the coast of Ireland, Where he is supposed to have turned Papist and afterwards he went into the French Service and was Captain of a little Man of War and employed against the Protestants. He was broke for some Misbehaviour and came over into England. Turned Gamester and having a good stock of assurance set up for Director General at Bath where he won a vast estate of Lord Howard and the Duke of Bedford and generously gave it up again upon condition that he should have a Rent Charge out of these estates £1300 pr. ann. for life. Upon which he set up his Chariot and 6 and keeps up the same Equipage and has a fine house a Bath and another in town, complemented by the Mayor and is in reality the Governor of the Place. At Tunbridge he does not assume so much Authority. He was formerly Rude and Saucy to strangers and specially Country Ladies that had not secrets to keep, no Intrigues to fear the Discovery of. At present he is much civiler. He playes with a good deal of Sedateness and Fairness. Is a man of tolerable good sense and well fitted for the station he is in. A trifling idle life. Looks now younger than he did about 20 years ago.

Gets up at 4 a clock in the morning, drinks little wine. He once danced both at Bath and Tunbridge the same day for a Piece of Galantry; from 4 a clock in the morning to 10 at night. Rode 15 horses.

THOMAS WILSON, 1736

30th

About 2 p.m. (as I was afterwards told) Mr Humphry Stafford, the Lady Mainwaring's second son (suspecting I should marry his mother) broke into my chamber, and had like to have killed me, but Christopher Smith withheld him by force; for which all persons exceedingly blamed him, in regard it was thought I was near death, and knew no body. God be blessed for this deliverance.

ELIAS ASHMOLE, 1647

31st

Up, and very betimes by six o'clock at Deptford, and there find Sir G. Carteret, and my Lady ready to go: I being in my new coloured silk suit, and coat trimmed with gold buttons and gold broad lace round my hands, very rich and fine. By water to the ferry, where, when we come, no coach there; and title of ebb so far spent on the horse-boat could not get off on the other side the river to bring away the coach. So we were fain to stay there in the unlucky Isle of Dogs, in a chill place, the morning cool, and wind fresh, above two, if not three hours, to our great discontent. Yet, being upon a pleasant errand, and seeing that it could not be helped, we did bear it very patiently; and it was worth my observing to see how, upon these two scores, Sir G. Carteret, the most passionate man in the world, and that was in greatest haste to be gone, did bear with it, and very pleasant all the while, at least not troubled so much as to fret and storm at it. Anon the coach comes: in the meantime, there coming a News thither with his horse to go over, that told us he did come from Islington this morning; and that Proctor, the vintner, of the Mitre, in Wood Street, and his son, are dead this morning there, of the plague: he having laid out abundance of money there, and was the greatest vintner for some time in London for great entertainments. We, fearing the canonical hour would be past before we got thither, did, with a great deal of unwillingness, send away the licence and wedding-ring. So that when we come, though we drove hard with six horses, yet we found them gone from home; and, going towards the church, met them coming from church, which troubled us. But, however, that trouble was soon over, hearing it was well done: they being both in their old clothes; my Lord Crewe giving her; there being three coachfuls of them. The young lady mighty sad, which troubled me; but yet I think it was only her gravity in a

little greater degree than usual. All saluted her, but I did not, till my Lady Sandwich did ask me whether I had saluted her or no. So to dinner, and very merry we were; but in such a sober way as never almost any wedding was in so great families: but it was much better. After dinner company divided, some to cards, others to talk. My Lady Sandwich and I up to settle accounts and pay her some money. And mighty kind she is to me, and would fain have had me gone down for company with her to Hinchingbroke; but for my life I cannot. At night to supper, and so talk; and which, methought, was the most extraordinary thing, all of us to prayers as usual, and the young bride and bridegroom too: and so, after prayers, soberly to bed; only I got into the bridegroom's chamber while he undressed himself, and there was very merry, till he was called to the bride's chamber, and into bed they went. I kissed the bride in bed, and so the curtains drawn with the greatest gravity that could be, and so good-night. But the modesty and gravity of this business was so decent, that it was to me indeed ten times more delightful than if it had been twenty times more merry and jovial. Whereas I feared I must have sat up all night, we did here all get good beds, and I lay in the same I did before, with Mr Brisband, who is a good scholar and sober man; and we lay in bed, getting him to give me an account of Rome, which is the most delightful talk a man can have of any traveller: and so to sleep. Thus I ended this month with the greatest joy that ever I did any in my life, because I have spent the greatest part of it with abundance of joy, and honour, and pleasant journeys, and brave entertainments, and without cost of money; and at last live to see the business ended with great content on all sides.

SAMUEL PEPYS, 1665

AUGUST

1st

The old cathedral might well have been repair'd, instead of building the present ballroom; at the back of which, is the Welsh chapel, but such is the decline of that language (soon to extinguish like the Cornish) that whereas, within a few years, the numbers were even, there are now but 7 or 8 people in the Welsh congregation. this change must necessarily happen from the great intercourse with England, and from their militia having dwelt in English camps. – Harping also is in the wane; tho' there is one gentleman of this country, Mr Gwynne, who is a very fine performer, and draws all the harpers to his house. –At my return, in which my horse gain shew'd symptoms of stumbling, I walk'd for some time with Mr Os; when we order'd a harper to attend us, (the first we have had,) who, if not of the neatest taste, rattled away to my amusement, (particularly Lady Townshends Delight) and was conversed with, in Welsh, by Mr Traherne; who eat some cold meat, and stay'd till eleven o'clock.

JOHN BYNG, 1789

2nd

You may have heard it wrong; I will concisely tell it right. His carriage had just stopped at the garden-door at St James's and he had just alighted from it, when a decently dressed woman, who had been waiting for him some time, approached him with a petition. It was rolled up, and had the usual superscription – For the King's Most Excellent Majesty. She presented it with her right hand; and, at the same moment that the King bent forward to take it, she drew from it, with her left hand, a knife, with which she aimed straight at his heart!

The fortunate awkwardness of taking the instrument with the left hand made her design perceived before it could be executed; the King started back, scarce believing the testimony of his own eyes; and the woman made a second thrust, which just touched his waistcoat before he had time to prevent her; and at that moment one of the attendants, seeing her horrible intent, wrenched the knife from her hand.

'Has she cut my waistcoat?' cried he, in telling it – 'Look! for I have had no time to examine.'

Thank heaven, however, the poor wretch had not gone quite so far. 'Though nothing,' added the King, in giving his relation, 'could have been sooner done, for there was nothing for her to go through but a thin linen and fat.'

While the guards and his own people now surrounded the King, the assassin was seized by the populace, who were tearing her away, no doubt to fall the instant sacrifice of her murtherous purpose, when the King, the only calm and moderate person then present, called aloud to the mob, 'The poor creature is mad! – Do not hurt her! She has not hurt me!'

He then came forward, and showed himself to all the people, declaring he was perfectly safe and unhurt; and then gave positive orders that the woman should be taken care of, and went into the palace, and had his levée.

There is something in the whole of his behaviour upon this occasion that strikes me As proof indisputable of a true and noble courage: for in a moment so extraordinary – an attack in this country, unheard of before – to settle so instantly that it was the effect of insanity, to feel no apprehension of private plot or latent conspiracy – to stay out, fearlessly, among his people, and so benevolently to see himself to the safety of one who had raised her arm against his life – these little traits, all impulsive, and therefore to be trusted, have given me an impression of respect and reverence that I can never forget, and never think of but with fresh admiration.

FANNY BURNEY, 1786

3rd

James Levitt has begun business at Hull, in partnership with a young man of the name of Kidd, son of Kidd of Dairy Coates near Hull, they carry on their business at 47 Dock Street. Young Barnard Cook lately had a fit, much likely brought on by drinking and intemperance, he is better now. – This is Mr Barnard's rent day. I have no doubt but his ears will be assailed by complaints, on the dry weather having such an injurious effect on the Crops both of grass, and spring corn; as for Wheat they cannot complain for the Crop is in general very good, and I hope it will be got, in good state. I hope he (Mr B) will not give them any thing again, for the Farmers beat all others with complaints, there is never a day in the year but they complain either of one thing or another.

ROBERT SHARP, 1826

4th

In the evening I began near Stockton market-place as usual. I had hardly finished the hymn, when I observed the people in great confusion, which was occasioned by a lieutenant of a man-of-war, who had chosen that time to bring his press-gang, and ordered them to take Joseph Jones and William Alwood. Joseph Jones telling him, 'Sir, I belong to Mr Wesley,' after a few words he let him go; as he did likewise William Alwood, after a few hours, understanding he was a licensed preacher. He likewise seized upon a young man of the town; but the women rescued him by main strength. They also broke the lieutenant's head; and so stoned both him and his men, that they ran away with all speed.

JOHN WESLEY, 1759

5th

Haslemere – very fine; Helen and I started about 3.30 to walk to Tennyson's, as invited. In the shady lane the carriage overtook us, T. had kindly called for us. He was in the carriage with his little grandson, Alfred, in his nurse's lap, and Mr Fields, an American guest. Little Alfred, aged three, had on the great Alfred's black sombrero, and the child's straw hat with a blue ribbon was stuck on the top of the poet's huge head, and so they drove gravely along.

WILLIAM ALLINGHAM, 1880

6th

Fell in, fortunately, with a dinner at Malone's. Found much satisfaction in such a restoration to better society, with the health of the country to qualify me to enjoy it. Proceeded to Nepean. Detained between his house and the office till near five o'clock, when I found a set of people going to a battle in Tothill Fields. Got some dinner at the tavern in Palace Yard, and proceeded thence to the scene of action, where, between six and seven, saw very commodiously from a dray, a smart battle between Jack Joseph, a soldier who showed upon his back floggings which he had received to a distinguished amount, and one Hardy, I think, a carpenter. Joseph was bulky, but old and corpulent, and not a match for the other in activity, but he fought most courageously, and after eleven times being either thrown or struck down, gave me a great persuasion that he would win, even if his antagonist had not give out suddenly, in a way very discreditable either to his courage or his honesty.

WILLIAM WINDHAM, 1787

7th

Finer day. We get berries before lunch. After lunch the motor comes very late and instead of going to Berkley castle we go to Malmesbury Abbey. We break down on the way back narrowly miss a Traction engine and a drunkard etc. etc.

John Knight (aged 12), 1912

8th

Went with Lord Hinton, who had never fished with a minnow before, and the trout ran so remarkably well that he caught 7 brace of the largest fish we had seen for the season in the space of an hour and half. I killed also one trout, while instructing him how to troll, which was the largest caught this year, weighing 2 lb.

Lord Hinton hooked a trout with a minnow, which was so large as to require nearly twenty minutes to get him to the top of the water; and while we were in the very act of landing him, we had the sad mortification to see him break the tackle and swim away. He was the largest trout I ever saw, and has defeated all the fishermen. I should guess his weight at about 7 lb.

Colonel Peter Hawker, 1811

9th

The Lord Molineux sent me a fat buck to Wigan; I dined there with Mr Mayor and the Recorder; went to the church to prayers. After dinner called at Mr Stanley's, and went to the Anchor at Preston, where I met my Lord Brandon, who supped with us, brought the Bayly of the town, and an impertinent doctor of physic.

Thomas Cartwright, 1687

10th

Satterday morning about ten of the clock came the King's trumpet back from Essex, and brought a letter directed for his highnes Prince Maurice and the Earle of Forth:

My Lords,

In the beginning of your lettre you express by what authority you send it. I having no authority to treat without the Parliament who have entrusted me, cannot doe it without breach of trust.

Your humble servant,

ESSEX

From Listithiel, Aug. 10. 1644

Newes about night that Sir Richard Grenvile was with his army at Bodman and had forced his entrance into the towne. This afternoone the King and his cavaliers went on to the hills upon Brodock Downe, where he saw many of the insolent rebells braving upon the adjoyning hill betwixt him and Listithiel: many horse mett on both sides, in piquering; none killed, few wounded, many of the rebells were.

RICHARD SYMONDS, 1644

11th

At dinner the conversation led to the alleged cause of Lord Byron's parting with Lady Byron, and some observations were made which occasioned me disagreeable sensations; being evidently perceived, it made me quite embarrassed, and I did not in consequence recover the tone of my mind all day, uncomfortable as to the impression my want of self-possession might have caused, for which there was no actual reason. In the same way I always became embarrassed and confused before I had children, when the want of them was alluded to. I am very weak in this respect.

WILLIAM MACREADY, 1835

12th

The weather no better, and as there seemed no hope of its improvement, we decided on starting at two o'clock, and proceeding either to *Loch Ryan* or *Lamlash*. Lord Adolphus read the service at half-past ten, at which the two eldest children were also present.

I intend to create Bertie "Earl of Dublin," as a compliment to the town and country; he has no Irish title, though he is *born* with several Scotch ones (belonging to the heirs to the Scotch throne, and which we have inherited from James VI. of Scotland and I. of England); and this was one of my father's titles.

The preparations on deck for the voyage were not encouraging; the boats hoisted up, the accommodation ladders drawn quite close up, every piece of carpet removed, and everything covered; and, indeed, my worst fears were realized. We started at two, and I went below and lay down shortly after, and directly we got out of the harbour the yacht began rolling for the first three-quarters of an hour, in a way which was dreadful, and there were two rolls, when the waves broke over the ship, which I never shall forget. It got gradually better, and at five we entered *Loch Ryan*, truly thankful to be at the end of our voyage. Albert came down to me and then I went up on deck, and he told me how awful it had been. The first great wave which came over the ship threw everybody down in every direction. Poor little Affie was thrown down and sent rolling over the deck, and was drenched, or the deck was swimming with water. Albert told me it was quite frightful to see the enormous waves rising like a wall above the sides of the ship. We did not anchor so high up in *Loch Ryan* as we had done two years ago; but it was a very safe quiet anchorage, and we were very glad to be there. Albert went on shore.

QUEEN VICTORIA, 1849

13th

There cannot be a cleanlier, civiller inn than this is; which bears all the marks of old gentility and of having been a manor house: walls very thick, floors oaken and wide, with a profusion of timber and the remains of much tapestry for carpeting, whereon was well-told, instructive church history. My bedroom was very large, with black oaken boards, a wrought ceiling, a wide cornice, with a lofty mantelpiece. In short, I appear'd to be in the grand bedchamber of an old family seat. In the kitchen hung a picture which appear'd to me the work of a great master (perhaps of Rubens), but the landlord, having had a hint of its value, did not seem inclined to part with it unless some foolish sum had been offer'd him.

Most inns will do during the summer's heat, but there are not ten endurable in the winter when you come out of London from register stoves and turkey carpets.

JOHN BYNG, 1789

14th

The Astrologers' Feast at Painters Hall, London.

This night about one a'clock, I fell ill of a surfeit, occasioned by drinking water after venison. I was greatly oppressed in my stomach; and next day Mr Saunders the astrologian sent me a piece of bryony root to hold in my hand, and within a quarter of an hour, my stomach was freed of that great oppression, which nothing which I took from Dr Wharton could do before.

ELIAS ASHMOLE, 1651

15th

After seeing [Bishopston] church I went along a narrow deep-hedged winding lane, and came to a magnificent walnut tree, the finest by far I ever saw; and opposite a nice-looking small old-fashioned house, at the gate of which were eight children, waiting about with no apparent object: presently I heard a rough, loud man's voice. I thought he was driving them off, but he was counting them: he was in shirt-sleeves, but had a well-dressed companion. They leant over the gate, the rough man called the children, and in his rude way, disguising kindness (ever since the fashioning of this eccentric island-people kindness has been a thing worn under a cloak), he distributed his plums, sending one to the brat in the 'cradle' (perambulating): he would not help me about my road till he had finished the dole. I had half a mind to stop and talk to him – indeed I began about the walnut-tree, and am indebted to him for knowing it is a walnut – but shyness, the plague of this eccentric English nation, broke off our budding acquaintance.

WILLIAM CORY, 1865

16th

My boys engaged to attend young Newnham and Langford fishing in the brook; their two companions, with young Peter Hoare, came to breakfast; the whole party went afterwards to fish in the Cam. On my return I found the lads had had good success with their fishing, but young Newnham only caught one, as he thought it cruel to use a worm, and only fished with paste. I really believe he is an excellent young man, although he may in some instances carry his ideas too far.

JOHN SKINNER, 1824

17th

I spent rather a feeble morning; a hot, damp south-west wind was blowing, and the mind was unstrung. I went out bicycling, and worked down against the wind to Burgess Hill, returning to Wivelsfield, and I saw many beautiful vignettes; a deserted byre, with a big stone-tiled barn, doors open, and a water-wagtail, with head on one side, looked curiously in to the raftered dark; a little timbered, ancient house, the front walls all scored with pale half-circles, where the roses swung to and fro; a deep, silent lane, overhung with close hazels, up which I went in gratified silence . . . . It has been a happy day, at least a contented one, in spite of a few sombre shadows which lie in the background of the mind, like big clouds, and from which a few scattered rain-drops seem at times to fall.

What odd tricks the mind plays. At Stanmore I saw in the church the grave of some good woman, who died on August 17, aged forty-three. I was seized with a mild presentiment that August 17 would bring me some fateful crisis. But it has passed without event, and I am still here.

A. C. BENSON, 1905

18th

To Cree Church, to see it how it is: but I find no alteration there, as they say there was, for my Lord Mayor and Aldermen to come to sermon, as they do every Sunday, as they did formerly to Paul's. There dined with me Mr Turner and his daughter Betty. Betty is grown a fine young lady as to carriage and discourse. We had a good haunch of venison, powdered and boiled, and a good dinner. I walked towards White Hall, but, being wearied, turned into St Dunstan's church, where I heard an able sermon of the minister of the place, and stood by a pretty, modest maid, whom I did labour to take by the hand, but she would not, but got further and further from me; and, at last, I could perceive her to take pins out of her pocket to prick me if I should touch her again – which, seeing, I did forbear, and was glad I did spy her design And then I fell to gaze upon another pretty maid, in a pew close to me, and she on me; and I did go about to take her by the hand, which she suffered a little, and then withdrew. So the sermon ended and the church broke up, and my amours ended also.

SAMUEL PEPYS, 1667

19th

The 19th August, 1622, being Monday, about one of the clock in the morning, the wind arose and blew so vehemently for six hours, that it brake down divers strong trees. It quealed [curled up] all hedges towards the south that they davered [withered] as if they had been scorched with lightning. It spoiled standing corn so, as in many places it seemed that all the corn (especially barley and oats) had been threshed or beaten out of the husks. By report there is 200*l.* loss and hurt done to corn in Axmouth only by the said wind.

WALTER YONGE, 1622

20th

We steamed past the various places on the beautiful coast of *Devonshire* which we had passed three years ago – *Seaton, Sidmouth,* off which we stopped for ten minutes, *Axmouth, Teignmouth,* &c.; – till we came to *Babbicombe,* a small bay, where we remained an hour. It is a beautiful spot, which before we had only passed at a distance. Red cliffs and rocks with wooded hills like *Italy,* and reminding one of a ballet or play where nymphs are to appear – such rocks and grottos, with the deepest sea, on which there was not a ripple. We intended to disembark and walk up the hill; but it came on to rain very much, and we could not do so. We tried to sketch the part looking towards *Torbay.* I never saw our good children looking better, or in higher spirits. I contrived to give Vicky a little lesson, by making her read in her English history.

We proceeded on our course again at half past on o'clock, and saw *Torquay* very plainly, which is very fine. The sea looked so stormy and the weather became so thick that it was thought best to give up *Plymouth* (for the third time), and to put into that beautiful *Dartmouth,* and we accordingly did so, in pouring rain, the deck swimming with water, and all of us with umbrellas; the children being most anxious to see everything. Notwithstanding the rain, this place is lovely, with its wooded rocks and church and castle at the entrance. It puts me much in mind of the beautiful *Rhine,* and its fine ruined castles, and *Lurlei.*

I am now below writing, and crowds of boats are surrounding us on all sides.

QUEEN VICTORIA, 1846

21st

Last night the Princess again went to sup at Mr Angerstein's, and unfortunately Lord and Lady Buckinghamshire were there. The latter behaved very rudely, and went away immediately after the Princess arrived. Whatever her opinions, political or moral, may be, I think that making a curtsy to the person invested with the rank of Princess of Wales, would be much better taste, and more like a lady, than turning her back and hurrying out of the room.

I wonder why the Princess treats the Dean of Windsor with such marked dislike, for he has always been respectful and attentive to her and her mother, the Duchess of Brunswick. It is vexatious to those who take an interest in her Royal Highness' welfare, to observe how she slights persons to whom it is of consequence for her to show civility; and how she mistakes in the choice of those on whom she lavishes her favour. The Princess is always seeking *amusement,* and unfortunately, often at the expense of prudence and propriety. She cannot endure a dull person: she has often said to me, 'I can forgive any fault but that'; and the anathema she frequently pronounces upon such persons is, – 'Mine Gott! dat is de dullest person Gott Almighty ever did born!'

LADY CHARLOTTE BURY, 1813

22nd

I had an awfully bad night, kept waking up at all hours, thanks to Clarke who snored and ground his teeth like a maniac all the night. This was the first time I had slept in the same room with Clarke, and I was very glad it was the last. We got up at 7, took towels, went across the bridge to the weir and bathed. It was very jolly, the river just there being very wide, and a tremendous rush of water from the weir. We went back to the Hotel and ordered breakfast, and after bullying the waiters and waiting nearly an hour, we got some. It was quite on a par with the supper we had the night before; everything

very bad and served in a most uncomfortable style. The coffee was about the substance of mud, the bread was stale and the ham was very salt. The three egg-cups which we used appeared to be the only ones the establishment possessed, as some other fellows that were having their breakfast at another table in the coffee room, had their eggs brought in wine glasses. We asked for a slop basin. The waiter looked as if he thought it quite an unnecessary luxury, and brought us a finger-glass, that, I suppose, being the nearest substitute he could find. After breakfast, whilst the other two packed up and got the boat ready, I walked to the town with my can, and bought half a gallon of milk.

HOWARD WILLIAMS, 1875

23rd

I was spectator of the most magnificent triumph that ever floated on the Thames considering the innumerable boats and vessels, dressed and adorned with all imaginable pomp, but, above all, the thrones, arches, pageants, and other representations, stately barges of the Lord Mayor and Companies, with various inventions, music and peals of ordnance both from the vessels and the shore, going to meet and conduct the new Queen from Hampton Court to Whitehall, at the first time of her coming to town. In my opinion, it far exceeded all the Venetian Bucentoras, etc., on the Ascension, when they go to espouse the Adriatic. His Majesty and the Queen came in an antique-shaped open vessel, covered with a state, or canopy, of cloth of gold, made in form of a cupola, supported with high Corinthian pillars, wreathed with flowers, festoons and garlands. I was in our new-built vessel, sailing amongst them.

JOHN EVELYN, 1662

24th

Comes Sympson, to set up my other new presses for my books, and so he and I fell in to the furnishing of my new closet and taking out the things out of my old. And I kept him with me all day, and he dined with me; and so all the afternoon, till it was quite dark, hanging things, that is, my maps and pictures and drafts, and setting up my books, and as much as we could do, to my most extraordinary satisfaction; so that I think it will be as noble a closet as any man hath, though, indeed, it would have been better to have had a little more light. This afternoon comes Mrs Barbary Sheldon, now Mrs Wood, to see my wife: I was so busy, I would not see her. But she come, it seems, mighty rich in rings and fine clothes, and like a lady, and says she is matched mighty well, at which I am very glad, but wonder at her good fortune and the folly of her husband.

SAMUEL PEPYS, 1666

25th

Heard of a famous dandy at Harrowgate of the name of Stewart, a relative of Lord Castlereagh, who being asked by the Master of Ceremonies to dance enquired of him if the lady he meant to introduce him to was handsome, and being told she was he enquired if she was rich, and being told she had a good fortune asked if she danced well and being answered in the affirmative said, 'Trot her out'. When he came to her he took out his quizzing glass and having eyed the lady some time through it says to the M. C. 'Trot her back again'.

BENJAMIN NEWTON, 1818

26th

This day to London. Got away about 11.40: a nice fine day, not so rough as sometimes.

Saw a young man on a tricycle in Kensington. Of course it was a very modern "tric", and he could travel too. I thought of days when I used them, in between whiles, for business and sometimes had such a load on carrier at rear that I, being a light weight myself, it has stood up on end going up hills, front wheel in the air and I on the road, which made me feel quite embarrassed (in the middle of town). Also the pedals would sometimes fly round without moving the "tric" off the tram track, through a "patent" free-wheel which was "free" both ways at times.

Another time, coat-tails caught tight in rear brake of a bicycle I was on in busy part of the town – also on tram track – and I could neither get off the bike nor move forward or backwards until I tore the tail of the overcoat away.

Some rather mirth-provoking incidents for *other* people.

Hyde Park Corner was in an uproar of road relaying, just where I wanted to steer into the right hand. Found traffic would not allow this so had to go all around the "merry-go-round" just to get into St George's Hospital.

Succeeded in getting in and had tea and transacted my affairs – with the bike safe and sound in the inner courtyard.

Having been somewhat "run down" of late (not in the road sense, I'm glad to say) have had certain tablets prescribed for me which I have great hopes of.

They may put a little more "pep" in my pottering around, and help fill my "mile bag" a little fuller.

Arrived in Kingston just in time to secure my special loaf and so home to tea. Tea over, I felt I had somehow not had near enough riding so got out again and did a dash round Leatherhead, Ashstead and Epsom in the 1½ hours daylight left me. Home at dusk, having done 28½ this afternoon and another 16½ this evening – 45 for the day.

Not so much wood-block road laying nowadays, but find they have again used this type of surface at Sheen (between Sheen and Richmond).

Think this is all for to-day (except that one of the dogs had a fit this evening, causing much ado).

'JOHN SOWERBY', 1938

27th

I went to-day into the city to thank Stratford for my books, and dine with him, and settle my affairs of my money in the bank, and receive a bill for Mrs Wesley, for some things to buy for her; and the d— a one of all these could I do. The merchants were all out of town, and I was forced to go to a little hedge place for my dinner. May my enemies live here in summer! and yet I am so unlucky, that I cannot possibly be out of the way at this juncture. People leave the town so late in summer, and return so late in winter, that they have almost inverted the seasons. It is autumn this good while in St James's Park; the limes have been losing their leaves, and those remaining on the trees are all parched. I hate this season, where every thing grows worse and worse. The only good thing of it is the fruit, and that I dare not eat.

JONATHAN SWIFT, 1711

28th

When the king was at supper, eating a pullet, and a piece of cheese, the room without was full, but the men's stomachs were empty for want of meat; the good-wife, troubled with the continual calling upon her or victuals, and haveing, it seems, but that one cheese, comes into the room where the king was, and very soberly asks if the king had done with the cheese, for that the gentlemen without desired it.

Henry Slingsby, 1646

29th

Other wild plants found here. Wild pansie, tansie, Hound's tongue, Bittersweet, Hellebor, Marjoram, Yellow Agrimone, Nettle-leaved bell flower and vipers' buglos. Berries of Lords and ladies found also berries of some bush which turn from green to red and red to black. Amunsden reached the South Pole and also Scott a short time ago. We saw some nasturtium growing right up a house intertwined with a vine. Patrick found a double daisy. There is a lot of Maidenhair fern growing all over Tintern Abbey. The floods in Norwich are awful and people have had to swim for their lives. At Monmouth they are bad. One waiter reached his house in a boat and found his family living on the top floor. Many farms have lost 100s of £ worth of goods. The harvest being hopeless and much hay lost in actual floods. The Wye is now very swift also the Monnell. We motored 79 miles on Thursday to Tintern via Monmouth . . . .

John Knight (aged 12), 1912

30th

Abroad, and met with Hadley, our clerk, who, upon my asking how the plague goes, told me it increases much, and much in our parish; 'for,' says he, 'there died nine this week, though I have returned but six': which is a very ill practice, and makes me think it is so in other places, and therefore the plague much greater than people take it to be. I went forth, and walked towards Moorfields to see, God forgive my presumption! whether I could see any dead corpse going to the grave; but, as God would have it, did not. But, Lord! how everybody's looks and discourse in the street is of death, and nothing else; and few people going up and down, that the town is like a place distressed and forsaken. To my great joy to find myself worth £2,180 and add beside plate and goods which I value at £250 more.

SAMUEL PEPYS, 1665

31st

I begin to be heartily tired of this place [Weymouth] for it is all sameness and dullness: a gentleman left it some days since, saying he would not stay in any place, where were neither wenching, drinking, or gaming; and neither of the three are practised here, as so many young men and officers are employ'd in camps or on foreign service. – Col. York dined with us at our scrambling meal, at which I carve, put on the dishes and wait: we sat long, prosing over the American War, in which Col. York serv'd till captur'd with Ld Cornwall's; as also on the fatal loss of the Royal George man of war, a calamity that affects every bosom, and shocks the most obdurate heart.

JOHN BYNG, 1782

SEPTEMBER

1st

War is on us this morning. Hitler has taken Dantzig: has attacked – or is attacking – Poland. Our P[arliament]t meets at 6 tonight. This after a day in London, submerged doubts & hopes. Last night we heard terms to Poland read. We then had some hope. Now at 1 I go to listen I suppose to the declaration of war.

A dull hot day. I dont know why I write this. or what I feel. or shall feel. Children may come at 2 – have told Mabel to come. All is hovering over us. And a grouse bought for John at Wimbledon for lunch & L. putting bags on fruit trees, & the man putting up our columns; & complete silence everywhere. 5 to 1.

VIRGINIA WOOLF, 1939

2nd

Soon as dined, I and Moone away, and walked through the City, the streets full of nothing but people; and horses and carts loaden with goods, ready to run over one another, and removing goods from one burned house to another. They now removing out of Cannon Street, which received goods in the morning, into Lombard Street, and further: and, among others, I now saw my little goldsmith Stocks, receiving some friend's goods, whose house itself was burned the day after. We parted at Paul's; he home, and I to Paul's Wharf, where I had appointed a boat to attend me, and took in Mr Carcasse and his brother, whom I met in the street, and carried them below and above bridge to and again to see the fire, which was now got further, both below and above, and no likelihood of stopping it. Met with the King and Duke of York in their barge, and with them to Queenhithe, and there called Sir Richard Browne to them. Their order was only to pull down houses apace, and so below bridge at the waterside; but little was or could be done, the fire coming upon them so fast. Good hopes there was of stopping it at the Three Cranes above, and at Botolph's Wharf below bridge, if care be used; but the wind carries it into the City, so as we know not, by the wateside, what it do there. River full of lighters and boats taking in goods, and good swimming in the water; and only, I observed that hardly one lighter or boat in three that had the goods of a house in, but there was a pair of virginals in it. Having seen as much as I could now, I away to White Hall by appointment, and there walked to St James's Park; and there met my wife and Creed, and Wood and his wife, and walked to my boat; and there upon the water again, and to the fire up and down, it still increasing, and the wind great. So near the fire as we could for smoke; and all over the Thames, with one's face in the wind, you were almost burned with a shower of fire-drops. This is very true: so as houses were burned by these drops and flakes of fire, three or four, nay, five or six houses, one from another. When we could endure no more upon the water, we to a little alehouse on the Bankside, over against the Three Cranes, and there stayed till it was dark almost, and saw the fire grow; and, as it grew darker, appeared more and more; and in corners and upon steeples, and between churches and houses, as far as we could see up the hill of the City, in a most horrid, malicious, bloody flame, not like the fine flame of an ordinary fire. Barbary and her husband away before us. We stayed till, it being darkish, we saw the fire as only one entire arch of fire

from this to the other side the bridge, and in a bow up the hill for an arch of above a mile long: it made me weep to see it. The churches, houses, and all on fire, and flaming at once; and a horrid noise the flames made, and the cracking of houses at their ruin. So home wth a sad heart, and there find everybody discoursing and lamenting the fire; and poor Tom Hater came with some few of his goods saved out of his house, which was burned upon Fish Street Hill. I invited him to lie at my house, and did receive his goods; but was deceived in his lying there, the news coming every moment of the growth of the fire; so as we were forced to begin to pack up our own goods,and prepare for their removal.

SAMUEL PEPYS, 1666

3rd

We passed the river Ribble (which rises in the Yorkshire hills) to Preston, which was now extremely crowded with the gentry as well as commonalty, from all parts to the Jubilee, as we call it, but more rightly the Guild: we were too late to see the formalities, (the several companies in their order, attending the Mayor, &c. to church; and thence after sermon, to the Guild-house, to the feast, &c.) at the opening of the Guild, but were in time enough for the appendices, the pageant, &c. at the bringing in the harvest, ushered in by two gladiators in armour, on horseback, &c. The Queen discharged her part well, but the King was too effeminate. I was best pleased with a good providence that attended a fellow clad with bears' skins, &c., who running amongst the mob in the Low-street, by the church-yard, happily chased them away just before the wall fell, whereby their lives were saved. Had afterwards the company of several Yorkshire and Lancashire justices, with whom went to see the posture-master, who not only performed several uncommon feats of activity, but put his body instantly into so strange and misshapen postures, as are scarce credible, &c. Disturbed with the music, &c., and got little rest till three in the morning.

RALPH THORESBY, 1702

4th

At dinner was a sensible and cultivated General Smith, to whom I was introduced by his contemporary Mr Barnard, a charming representative of the Regency and the nankins . . . He left the navy, for which he still retains a preference, and went into an infantry regiment. When the Waterloo campaign began, the headquarters with three companies were on their way from the West Indies. The battalion was made up at home, and was sent up from Brussels to the field, arriving at 11 o'clock – 702 men; fifteen officers, of whom seven were wounded. They were under General Lambert. They remained stationary till 6 p.m., when Smith was cut over in the leg, and had to hobble to the rear. He got upon a return tumbril; was helped up by an officer of the Light Division, who had an arm in a sling, and was very civil. They went very slowly through the forest of Soignes; the sides of the road were deep mud, pavement in the middle. A staff-officer rode up and asked the man with the arm in sling whether he really was so badly wounded as not to be able to return to duty: he said he was; the staff officer said he was sorry to hear it. Smith ascertained after they got to Brussels that it was a sham. I asked him these questions: Did the men complain of the inefficiency of their muskets? – No. Did they see what was going on? – No. Could you see what was going on elsewhere, as for instance at Hougoumont? – No. We could see ears of corn cut off one after another; then we heard the bullet. Did you observe wounded men lying close to you, whom you could not leave your ranks to help? – No. Did you receive any supplies of ammunition? – No. Did any staff-officer come to you? – If they did, it was only to the brigadier. Nothing was said to us about the progress of the battle by any one. Did you get any food? – No. Most of the men had never been in action before; unconscious of danger. I have hastened to put this down for fear I should forget the previous evidence of an eye (and leg) witness about Waterloo. Perhaps I may never have another chance of questioning another man who was there.

WILLIAM CORY, 1864

5th

Mamma wrote to C. J. telling him his conduct was very foolish (of which I should think he is the best judge) and refusing to let me accept his proposals on account of his poverty, & not knowing him sufficiently to be able to judge of his character – which I think is very hard that just because she does not know what his life has been in the Navy, she supposes he has come home in ill health brought on by dissipation, which I never never will believe. I am more miserable than I have been since dear Papa died – this certainly is a weary world; money matters always standing in the way of happiness. I must look higher than earth for happiness.

A 'YOUNG LADY', 1867

6th

Mr Richard Cromwell his [Oliver Cromwell's] son was proclaimed Protector at Oxon at the usual places where kings have been proclaimed. While he was proclaiming before S. Marie's church dore, the mayor, recorder, townclerk, &c. accompanied by col. Unton Croke and his troopers, were pelted with carret and turnip-tops by yong scholars and others who stood at a distance.

ANTHONY WOOD, 1658

7th

Woodyates Inn may do well enough for a bait, [somewhere to stop for a bite to eat] but never for a place of nightly rest; for the bedrooms are miserable and the beds shocking: with mine I was so discontented that I awoke every hour, wishing for morning; of which I took the advantage, for I was on my horse by half-past six o'clock, having much difficulty to call the waiter to receive the bill.

Most refreshing was the ride to Sarum, [Salisbury] the air so cool and so sweet; and by the way I saw several deer upon the edge of the chase. I was at Sarum in time for the hot rolls and was receiv'd at the White Hart civilly and attentively, there shaved and dressed, drank coffee and then went to survey the cathedral. The close is comfortable and the divines well seated; but the house of God is kept in sad order, to the disgrace of our Church and of Christianity. Whenever I see these things, I wish for the return of the authority and Church government of a Land. The churchyard is like a cow-common, as dirty and as neglected, and thro' the centre stagnates a boggy ditch.

I hope that when the new bishop arrives, who is a scholar and a gentleman, he will be shock'd at the dilapidations of the beautiful old chapter-house and the cloisters, thro' the rubbish of which they are now making a passage for his new Lordship's installation in the chapter-house.

Salisbury has the advantage of a stream running thro' every street of the town, which must conduce to comfort, health and cleanliness; but I should fancy, from its being deeply brick'd up, must be often productive of accidents.

JOHN BYNG, 1782

8th

Upon thursday Sept 8 1673 there came to my house a poor ragged man in black, tho he had a good stuffe coat over all, my wife called out of my study to speak to him, he told me he made bold to call of me I askt him what profession he was of, he told me that he was a preacher, that his name was Hulmes, that he came from beyond Ripley, had been upon the Walls beyond York. – I askt him if he understood greek, he answered, no, I askt him what authours he read, he told me, authours enew, but he needed no papers, for he carryed his bible with him, I further discoursed with him, but found him a pittiful ignoramus, understood no latine, talkt impertinently, would haue begged a pair of Stockings of me – I admonisht him for pretending to so high a profession without gifts or call, he sd he had sure gifts that had used it 16 yeares – I left him, Mr Furnace admitted

this man to preach at Coley chappel Sept 21, when he had done he desired church-wardens to collect something for him, but they not going, he went himself from seat to seat and gathered for himself some 7sh amongst people –

OLIVER HEYWOOD, 1673

9th

We also passed shops where animals were for sale, which goods were both novel to us and comical. Peacocks were placed on pretty perches, bright cages with songsters hanging in between; there were cases of monkeys, large bird-cages containing turtle-doves, others with fine domestic fowls; lap-dogs of every type followed in nicely padded kennels; pointers lay at the bottom on leads, and by their side baskets of all kinds of game – all grouped so artistically that the whole made a charming picture. With like views and discussions we arrived at the northern end of the town, at the playhouse dedicated to the small middle-class Sadler's Wells. This district is very lovely: large meadows alive with herds of excellent cows; lakes with trees in front of the house itself, numerous avenues with delightful tables and benches for visitors, under trees hung with tiny lamps. In the open temple lower-class lasses, sailors and other young people were dancing. We were astonished at the handsome building and illumination of the hall, consisting of some hundred splendid Argand lamps which were bright as sunlight, and proved at the same time that such lamps do not smoke one little bit.

The scenes in the pit and boxes we found as strange as the ten-fold comedy itself. In the pit there is a shelf running along the back of the seats on which the occupants order bottles of wine, glasses, ham, cold chops and pasties to be placed, which they consume with their wives and children, partaking while they watch the play. The front seats of the boxes are just the same. In three hours we witnessed nine kinds of stage craft. First, a comedy, then a ballet, followed by a rope-walker, after this a pantomime, next some balancing tricks, an operette, and the most miraculous feats by a strong man; another comedy, and finally a second operette. All the decorations were exceedingly well painted, the dresses very fine and the music good.

The producers go to great expense and yet always make fifteen to twenty thousand guilders profit. The box next to ours was occupied by eight so-called light girls, all with fine, blooming figures, well dressed and true to their name, the most obvious gaiety in their eyes and faces. Not one of them looked older than twenty, and everyone so made that the best father or husband would be proud of having a virtuous daughter or wife with such stature and good features. We were sorry to think that Mr Archenholz had counted fifty thousand of these surely unhappy creatures. On our homeward path we saw the crowd of lamps along the roads, as Sadler's Wells lies on higher ground, and admired the splendid lighting of the city and its squares; but it was almost eleven o'clock before we reached home.

SOPHIE V. DE LA ROCHE, 1786

10th

Mama, and her lady and gentleman, to dinner. All were in constant expectation of more telegraphic despatches. At half-past ten o'clock two arrived – on for me, and one for Lord Granville. I began reading mine, which was from Lord Clarendon, with details from Marshal Pélissier of the further destruction of the Russian ships; and Lord Granville said, 'I have still better news;' on which he read, "From General Simpson – *Sevastopol is in the hands of the Allies*." God be praised for it! Our delight was great; but we could hardly believe the good news, and from having so long, so anxiously expected it, one could not realize the actual fact.

Albert said they should go at once and light the bonfire which had been prepared when the false report of the fall of the town arrived last year, and had remained ever since, waiting to be lit. On the 5th of November, the day of the battle of *Inkermann,* the wind upset it, strange to say; and now again, most strangely, it only seemed to *wait* for our return to be lit.

The new house seems to be lucky, indeed; for, from the first moment of our arrival, we have had good news. In a few minutes, Albert and all the gentlemen, in every species of attire, sallied forth, followed by all the servants, and gradually by all the population of the village – keepers, gillies, workmen – up to the top of the cairn. We waited, and saw them light it; accompanied by general cheering. The bonfire blazed forth brilliantly, and we could see the numerous figures surrounding it – some dancing, all shouting; – Ross playing his pipes, and Grant and Macdonald firing off guns continually; while poor old François d'Albertançon lighted a number of squibs below, the greater

part of which would not go off. About three-quarters of an hour after, Albert came down, and said the scene had been wild and exciting beyond everything. The people had been drinking healths in whisky, and were in great ecstasy. The whole house seemed in a wonderful state of excitement. The boys were with difficulty awakened, and when at last this was the case, they begged leave to go up to the top of the cairn.

QUEEN VICTORIA, 1855

11th

Sick of pictures, town, nobility, King, Lords and Commons, I set off by a steamer to Broadstairs. Came in stewed by steam and broiled by sun. I fagged about till sick, and got lodgings for my dears for a short breath of sea air.

Slept at an inn in a smallroom, fried till morning, got up at half-past five, took a delicious dip and swam exulting like a bull in June, ate a breakfast worthy of an elephant; put off and joined the Ramsgate steamer, and was in town again by half-past four. To-day I am fatigued, and to-morrow I take all my dears down. It is six years since they have changed air but for a day or two. I hope it will do them all good.

B. R. HAYDON, 1832

12th

Professor [Charles] Wheatstone, the Davies Gilberts, and Professor Powell were ushered in, and joined our party. Wheatstone was most interesting at dinner; he knows John Martin intimately, and says he is exactly like his pictures – all enthusiasm and sublimity, amazingly self-opinionated, and has lately taken a mechanical turn. He thinks him a man of great but misdirected genius. He gave some instances of monomania, and mentioned one extraordinary trance case of a man who was chopping down trees in a wood, and laid down and slept much longer than usual; when he awoke life was a blank; he was not in a state of idiotcy, but all his acquired knowledge was obliterated. He learned to read again quickly, but all that had passed previously to his trance was entirely swept away from his memory. At the age of fifty he slept again an unusual time; on awaking, his first act was to go to the tree which he had been felling on the former occasion to look for his hatchet; the medium life was now forgotten, and the former returned in its distinct reality. This is well authenticated.

CAROLINE FOX, 1836

13th

Rode through a most beautiful country to Otley. The roads in many places for a mile or two scarcely passable, the first four miles from Rochdale excessively bad, two miles in the middle between Halifax and Bradford very bad, a mile down to the bridge over the Aire between Bradford and Otley, these parts are the worst, but it is a matter of great surprize that the whole of the road should be in such indifferent repair and some execrably bad through the whole of this manufacturing district, that the whole and sole cause where the road is not pitched is the not letting the water off or breaking the stones and that the whole distance from Congleton to Otley there were not 20 persons employed in either of these occupations, notwithstanding they tell you half the people are out of employ and every three miles at furthest there is a shilling turnpike for chaise and pair. The environs of Rochdale, Ripponden, Halifax, Bradford, the bridge over the Aire and Otley are beautiful in the extreme and were it not for the reflection that the greatness of Great Britain depended I may say principally on the defacing of the hand of nature in these parts by the hand of man, which produces not only riches in every way from exportation and taxation at home and raises in time of war an innumerable population which is seen over the whole district for the armies, one could not help regretting that scenes so romantic and lovely should be impaired and destroyed by the black steam engines, but the yarn, the cloth, the cotton, the morals of the people destroyed by being crowded together and the hammers of the water engines perpetually affrighting quiet and comfort from vallies which at first view one would imagine were placed by nature in the most remote and sequestered situations for the peculiar residence of innocence and peace. The seats or rather the villas of the manufacturers like the citizens in the neighbourhood of London have neatness to recommend them but scarcely any character through the whole district that distinguishes one very much from another.

BENJAMIN NEWTON, 1816

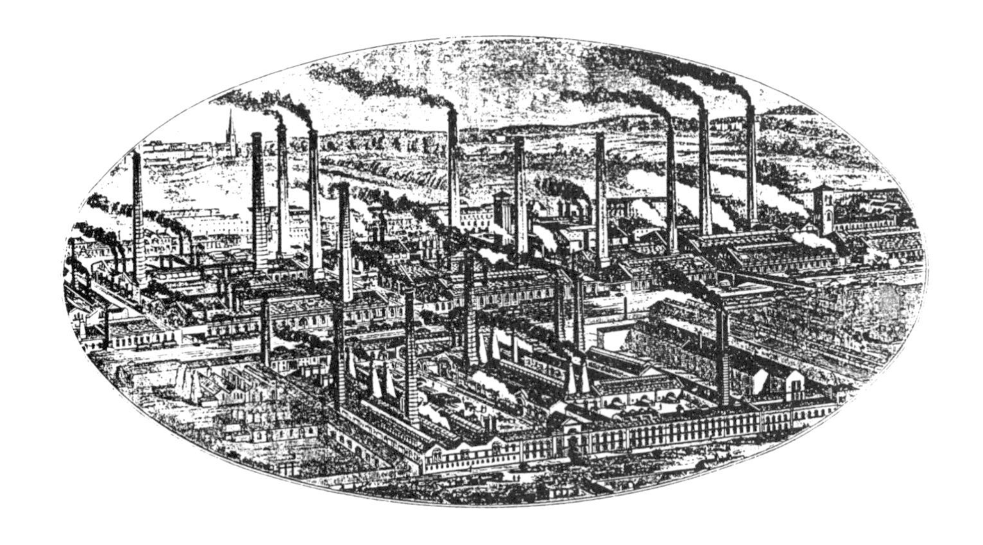

14th

Fine, warm, windy. Trip in steamer. On board a blind man singing to a harmonium played by a woman: 'Became blind at fifteen.' 'Those feel it less who are born blind,' I suggested. 'Perhaps,' he answered, 'but I am glad to have seen the world.' We ran past the Needles, touched at Bournemouth Pier and took in new passengers, then came the cliffs of Swanage Bay, the Old Harry rock, with tossing and sea-sickness. Landed at Swanage, an out-of-the-world place, houses roofed with large gray stones, narrow crooked street. Many stone-masons here. Beyond, a valley with trees and brook. Lunched at 'The Ship', kept by Mrs Diddlecomb, and back to steamer - more tossing and discomfort, of which I had a little.

On deck made friends with a quick bright Boy of seven, whose father sat grave and silent reading letters in a female hand. Boy and I talked oceans of nonsense. Passengers got out at Bournemouth and Yarmouth; then we ran for Lymington by starlight, missed the channel, and stuck in the mud. We had to land by boat, some of the women frightened; one, a smooth fair woman, 'going to Leicester to-morrow,' threw her arms round me, which was some compensation. The oars sparkled as they dipped. Landed at the Bath, with wet feet; to Custom House, and home to dinner.

WILLIAM ALLINGHAM, 1865

15th

Sow'd Rye & Turnip on Church Hill for the Sheep in Spring. Went to the Baldwin Taylor for my coat. B [breakfast] at Oxford & left Leather Breeches to be wash'd. Neice was gone to Heddington. A Duck for Din. Lord & Lady Harcourt drank Tea with Me. Lady Harcourt was stung by a Whasp. Finish'd thatching Bean Ricks.

JAMES NEWTON, 1759

16th

A 6 o'clock this evening a large balloon, striped red and blue, passed over this house very high in the air, almost a mile high it was said. It looked very small and we could not see the car. There was one man in it and he kept on sending down parachutes and emptying sandbags. The balloon was rapidly travelling eastwards in a straight line, but it had previously been veering about a good deal in various currents of air, passing over the Plough before it came to us. The balloon started from Bristol where there was a great Conservative demonstration and came down at Yatesbury.

The Yatesbury people were terrified when they saw the balloon descending and some ran away and some stared. But the aeronaut could get no one to help him or catch hold of the grappling ropes to steady the balloon, so it came down bump and bounced up again. At last it was secured and packed, and the aeronaut found board and bed at the Parsonage. It was said that he had made 30 ascents before.

FRANCIS KILVERT, 1871

17th

Dearest Mary and I were so set agog by Richmond, that I said, as we awoke, 'Let us go to Windsor.' She agreed, and away we went with barely money enough, but full of spirits. We got there, at six dined at the White Swan, evidently the remains of an ancient inn, and sallied forth to the castle, so full of spirits that we laughed at an odd-shaped stone or anything that would excuse a jest. The White Swan became so full and noisy, we went to the White Hart – clean, neat inn, and were in comfort. We walked to Eton, and sat and lounged in the shade of its classical playground. Our money lasted well, but, unfortunately, a barber who shaved me, as he was lathering, so praised his Windsor soap, that I, victim as I was, took six cakes, spent four shillings out of the regular course, and thus crippled our resources. The great thing was now whether we should pay the inn bill, or pay our fare to town, and leave part of the bill to be sent. Mary was for paying the bill, and part of the fare, and paying the rest when we arrived. We did this, and I was reduced to sixpence when

we took our places on the top. Before the coach set off I took out the sixpence, as if I had £50 in my pocket, and said; 'Porter, here's sixpence for you'; flinging it so that it rang on the pavement. The porter, unused to such a present for looking after luggage, bowed and thanked me so much that all the passengers saw it, and without sixpence in my pocket I got as much respect all the way home as if I had £100.

B. R. HAYDON, 1822

18th

We enter'd Aylesford by a steep old Stone Bridge; and so to The Anchor Ale House, as bad a stop as could be, with most miserable stabling. The Day was so gay that any misery was to be Endured – so we attempted to be happy over our bad mutton chops and a Pudding with Brandy and Water. We saw, whilst at Dinner, a Gang of well-mounted smugglers pass by: How often have I wish'd to be able to purchase a Horse from their excellent Stables. – No Dinner could be worse than ours; nor could a stupider Inn Keeper be found! But we were highly gratified by our walk after Dinner; first to the church yard, then to the beautiful walk towards the Friars where The Dowager Lady Aylesford Resides . . . The View, from below The Elms, of the River, the Town, and Preston Hills of a well-wooded rich Country, screen'd from the North by the Hollingburn Hills is composed of the loveliest scenery. The Bridge must be one of the oldest extant. Our landlord was a surly ignorant Brute; nor would answer to any of our Questions about Harvest, Hop Picking, &c. &c.

After this hot walk tho' so much to our satisfaction we hasten'd to go: Recrossing The Bridge we turn'd to the Left over fields, (the Gates of which were luckily unlocked) near The River, to Allington Castle: near to which is much made Ground, and highly raised mounds.

Allington Castle is as concealed a Spot and of as much curiosity as can be found; In it resides a Farmers Family and Cottagers. It should be a survey of 3 Hours: – but all Tourists hurry Thence to Langher; and so to Barsted; where we came, at the Coll's desire to hunt Family antiquities. – At a small Inn having taken Tea, we walk'd to The Church; but our search was in vain as to Bertie monuments.

The Twilight now came on, and our Road lay thro Hop Grounds, where every creature (even at that hour) was employ'd in Picking Hops, with their whole Families; For the little Children in their Cradles (a pleasant and novel sight) were strew'd, dispersedly amidst The Hop Gardens: – The Twinkling Lights aided the Imagination and made me fancy it like a scene in a Pantomime Dance. – Ld. Romney's Seat, The Mote, which we pass'd by appeared to advantage by moon Light.

JOHN BYNG, 1790

19th

Between twelve and one, I preached at Freshford; and on White's Hill, near Bradford, in the evening. By this means many had an opportunity of hearing, who would not have come to the room. I had designed to preach there again the next evening; but a gentleman in the town desired me to preach at his door. The beasts of the people were tolerably quiet till I had nearly finished my sermon. They then lifted up their voice, especially one, called a gentleman, who had filled his pocket with rotten eggs: but, a young man coming unawares, clapped his hands on each side, and mashed them all at one. In an instant he was perfume all over; though it was not so sweet as balsam.

JOHN WESLEY, 1769

20th

Yesterday was a great Foot-race at Woodstock, for 1400 libs., between a running Footman of the D. of Wharton's and a running Footman of Mr Diston's of Woodstock, round the 4 Mile course. Mr Diston's Man, being about 25 years of Age (& the Duke's about 45), got it with ease, outdistancing the Duke's near half a Mile. They both ran naked, there being not the least scrap of any thing to cover them, not so much as Shoes or Pumps, wich was look'd upon deservedly as ye Height of Impudence, & the greatest Affront to the Ladies, of wich there was a very great Number.

THOMAS HEARNE, 1720

21st

8.50 p.m. Not long in from a very wet ride round Woking, Chobham, Bagshot and Staines – at least, it was pretty wet for 30 miles or so. But enveloped in cape and leggings I set out down the Portsmouth road, down through Ripley – steady rain – had to keep stopping to wipe glasses – everything a blur through wet specs.

Tried the sou'wester once more, found the elastic under chin interferes with side arms of glasses – this won't do, cannot risk glasses being dragged off. Tried sou'wester without chin strap. Would it keep on? Oh no, not for many yards.

It suddenly floated off my head like a balloon – flew away. Had to stop, go back, retrieve it (not that it's really worth the trouble). Decided it was no good anyway and put it away. Substituted beret. Still half blind with rain on glasses, but got on with it.

The old bike after a couple of weeks' rest, is a wonderful change, and glides along so silently and takes the hills very easily (think all the 3-gears must be a good bit lower than the new one. Rather a pity the gears of the two bikes work in opposite directions. After 14 1/2 years of B.S.A. 3-speed, I found myself working the new (Sturmey-Archer) in the same way and at the last gasp on very steep hills let it forward only to find myself come to a standstill – on top gear.

'JOHN SOWERBY', 1938

22nd

I saw an *affiche* [poster] of Mr Cathcart's running away £9 in the manager's debt stuck up in the green-room!! This man seems utterly despicable! Walked round the market-place, and so home by the church – examining the wooden spire, curious and unsightly, observed the date 1003 upon the porch. Laid out my clothes, sent for a play-bill and a History of Chesterfield – not very interesting. Wish to see Hardwick and Chatsworth, if practicable. Read a little of *Hamlet,* which I acted to the dullest, most insensible audience, and among the most brutish I ever yet had to endure. I did my best, but occasionally felt the lethargy of the audience steal over me. My friend Horatio did everything at night contrary to what I had requested in the morning, but I think I never either looked or offered an ill-natured thing. Was tired, and beginning to grow *home-sick.*

WILLIAM MACREADY, 1834

23rd

Lord Desart has a very large and noble Newfoundland dog, black and white. The head is entirely black, and has a strange protuberance at the back of it. He is very powerful and courageous, and very faithful to his master. He always goes with the gentlemen when they bathe, and makes himself quite troublesome by attempting to drag them or Richard from the water, under the apprehension that they are drowning. He was brought up to-day into mamma's room, for the second time, to amuse her. He is not fond of ladies, and, indeed, cares for few people besides Lord Desart. However, he received some bread and toast very graciously, and laid his paws very heavily, with a great bounce, on mamma's bed. He conducted himself very independently and unceremoniously, and by no means courts caresses.

EMILY SHORE (AGED 13), 1833

24th

Worked in the morning as usual, and sent off the proofs and copy. Something of the black dog still hanging about me; but I will shake him off. I generally affect good spirits in company of my family, whether I am enjoying them or not. It is too severe to sadden the harmless mirth of others by suffering your own causeless melancholy to be seen; and this species of exertion is, like virtue, its own reward; for the good spirits, which are at first simulated, become at length real.

SIR WALTER SCOTT, 1828

25th

Went to see the young Widow Self got acquainted with at Islington Wells & She lives with her Brother a hedge Schoolmaster near More Fields, & she seem'd to be pleas'd with my Company & invited me to come & drink Tea with Her. Call'd on Mrs Pickering & threaten'd to seize Challiners Goods if he did not pay One guinea by next Saturday se'nnight. Got home before Din & view'd my Lord Foley's Garden. Sisters went to Chelsea in my Landau & Self went with Hetty over the Stones. Went to St George's Church but did not stay till Prayers begun having an Occasion to make Water often with some small sort of Pain & also a tendency to go to stool.

JAMES NEWTON, 1761

26th

Doctor's Consulting Rooms – my life has been spent in them! Medical specialists – Harley Street men – I have seen four and all to no purpose. M – wrote me the other day, –

'Come along and see me on Tuesday; some day I dare say we shall find something we can patch.'

He regards me with the most obvious commiseration and always when I come away after a visit he shakes me warmly by the hand and says, 'Good-bye, old man, and good luck.' More luck than the pharmacopoeia.

My life has always been a continuous struggle with ill-health and ambition, and I have mastered neither. I try to reassure myself that this accursed ill-health will not affect my career. I keep flogging my will in the hope of winning thro' in the end. Yet at the back of my mind there is the great improbability that I shall ever live long enough to realise myself. For a long time past my hope has simply been to last long enough to convince others of what I might have done – had I lived. That will be something. But even to do that I will not allow that I have overmuch time. I have never at any time lived with any sense of security. I have never felt permanently settled in this life – nothing more than a shadowy *locum tenens*, a wraith, a festoon of mist likely to disappear any moment.

W. N. P. BARBELLION, 1914

27th

Tolerably tired we both were and in equal haste for dinner. Mrs B had been long return'd. – A curricle drove in with some Irish acquaintance of Mrs B's; a visit was unavoidable tho particularly avoided by me as neither understanding their breeding or language.

This was a loss of evening to me for I was dragg'd to see his coach horses drink warm water and then be swaddled up in cloathes. When we retired to our old fashioned hour of supper, they call'd for tea for she is most tediously fine and he is aquiescent: They have just finish'd a cold autumnal tour to the Lakes, because nobody of elegance can quit London during all the heat and stinks of a metropolis. I being tired at an unfashionable hour, hurry'd to bed.

JOHN BYNG, 1794

28th

To-day we visited Mr Boydell's shop, London's most famous print dealer. What an immense stock, containing heaps and heaps of articles! The shop is on the Strand, one of the city's most populous thoroughfares, and has a view either side.

Here again I was struck by the excellent arrangement and system which the love of gain and the national good taste have combined in producing, particularly in the elegant dressing of large shop-windows, not merely in order to ornament the streets and lure purchasers, but to make known the thousands of inventions and ideas, and spread good taste about, for the excellent pavements made for pedestrians enable crowds of people to stop and inspect the new exhibits. Many a genius is assuredly awakened in this way; many a labour improved by competition, while many people enjoy the pleasure of seeing something fresh – besides gaining an idea of the scope of human ability and industry.

I stayed inside for some time so as to watch the expressions of those outside: to a number of them Voltaire's statement – that they stare without seeing anything – certainly applied; but I really saw a great many reflective faces, interestedly pointing out this or that object to the rest.

SOPHIE V. DE LA ROCHE, 1786

29th

M., being Mich(aelmas) day, severall schollers went to steale geese at Wulgercote [Wolvercote]; but being discovered they were pursued; and in the pursuit one scholler was thrust in the arme with a prong, another taken. He that was taken they had to Wulvercote and set him in the stocks in is gowne; but the rest rallying up forces to the number of 40, came and rescued the man, broke all the windows in Wulvercote, and took a goose and stuck him on the end of a long staff, and soe marched through the town and home in triumph.

ANTHONY WOOD, 1662

30th

Dined at the Athenaeum, and was complimented on my good looks, but found my loss of memory of a very alarming kind. Having dined, and my spectacle-case being brought me, I took a nap in the drawing-room. Thought it some room belonging to magistrates and quarter sessions, and took the book-racks at a distance for the court. Everything seemed bigger and older. I at length was spoken to by some one, and asked him where I was. This is worse than anything that ever occurred. There is no doctoring for a case like this; nor can the patient minister to himself.

HENRY CRABB ROBINSON, 1863

OCTOBER

1st

Thursday, the 1st. E.M.P. [evening and morning prayers] St James's. Bought Brass Handles for the Locks. Saw the learned Canary Bird & heard two men play several Tunes on Glasses about half full of Water. At this Performance Self convers'd with a Lady in Mourning with two Children & could take her to be my Wife if she was willing to have me for her Husband. Mrs Ridly drank Tea here. Waited on Admiral Long & he expected me in the Morning at his House to write a Letter for Him.

JAMES NEWTON, 1761

2nd

A gale of wind all day, with a drizzling rain and sometimes a heavy pour. Up at five, and, as I said would be the case, found no pheasants where I was the day before, as they seldom return the next day. Came home wet to the skin at eleven. Out again at one: went fly fishing; bagged at the same time 1 jack snipe, 1 hare, 1 cock pheasant, and 2 partridges, and had capital sport pulling out the trout. Returned (wet through again) by four o'clock with fish, flesh, and fowl in plenty.

COLONEL PETER HAWKER, 1816

3rd

The Bow Street officers are still hovering about the county in disguise, in hopes of arresting Page himself. Papa met them to-day while riding; one was dressed like a gamekeeper, the other like a tinker. Papa knew them at once, and spoke, not knowing that they wished to be concealed.

Papa. "Well, what sort of success have you had?"

Officer (in a low voice). "None yet. We are going about in this disguise that it may not be known we are here."

(*Aloud, as papa was going on*) "We'll take the letter for you, sir."

Papa. "Oh, thank you."

This was to blind a carter who was a little behind them, and might find them out.

EMILY SHORE (AGED 15), 1835

4th

Gale raging like fury all night and all to-day up to evening. But having given into it yesterday, letting it drive me home with only 6 miles for the book, I felt I really must fight it to-day so as to get *somewhere* for tea. Put on a few extra shirts and pullovers, the beret and the "shorts" (tried trousers and felt all at sea in *them* after the whole summer in the "shorts"). Went off down the by-pass about 2 p.m. in the teeth of the wind.

I don't know how many times it beat me to a standstill (to regain my breath) before I got even to the Portsmouth road. Felt like a mere straw on the road, blown all ways at once. Eddies of wind every way; job to hold the bike straight at all.

Still I progressed. Having gained the Portsmouth road still alive and kicking, I turned a little more south, going off a point or two from the direct force of the wind. But even so had a job to keep moving. Got through Cobham, then had a few moments' rest on the heather (Wisley Common), where the sun was showing lovely. Got on through Ripley. Heavy shower. Put on cape. Wind so strong rain could not last: it was blown miles away in a few minutes.

Away with the cape again. Most difficult trying to ride in a cape in such a tempest. Got on finely into Guildford, no stop; down the steep cobbles. Sun and wind in my eyes, had difficulty to see the scout's signal here, or even see the "Scout", although I knew he was there. Then overran the "red" at the bottom of the town ere I realized there *is* signal there also. Stopped with great jerk part way over.

On up the hill out of the town and on towards Godalming, but not right into it, stopping at Peasmarsh (*the* tea hut), halfway between Guildford and Godalming.

I found my usual "hostess" missing, as she is gone to the "pictures", and her deputy "carrying on". So had 1 tea, 1 sausage roll and 1 butter roll for 5½d. (and felt I needed it as I had shoved 20 miles against the gale). Whilst there, a real deluge came on, which meant I had to fish out the old cape to put over the bike out there in the wet. I was all right in the tea hut – very nice in there sipping tea, smoking and having a little conversation with certain motor people in and out of the place.

No cyclists at all on the road anywhere to-day except "locals" riding home from work, and some of *them* walking bikes. Stayed a good while in the jolly old hut and rain went off. Sun came out. I went out, packed up cape, got on bike and rode *with* the wind the 20 miles home. Fine going too. Grand. Not caught by the "dark" until nearly to Cobham.

Thank goodness it is such a good road, and had a white kerb all the way which is a great help. Halted near Cobham, and again (on a seat) at Esher. It was such a delightful evening, moon sailing high, I really had to dawdle about somewhere. Cut out the by-pass and came home Ditton way, having totalled exactly 40 miles down and back. Bike going fine, silent as the grave, and takes no notice of hills (going up with the wind). Altogether a beautiful little ride, and well worth fighting the gale to get it in.

Spent 5½d this journey.

'JOHN SOWERBY', 1938

5th

To my tailor's, and there took up with my friend Willett, and to the King's House: and there, going in, met with Knipp, and she took us up into the tiring-rooms and to the women's shift, where Nell was dressing herself, and was all unready, and is very pretty, prettier than I thought. And so walked all up and down the house above,and then below into the scene-room, and there sat down, and she gave us fruit: and here I read the questions to Knipp, while she answered me, through all her part of 'Flora's Figaries' which was acted today. But, Lord! to see how they were both painted would make a man mad, and did make me loathe them; and what base company of men comes among them, and how lewdly they talk! and how poor the men are in clothes, and yet what a show they make on the stage by candle-light, is very observable. But to see how Nell cursed, for having so few people in the pit, was pretty; the other house carrying away all the people at the new play, and is said, nowadays, to have generally most company, as being better players. By and by into the pit, and there saw the play, which is pretty good.

SAMUEL PEPYS, 1667

6th

Lord Dudley's place is in this hideous region, one mile on the London side of Basingstoke, our fourth stage, at which we arrived at thirteen minutes to two. Here we dined. Now, I had a great horror of Basingstoke, because when papa and mamma went to Devonshire five years ago, they stopped here at a most horrid inn, and could get nothing to eat but putrid chops; the whole place, too, they described as filthy, abounding with bad smells. So that we rather dreaded dining here; but we were agreeably disappointed. I cannot deny that every street was flanked by two open drains nearly overflowing, nor that the horses marched to their stables through the same passage by which we walked to dinner, and that the only reason we smelt no bad smells might have been that we had no leisure so to do. But when we entered the dining-room, a large apartment, we discovered the following goodly apparitions: at the top a round of beef, at the bottom a fillet of veal, in the centre a ham, chicken, potatoes, bread, and butter; the whole forming a capital cold dinner. Mamma and I, with a very good appetite, fell on the fowl. One of his wings was already gone; we took the other, and stripped him besides of his breast, and a portion of one leg. In about a quarter of an hour we were summoned back to the coach, and left Basingstoke greatly raised in our esteem . . .

EMILY SHORE (AGED 16), 1836

7th

Dr Lardner came into my room, and chatted with me for some time; among other things, in speaking of the tour he had made through Scotland and by the lakes, he mentioned his visit to Southey at Keswick. On passing the drawing-room he noticed several ladies apparently in a very cheerful mood; on giving his name, after waiting about five minutes, Southey came to him, the very image of distraction, took his hand and led him into his study. For a long time he remained silent – at length told him he believed he must dismiss him; in fine he disclosed to him that within the last five minutes, since he rang the bell at the lawn gate, Mrs Southey had, without previous indication or symptom, gone raving made, and to that hopeless degree that within an hour he must take her to an asylum. These are the cruel liabilities of our nature, which no human power can cure, but which only resignation and the hope that religion offers can alleviate and soothe.

WILLIAM MACREADY, 1834

8th

The 8th October, my uncle Houghton's birthday, went to Baguley with cousin Brearcliffe, Mr Cattell, Mr Thyer, Mr Greaves, Mr Egerton, my papa and mamma, stayed two nights; everybody in hiding for fear of the rebels [Bonnie Prince Charlie's rebel forces advancing into the North of England]; two regiments gone through this town.

I bought a blue and white gown off Mr Starkey, gave 12s for it. The Presbyterians are sending everything that's valuable away, wives, children, and all, for fear of the rebels.

ELIZABETH BYROM, 1745

9th

Self Br [breakfast] with Mrs Dellafey & then waited on Her to Kew Gardens where we were much entertained, tho' it remained doubtfull for some time whether the Gardiner would let us see them, till I talk'd about giving him a Shilling. The Chinese Pagoda ten story hight & the two heathen Temples on each Side of it, are striking Things. The Temple of the Sun & the Temple of Fame are very well worth seeing. The Ruins also are very natural. The Chinese Temple by the Water is very delightfull. The Flower Garden & the Avery as well as the Gold & Silver Fishes are very entertaining. The Chinese Parteridges are vastly Beautifull. Call'd on Mr Arnold. Din'd at the Pack horse at Turnham Green. Drank Tea Evening at Mrs Dellafeys & then return'd Home.

JAMES NEWTON, 1761

10th

Read Cunningham's Morning Thoughts. The weather so dreadful that we could not get to church – still less could I return to the cottage, in consequence of which I was seized with a real fit of the fidgets.

Prayers at home – the gentlemen returned from Cork – in the evening read some of Paley's Evidences – a most valuable work.

Saw in the papers that the expedition from Calcutta had sailed on the 12th April and with it, I fear, my best beloved brother! May God protect him!

Visited a wretched family who are actually living in a *hole* made between the angles of a hedge and covered with straw – the poor woman within three weeks of her confinement, her sick child stretched by her side. We hear of misery – we talk of it – but we know not what it is until we have seen it exemplified in *Ireland!* In the afternoon Mr Hare came from Cove to pay us a visit and brought with him the news of the expedition having succeeded. Oh how I long for to-morrow's news.

Clarissa Trant, 1824

11th

After luncheon, Albert decided to walk through the wood for the last time, to have a last chance, and allowed Vicky and me to go with him. At half-past three o'clock we started, got out at Grant's, and walked up part of *Carrop,* intending to go along the upper path, when a stag was heard to roar, and we all turned into the wood. We crept along, and got into the middle path. Albert soon left us to go lower, and we sat down to wait for him; presently we heard a shot – then complete silence – and, after another pause of some little time, three more shots. This was again succeeded by complete silence. We sent some one to look, who shortly after returned, saying the stag had been twice hit and they were after him. Macdonald next went, and in about five minutes we heare "Solomon" give tongue, and knew he had the stag at bay. We listened a little while, and then began moving down hoping to arrive in time; but the barking had ceased, and Albert had already killed the stag; and on the road he lay, a little way beyond *Invergelder* – the beauty that we had admired yesterday evening.

QUEEN VICTORIA, 1852

12th

A handsome maid living in Catstreet, being deeply in love with Joseph Godwin, a junior fellow of New Coll., poyson'd herself with rats-bane. This is mention'd because it made a great wonder that a maid should be in love with such a person as he, who had a curl'd shag-pate, was squint-ey'd and purblind, and much deform'd with the smal pox.

ANTHONY WOOD, 1655

13th

I went out to Charing Cross to see Major-General Harrison hanged, drawn, and quartered; which was done there, he looking as cheerful as any man could do in that condition. He was presently cut down, and his head and heart shown to the people, at which there was great shouts of joy. It is said, that he said that he was sure to come shortly at the right hand of Christ to judge them that now had judged him and that his wife do expect his coming again. Thus it was my chance to see the King beheaded at White Hall, and to see the first blood shed in revenge for the King at Charing Cross. I went by water home, where I was angry with my wife for her things lying about, and in my passion kicked the little fine basket which I bought her in Holland, and broke it, which troubled me after I had done it.

SAMUEL PEPYS, 1660

14th

Wet morn. I thought it very uncertain that Mr Bramston would come; however he did come – just as I had risen from my prayers and prayed that God would direct me, I saw him riding up to the house. Lady Cork's conversation had made me feel quite *conscious* and foolish, altho' indeed I can hardly believe what she told me; it is too flattering, even to my vanity. I felt my cheeks burning with awkwardness when I had to make my appearance in the Drawing Room.

Lord Mount Sandford was not up – it was reported that he had over-slept himself – but I have always suspected and I believe with truth that it was a *fox's sleep* – that he wished to give us an opportunity of chatting comfortably and quietly in the Drawing Room before breakfast.

Yet there was something so ridiculous in the circumstance attending our first and last meeting in 1828, the grunting of 700 pigs and the smell of steam and the horrors of seasickness were so blended with my recollections of his pleasant conversation that I could hardly help laughing. I found him as I expected very pleasing and gentlemanlike. We shall perhaps meet again.

CLARISSA TRANT, 1831

15th

This is the day on which I was married and it is now three years since. Doubtless many have been the disputes which have happened between my wife and myself during the time, and many have been the afflictions which it has pleased GOD to lay upon us, and which we have justly deserved by the many anemosityes and desentions which have been continually fermented between us and our friends, from allmost the very day of our marriage; but I may now say with the holy Psalmist, 'It is good for us that we have been afflicted'; for, thanks be to GOD, we now begin to live happy; and I am thoroughly persuaded, if I know my own mind, that if I was single again, and at liberty to make another choice, I should do the same – I mean make her my wife who is so now.

THOMAS TURNER, 1756

16th

Considered the servant problem. Mrs Newsholm had said that Sandy having left she would not mind coming back. Margaret said Mrs Newsholm was conscientious and well disposed but prejudiced and inclined to listen to tales. Mrs N. said that Sandy's language was shameful and unfit for young girl's to hear and he neither could, nor did work, leaving all to the footmen to do. Ann said for long servants had set one another against the place. Even Keen was unsettled the first year he was here, and told her he had heard tales enough to induce him to leave ten times. Tothill, although a good worker, had never been a friend of the family and never lost an opportunity of saying and hinting and insinuating things against us, and there was no love lost between Tothill and me. He was very ungrateful, Mrs Newsholm did not think Emily exactly put her in her right place in reference to underlings, and especially the housemaid whom she sometimes took into the storeroom.

DEARMAN BIRCHALL, 1876

17th

Dined at Hollin Hall, met Mr and Mrs Faber, Mr Powell Guise, Mr Bernard Gilpin. On my complaining of the toothache Mr Faber (the writer on Prophecy) said he heard the toothache accounted for in the following manner by a friend of his and he gave the account as if he believed it. He said that certain minute epemerae of the butterfly species flying about are accidentally taken into the mouth and that they then make a nidus in a rotten tooth where they deposit their eggs which in process of time are hatched and produce minute grub which immediately begin feeding on the nerves of the tooth and cause the intolerable pain which is experienced and that the remedy applied by his friend was to procure the seeds of henbane, make them very dry and then set them on fire under a tin funnel, the small end of which is to be directed so that the smoke may issue against the offending tooth which will immediately kill the grubs, and that the friend had ejected several in the saliva after the operation and seen them very distinctly with a lens.

BENJAMIN NEWTON, 1816

18th

On Oct. 18th. occurred the death of *Poor Miss Mouse*, otherwise *Xarifa*. I was very much distressed, because she had been so sensible about taking medicine that I thought she would get through, but the asthma got over her one night, and she laid herself out in my hand and died. Poor little thing, I thought at one time she would last as long as myself.

I believe she was a great age. Her nose and eyebrows were white, and towards the end of her life she was quite blind, but affectionate and apparently happy. I wonder if ever another doormouse had so many acquaintances, Mr Bright, Mr J. Millais, and Mr Leigh Smith had admired and stroked her, amongst others. I think she was in many respects the sweetest little animal I ever knew.

BEATRIX POTTER, 1886

19th

To business all day. Gracie went off to Hounslow to stop a few days to try and cheer up the old people after Katie's departure. The day was wretched but Bessie thought it would be an act of kindness and Grace was delighted to go. The Guards passed the

Dockyard on a splendid steamer this afternoon from Egypt and are to have a triumphant entry into London tomorrow. It seems but a few days time since we were all in a bustle and preparation to sent them away, indeed we have not yet got even straight after their departure – and now the farce (?) or tragedy (?) is ended and the performers are being called before the curtain to receive the applause of the audience. Plaudite!

CHARLES COMPTON, 1882

20th

My exquisite wedding bouquet was a present from dear Princess Christian, as well as the lace veil which I wore. When I was dressed and waiting, the band of the Scots Fusiliers marched past. It was a most curious coincidence, like a greeting from my dearest father, and it brought tears to my eyes. Martin Smith was most kind, and came to fetch me when all was ready. Of course Uncle Frederick Barne, who gave me away, behaved in an eccentric manner; but my bridesmaids were all there to time, and looked very pretty and nice in their pink frocks. They were Fanny Corbet, Tina Montgomery, Susan Rowley, Julia Angerstein, Evelyn Bathurst, Helen Ellice, Frances Vanneck, Caroline Duncombe, and Mina Nugent. I had a long time to wait first for Rainald and then for Mr Knightley and Mr Story, who married us; but I did not regret this, as it gave me plenty of time to collect my thoughts. Dear Rainald was very nervous, Mr Knightley still more so. I felt so perfectly happy in my choice that I could repeat the solemn words quite steadily, although Mr Knightley went so fast, it was very difficult. It was very soon over, and Mamma, Uncle Frederick, Charley Newdegate, Mr Gage, and Sir Thomas Munro witnessed the marriage. The next half-hour was rather trying, going about talking to people. I seem to have seen most of

my old Sotterley friends - Adèle Arnold, Lucy Wormald, and St. John. At one they all went in to breakfast, and we retire to a snug little luncheon upstairs. At 2 p.m. we went down, took leave of a few, very few, people, my darling mother bearing up beautifully and dear Tina being most helpful – and were off, the group of pink bridesmaids looking so pretty on the steps. The N.W.R. were most polite, giving us a saloon carriage all to ourselves. Lord Denbigh came and congratulated as we started, which also recalled dear Papa, and then away we sped to Blisworth, where a special engine brought us to Weedon. Here our new carriage was awaiting us, and at Dodford the Daventry volunteer corps was drawn up and gave us a hearty cheer. Our progress through Newnham was a small triumph, bands playing, bells ringing, arches of evergreens and flags and loud cheers all he way. The tenants, about thirty in number, very well mounted, were drawn up at the park gates, and escorted us to the house, the foot-people racing alongside, tumbling over each other in the fern in all directions. The bells of the dear little church that we love so well rang merrily, and all the school-children were drawn up in front of the house. As the carriage stopped, the tenants formed up outside the portico, and a very pretty and touching address was read. My darling husband spoke well and clearly in reply, and did not break down as I feared he would, for he felt it deeply, and his golden heart was indeed touched. The children strewed flowers at my feet as I stepped out of the carriage and we passed in, and so ended the long, trying, but happy day, and Rainald and I entered on our new life in our own home. May God bless it to us!

LADY KNIGHTLEY OF FAWSLEY, 1869

21st

Forty-five minutes past six. Too idle in bed to-day. O flesh, thou clog!

DR JOHN RUTTY, 1764

22nd

It rained so hard that we were not able to go to the well, we remained in doors, moping over our books until three o'clock when we were determined to walk out as it did not rain but the pavement was wretchedly dirty; we had eat a quantity of rotten Oysters for Luncheon and this made me quite sick. We called on Mrs Sheldon, Catherine we saw afterwards out of walking, she is the only one who goes to the ball. We put on our new gowns and drunk with the Miss Rushouts, Lord Nantwich and Mr Bowles, Lady Northwich, they being very ill and at ten we proceeded to the ball, the carriage had three journies, as Lord Northwich did not like going four in the charriot and fearing it would be improper for him and one of us to go alone, Justine and I had to make our debut alone in the ball room. Lady Mary was dressed in yellow, and had her diamonds, as for Lady Kenmare she looked beautiful. We payed out Lady Lloyd who spoke to us, we sat down, and I amused myself laughing at the dancers, Mr Blackwell (Lady Banbury's brother) was all civility he handed *me* to the carriage, the Servants when we passed, bawled out, *there goes* the dwarfs. I liked it better than the last although I did not dance, and did not speak to a soul. Mrs Corbett of Linslade looks most horridly large.

HARRIET WYNNE, 1804

23rd

Witnessed a strange scene in the House of Commons this afternoon. About four o'clock there was a rush of women into the outer lobby. They attempted to hold a meeting, and for more than a quarter of an hour there was a desperate fight between the police and the women, who were led by little Mrs Pankhurst, Miss Annie Kenney, and Miss Billington. These are the same women who created a scene some months ago.

Eventually they were cleared from the House of Commons, after reinforcements of police had been brought up. There was a good deal of rough treatment and considerable horse-play, but the frail women could not resist the stronger policemen. Nevertheless, a good many police were scratched and torn.

Ten of the viragos were taken to the police station, and were charged with rioting in the House of Commons. I suppose to-day they will be taken to prison, where they will, of course, threaten to go on hunger strike.

Why they should go on in this fashion remains a mystery, because they know that the House of Commons will not give women votes if it can help it.

R. D. BLUMENFELD, 1906

24th

"Up, Bfkt. had scarce done when Mr Hotham came, but could not stay he said, routed out a Bass and played to us, well. Then he staid to dinner, but was to go before dark, then it misled, then it grew darkish, then wrote and sent home instead of going, soon very facetious, pretty good friends, romped, but not all that, supped, had a long argument, he and I, concerning matrimony, managing wives, what degree of learning a woman ought to have etc. etc., liked my conversation very well and believe he did not dislike it, both agreed, though both differed. Not in bed till one. N. B. Miss Cleeve and I dressed up a Joan and put it in his bed."

ELIZABETH DRAPER, 1758

25th

After Br [breakfast] Self went to the Auction at Ditcot intending to have bought a speaking Trumpet, but it was sold before I got there & the old shabby Goods sold very well. Reach'd Wantage by Dinner time. Drank strong Beer at Mr Price's House, & Tea with the general Receiver of the Land Tax at Wantage. A Welsh Rabbit for Supper in the little Room near the Kitchen, & was pleasantly enough entertained with the People there, particularly Mr Oldworth, an elderly Man & a drunken Millar.

JAMES NEWTON, 1759

26th

Divers being at an invective sermon at the French ambassador's lodging in the Blackfriars, in London, part of the room wherein they were fell down, and killed about 80 or 92 persons, as it is reported.

The preacher was one Drury, a converted Protestant. He inveighed bitterly against Luther, Calvin, and Doctor Sutton, a reverent preacher sometime of St Mary Overy's in London, who, travelling beyond the seas, was drowned. This preacher said that the sea swallowed him because he was not worthy the earth should receive him. At which words the house sank. The report is strong that they have drawn out of the house 92 persons; and divers more are slain, with very many more grievously hurt.

WALTER YONGE, 1623

27th

I received several visits in the morning from Sir John Lowther, Sir Richard Allebone, Sir William Stich, and others; made up my accounts with Sir Edmund Wiseman; dined with Mr De Puy and Mr Ashton; took my leave of my Lord Treconnel, who promised to make the palace at Chester his way to Ireland, and said he hoped to live to see me Archbishop of Canterbury; and kissed the Queen's hand in her bed-chamber, where she told me she nor the King would never forget my services to them before they were so, nor should I ever want a friend so long as she lived. I had my sons John, Gervas, and Richard, with me at supper, Sir William Meredith, Mr Brooks, Dr Yonger, &c.,

THOMAS CARTWRIGHT, 1868

28th

Donegal. Set out for Lochrus on Customs duty. Outside car, moors and bare mountains to Ardara, when the groves of Woodhill give a softening. The sun sets into a jagged cloud breathing flame from its openings, rested on the dark mountains, disappeared, leaving a gloomy memory which soon faded too. Then the wind blew colder, the road became indistinct, the moors blended into a dim waste. Dine at Ardara, snug little room, adorned with pictures of Christ entering Jerusalem, Mary Queen of Scots, and Byron in a very large turn-down collar, with his arm round the waist of a lady with dark eyes and ringlets. A young naval officer in another room, who

smokes cigars. Biddy says with pride, 'O, Ardara's never without a stranger!' Driving back – in calm cold air, the stars shone in intense points of light all over the sky, the Heavenly Plough at rest in the unfurrowed air, the Pleiades glittering in the east, and we travelling straight south from the Polar Star. Then the moon-dawn spread up the sky, and above a low black outline of hills was lifted the bright snow-cold Presence, showing the solitary road and ghostly brown moorland stretching away on either side.

WILLIAM ALLINGHAM, 1847

29th

One evening while [imprisoned for debt] I was sitting by myself came a knock. I opened the door, and the head turnkey (who is a worthy man, for I have found him feeding the poor prisoners from his own table), after making sundry apologies, begged a few minutes' conversation. He sidled in and sat down, big with something. 'Perhaps, sir,' said he, taking out and putting across his knee a blue cotton handkerchief, 'you would scarcely suppose that from seven years old divinity and medicine have been my passions.' 'Certainly not, Mr Colwell.' 'Ah, sir, 'tis true, and I know, I assure you, much more than most of the doctors or parsons. Why, sir, you would little think I always cured the cholera. You may wonder, but it is a fact. I never lost a case, and in twenty-four hours they were well as ever. I do it all by *harbs,* Mr Haydon, by harbs. You are a public man – a man of genius, as they say, and perhaps you will laugh at a man like me knowing anything. But, sir,' said he, looking peculiarly sagacious and half knowing, yet trembling lest I should quiz, 'I gather my plants under the planets – aye, and it is wonderful the cures I perform. Why there is Lord Wynford, he is as bent as an old oak, and if he'd listen to me I'd make him as straight as a poplar.' 'No, Mr Colwell!' 'I would though,' he said in a loud voice, reassured on finding I did not laugh.

'By this time he had got courage. He assured me that he was blessed in a wife who believed in him, and that he had cured her often and often, and here his weather-beaten face quivered. 'Ah, Mr Colwell,' said I, 'your wife is a good, motherly woman. It's a comfort to me to see her face among the others here.' Colwell got solemn; assured me he had out-argued Taylor, the atheist, before the people; that he had undoubted evidence Joseph of Aramathea landed at Glastonbury, for at that time the sea came all up to the abbey, and what was to hinder him? 'And,' said he, 'Mr Haydon, would you believe it?' – drawing his chair closer, and wiping his mouth with his blue handkerchief, which he spread over his short thighs, that poked out, as it were, from under his belly – 'would you believe it, I can prove Abraham was circumcised the very day before Sodom and Gomorrah were burnt!'

"'Will you take a glass of wine, Mr Colwell?'" I replied. Colwell had no objection, and smacking his lips as he rose, said he would look in again, and bring me some books which would tell me all; but now he must go to 14 in 10 to give the gentleman his chum-ticket. I attended my guest to my little entrance, and he wished me good-night, looking an inch taller, perfectly convinced he had made an impression and would certainly have a convert.

B. R. HAYDON, 1836

30th

My reason for stopping at Penrith was to see Ulswater, one of the finest of the lakes, and the only one I could reach without going nearly forty miles out of my way. I hired a gig, and got a weaver's boy for a pilot; and, in six miles, reached the village of Pooley, at the foot of the lake. Nothing can be more romantically beautiful than the richly wooded hills that form the side scenery, and the majestic heights which compose the background of this landscape; in a word, the view creates a sort of sensation which we feel on hearing Mozart's music, seeing Shakespeare's tragedies, hearing Braham sing, or seeing ourselves surrounded by a good evening flight of wild fowl.

COLONEL PETER HAWKER, 1812

31st

On Saturday October 31 1674 being Wakefield fair, Mr Silvanus Rich, of Bulloughs in Peniston parish, being in Wakefield, with Mr Sottwel – and others and hauing drunk too liberally, in the night being dark they were getting on horsback, but Mr Rich being mounted on a good mare, outrid his company, and came down towards Wakefield bridge there was a great flood, waters were lying out so they ride deep before they came to the bridge, he being alone, his mare missed the bridge, and went below it into the main river, wch some imagine was 5 others 7 yards deep, his mare swam, he kept on, tho sometimes almost off, they were both taken doun a quarter of a mile doun the water, at last she came to the other side in the fields, where being to mount out of the water the mare could not, he got hold of a bough so parted from his beast, the bough failed him, he got hold of another, stuck there and at last got out, and at last he spyed his mare got into a field, he went to her, got on rode towards Ponfret forwards home, light of a house, went to bed got his cloathes dryed, so came home on Sabboth day – a miraculous providence, and fair warning! I pray god it may awaken conscience, this man hath made a profession, entertained ministers and meetings at his house, but of late hath given over, often stays out late, comes home in the night, ventures through dangerous waters, Lord strike home by this providence, –

OLIVER HEYWOOD, 1674

November

1st

My cousin, Sarah Swift Dew, who lives with us went by the first train for a situation in Devonshire – Winscott, near Torrington.

At noon today tolls ceased to be payable at both the Lower Heyford Turnpike Gates, & Bicester King's End gate (Bicester & Enstone Turnpike Trusts), & at Kirtlington Gate; & at Souldern Gate. The Heyford gates were removed today. The Commissioners of the Bicester & Enstone turnpike road have agreed to sell the Heyford Bridge Toll House & garden & the site of the Heyford Town Gate House & garden both in the parish of Lower Heyford, to Corpus Christi College, Oxford, for the sum of £60. Turnpike roads undoubtedly have done good service in times past, but their day seems to be over. The pulling down of these Turnpike Gates, or rather however the extinction of these Turnpike Trusts, will save me tenpence every Monday. I copied the Inscription on the Board at Souldern Gate which was as follows :- 'Souldern Gate. Tolls Payable at this Gate. For every Horse, Mare, Gelding, Mule, Ass, Ox, Bullock, & other Beast of Draught drawing in Carriage, not exceeding 5 Pence. For every Horse, Mare, Gelding, Mule, or Ass, not drawing, a sum not exceeding 1d. For every drove of Oxen, Cows, or neat [bovine] Cattle, a sum not exceeding 12 Pence per Score, and so on in proportion for any greater or less number 12 Pence. For every Drove of Calves, Pigs, Sheep, or Lambs, a sum not exceeding 6 Pence per Score, and so on in proportion for any greater or less number 6d. Double Toll on Sundays.'

George James Dew, 1877

2nd

This day I was with one Mr Fiddis, a minister at Holderness, who told me that, about six years ago, going to bed at a friend's house, some had out of roguery fixed a long band to the bedclose where he lay. About half an houer after he was got to bed they begun to pull, which, drawing the bedclose of by degrees put him into a suddain fright, and, looking up, he did really think and believe that he saw two or three spirits stirring and moveing about the bed, and says but that he discovered the string, and the partys confessing the fraud, he durst almost have sworn that he really saw strang things, which shews the effects of suddain frights.

ABRAHAM DE LA PRYME, 1698

3rd

I home, and by and by comes Chapman, the periwig-maker, and upon my liking it, without more ado I went up, and there he cut off my hair, which went a little to my heart at present to part with it; but, it being over, and my periwig on, I paid him £3 for it; and away went he, with my own hair, to make up another of; and I, by and by, went abroad, after I had caused all my maids to look upon it; and they conclude it do become me, though Jane was mightily troubled for my parting of my own hair, and so was Bess. I went to Sir W. Pen, who observed mightily, and discoursed much upon my cutting off my hair, as he do of everything that concerns me; but it is over, and so I perceive after a day or two it will be no great matter.

SAMUEL PEPYS, 1663

4th

Endured an hour's torture of indecision to-night asking myself whether I should go over to ask her to be my wife or should I go to the Fabian Society and hear Bernard Shaw. Kept putting off the decision even till after dinner. If I went to the flat, I must shave; to shave required hot water – the landlady had already cleared the table and was rapidly retreating. Something must be done and at once. I called the old thing back impulsively and ordered shaving water, consoling myself with the reflection that it was still unnecessary to decide; the hot water could be at hand in case the worst happened. If I decided on matrimony I could shave forthwith. Should I? (After dark I always shave in the sitting-room because of the better gaslight.)

Drank some coffee and next found myself slowly, mournfully putting on hat and coat. You can't shave in hat and coat so I concluded I had decided on Shaw. Slowly undid the front door latch and went off.

Shaw bored me. He is mid-Victorian. Sat beside a bulgy-eyed youth reading the *Freethinker.*

W. N. P. BARBELLION, 1914

5th

It being an extraordinary wett morning, and myself indisposed by a very greate rheume, I did not go to church, to my very great sorrow, it being the first Gunpowder Conspiracy anniversary that had ben kept now these 80 yeares under a prince of the Roman religion. Bonfires were forbidden on this day; what does this portend!

JOHN EVELYN, 1685

6th

Wednesday, a generall rendesvouz of all the King's armyes upon Shottover Greene.

This rendesvouz consisted of his Majesties owne army, Prince

Maurice, Prince Rupert's, Generall Gerard's, and Colonel Sir [Henry] Gage, who commanded the Queenes regiment of foot out of Oxford, and Colonel Hawkins his regiment. Toto 15,000 horse and foot.

At his Majesties being at Oxford this time, Prince Rupert was made Leift.-Generall of all the King's armyes under Prince Charles, and the Lord Generall Ruthyn, Earl of Brainford [Brentford], was made Lord Chamberlayne to Prince Charles, Sir William Bronkard [Brounker] Vice-Chamberlayne.

His Majestie returned to Oxford on Wednesday night; the army marched on towards Wallingford. This night Lord Brainford lost most of his ledd-horse; taken by the enemy.

RICHARD SYMONDS, 1644

7th

I was much alarmed by *Nelly's ghastly* appearance immediately after breakfast, who came in to say Dudley had brought from Winslow the account that a most dreadful action had been fought of Cadiz, Nelson & several Captains killed, & twenty ships were taken. I really felt undescribable misery until the arrival of the Post, but was relieved from such a wretched state of anxious suspence by a Letter from Lord Garlies, who congratulated me on Fremantle's safety & the conspicuous share he had in the Victory gained on the 21st off Cadiz. He adds poor Nelson was no more, he lived to take the Spanish Admiral his opponent & to know he was victorious. In the midst of my delight to hear Fremantle had been preserved in this severe action, I could not help feeling greatly distressed for the Fate of poor *Nelson*

whose loss is irreparable. The papers give an account of this grand victory, twenty ships have been captured but one had blown up in the action. In my way to Addington *[sic]* I met a Servant from Stowe with a most kind *mot* from Lord Buckingham & one from Lady Buckingham, he sent me the Gazettes in which I found the full detail of the action. Nelson's Fleet consisted of twenty seven ships, the French & Spaniards thirty three, came out of Cadiz the 19th & were over taken the 21st off Cape Trafalgar where the action was fought & appears to have been very severe. A violent gale of wind had obliged Admiral Collingwood to sink almost all the Prizes & he mentions in his last Letter the *Capt.* of the *Neptune* who had cleared & sunk the *Santissima Trinidada.* Capt. Duff & Cook were killed, & I fear the number of the killed & wounded will be very great when the returns are sent. How thankful I am Fremantle has once more escaped unhurt. The accounts greatly shook my nerves.

BETSY FREMANTLE, 1805

8th

We could not but stop frequently, both in going and returning, to look at the exquisite beauty of the woods opposite. The general colour of the trees was dark-brown rather than of ripe hazel-nuts; but towards the water there were yet beds of green, and in some of the hollow places in the highest part of the woods the trees were of a yellow colour, and through the glittering light they looked like masses of clouds as you see them gathered together in the west, and tinged with the golden light of the sun. After dinner we walked with Mrs Luff up the vale; I had never had an idea of the extent and width of it, in passing through along the road, on the other side. We walked along the path which leads from house to house; two or three times it took us through some of those copses or groves that cover every little hillock in the middle of the lower part of the vale, making an intricate and beautiful intermixture of lawn and woodland. We left William to prolong his walk, and when he came into the house he told us that he had pitched upon the spot where he should like to build a house better than in any other he had ever yet seen. Mrs Luff went with him by moonlight to view it. The vale looked as if it were filled with white light when the moon had climbed up to the middle of the sky; but long before we could see her face a while all the eastern hills were in black shade, those on the opposite side were almost as bright as snow.

DOROTHY WORDSWORTH, 1805

9th

I breakfasted, dined, &c. again at home. Nancy breakfasted, dined, &c, again at home. Mrs Jeans, her two Daughters and Nurse breakfasted, dined, supped and slept again at Weston Parsonage. At Noon put on my common Shoe on my right foot, it being almost quite well and swelling gone. Mr Du Quesne called here about one o'clock stayed about an Hour with us and then went home, as he came, on horseback, on old Fox. I asked him to dine with us, but there being no Moon, he could not. Dinner to day hash-Mutton and Suet Pudding – Mutton Stakes and a rost Goose &c. No tidings of Mr Jeans as yet, how long they stay with us cannot tell, they only begged to be taken in for 3. or 4. Days and now it is more than a Week – The Children particularly the smallest very great trouble, continually a fire above Stairs, washing, &c. &c.

JAMES WOODFORDE, 1792

10th

Walked over with the little girl Pritchard to Camden Town and had the pleasure of seeing some very beautiful water colour drawings etc. Back and read a little of Froude's England till 4 o'clock when I went down to Mount Street and had tea with James Green and his four daughters. Afterwards we had some music and Evelyn played on the piano on which she is very proficient, and gave also a song or two. I stopped there till 8 o'clock then went up and supped with friend Short at Kilburn.

CHARLES COMPTON, 1882

11th

Rain last night too and the morning not very promising, tis surely dreadful weather. Briffet is here to kill the sow. A horrible looking fellow, his very countenance is sufficient to kill anything, a large hulky fellow, a face absolutely furrowed with the small pox (a very uncommon thing in these days of innoculations) two ferret eyes and a little turned up nose with a mouth as wide as a barn door and lips as thick and projecting they look like two rollers of raw beef bolstered up to guard against, as it were, the approach to his nasty ragged rotten teeth. However he is a good pig killer.

WILLIAM HOLLAND, 1799

12th

This afternoon, going toward Westminster, Creed and I did step in (the Duke of York being just going away from seeing of it) at Pauls, and in the Convocation house yard did there see the body of Robt. Braybrooke, Bishop of London, that died 1404. He fell down in his tomb out of the great church into St Fayths this late Fire, and is here seen his Skeleton with the flesh on; but all tough and dry like a spongy dry leather or Touchwood all upon his bones. His head turned aside. A great man in his time, and Lord Chancellor – and now exposed to be handled and derided by some, though admired for its duration by others. Many flocking to see it.

SAMUEL PEPYS, 1666

13th

Fair weather, but a cross-wind. This day dined with us two fire-ships' Captains, and Captain Petts of the store-ship. We had an aitchbone of good beef and cabbage; a hinder-quarter of mutton and turnips; a hog's head and haslett roasted; three tarts, three plates of apples, two sorts of excellent cheese: this is our short-commons at sea. But we had like to have had a bad supper; for a little before 7 the

Master left his candle burning in his cabin, which fired a bunch of rosemary, and had like to have fired the ship: and this also I take to be an ill-omen of a bad, troublesome voyage.

HENRY TEONGUE, 1678

14th

Proclamations published at Carfax:

1. Prohibiting the landing of men or goods, coming fro*m* the parts of France & the Low Countries now infected.
2. Prohibiting carriages of great weight whereby ye wayes decayed.
3. Prohibiting the Importa*ti*on of glasses fro*m* other Countries into England.

THOMAS CROSFIELD, 1635

15th

There happened this week so thick a mist and fog, that people lost their way in the streets, it being so intense that no light of candles, or torches, yielded any (or but very little) direction. I was in it, and in danger. Robberies were committed between the very lights which were fixed between London and Kensington on both sides, and whilst coaches and travellers were passing. It began about four in the afternoon, and was quite gone by eight, without any wind to disperse it. At the Thames, they beat drums to direct the watermen to make the shore.

JOHN EVELYN, 1699

16th

This is Cave Sittings Day very fine and Sunshining. A Town's Meeting last night at Tindale's where there was the most quarrelling I ever knew at a meeting of this kind but not at all on the Town's affairs[.] Wm. Cousens & Matt. Pickering begun the fray Pickering having two Guineas a year less licence to pay than Cousens on account of his house not being rated so high, they called each other every thing but respected friends – Then Ths. Levitt and old Loncaster began, so fierce that one would have thought that it would have soon been over but it was kept up with spirit a long time. Ths. Levitt told Loncaster he was the town's fool, and the town was not very wise or else they would not have appointed a real fool Constable. There were several people drunk, but I enjoyed nay saw it quite composed as I take care never to drink so much as to lose the little sense I possess. I came away about half past ten. Several staid until four or five O'clock the next morning.

ROBERT SHARP, 1826

17th

There was a very damp fog, and the trees being drenched with wet a sharp frost which followed in the night candied them with ice. Before the sun, which melted the ice and dried the trees altogether, had struck it I looked at the cedar on the left of the portico and found every needle edged with a blade of ice made of fine horizontal bars or spars all pointing one way, N. and S. (if I am not mistaken, all on the S. side of the needles). There was also an edging of frost on the clematis up the railings and, what is very striking, the little bars of which the blades or pieces of frost were made up though they lay all along the hairy threads with which the seed-vessels of the clematis are set did not turn with their turnings but lay all in parallels N. and S.

GERARD MANLEY HOPKINS, 1869

18th

The weather has alternated wet and dry all the last week and yesterday morning and night it froze very sharp indeed but wet this morning and all day. I finished getting all the potatoes up yesterday – boiled some little ones. These appear full and very good ones too and the pigs eat them and are doing well now. I gave them the last of the beans yesterday and I shall give them no more. Took up 5 doz. of celery for Saturday – wants going now. Apples awful bad trade – no sale for anything and our Markets are up again and bread will rise again no doubt as there has been so much wet that there is no chance of a good crop next year. Had our coal home last week. It cost £2. 10. 0. Paid. Baker and I settled up last Friday. He done me as usual but I will have it straight with him now if he don't look out. Saw A. H. at the meet on Wednesday night and she just came up here now but didn't stop and I went down home with her and back again. I went down to Sellars last week, had shoes . . . and saw Tom. He is better but still very bad, a awful leg and the result is doubtful yet, I think. Rogers preached a good sermon today. Not many there. Finished sorting the apples. Pigs very cheap indeed £10 6/2 each. Nice pigs. Very little hunting now, shooting stays however.

JOSEPH TURRILL, 1866

19th

Having settled in the morning to go home, sent forward my horses, and was obliged, therefore, to adhere to my purpose, which the bad weather that came would have disposed me otherwise to change. It was a fall of rain and snow, with a south-east wind, which continued the whole way, and made my ride, both from the cold and uneasiness of the storm against my face, as unpleasant as any I recollect to have had. I continued, notwithstanding, to keep my mind tolerably well abstracted, and concluded a verse or two in some epigrams I was translating and settled a question about the increments of logarithms, from Sanderson, which had rather puzzled me.

WILLIAM WINDHAM, 1786

20th

Mr Custance told me this morning that he had a few Days ago about 80 Turkies, geese, Ducks, and Fowls stolen from [him] in one night – many of them that were fatting. This is the time of the year that many idle Fellows from Norwich go about the Country stealing Poultry to send them to London to make a Penny of them. I never had any stolen yet, but daily expect it. Burrows of Morton had but a few Days ago also taken from him Poultry to the Amount of 3 or 4 Pds value. We had Dinner to day one Fowl boiled and Piggs face, a Couple of Rabbitts smothered with Onions, a Piece of rost Beef and some Grape Tarts.

JAMES WOODFORDE, 1782

21st

Removed from the filthy lodging of Mrs Sheddon, 94 George Street, to the cleanest house I had seen since I left England, a Mrs Watson's in Clyde Buildings.

Mrs Sheddon having swore that I had engaged her lodgings for two months, when I particularly expressed, before witness, that I would not even engage them for more than a week, I was the previous evening served with the letter of a lawyer, which was brought me by a most assassin-like-looking fellow, with a hare lip, cut-throat face, and in a beadle's livery. Mrs Sheddon having this day refused to go before a magistrate (which in this country is optional), and she having preferred 'a suit at law,' to increase my trouble and expense, I was obliged to employ a Mr Donald, to enter on a regular lawsuit; and Mr Provost Hamilton was so kind as to stand bail, in order to get a certificate for the removal of my baggage, which had remained all the morning under quarantine. The action is of course going on.

This is a common species of imposition in Glasgow, Mr Donald having had many similar cases in hand.

COLONEL PETER HAWKER, 1812

22nd

Being Friday at night, about eight of the clock, being a very dark and misty night, the waves of the sea seemed to be flames of fire near about the Cobbe of Lyme, which in the fall and breaking thereof gave such a light that they might see the coast all along as far as Charmouth, as if it had been lightning. It was seen of an hundred people of Lyme, and confidently affirmed by Larcome, an honest man who saw the same. Among which a boy of the town being present went to the sea side and took up some of the water in a frying pan, and brought it to the Company, who pouring the same on the ground in falling seemed like to sparks of fire.

WALTER YONGE, 1616

23rd

The Bricklayer shot a Hare in my Premises & Self sent Him with a Cock & Carrots to my Sister Rock. Charles Scissel begun working for Me. The Bricklayer wanted to be paid for his Bricklayer's Work, but Self declin'd it. Got the Bottle Rack into the Brewhouse Court. Self & Giles went with the Materials of my Surtut Coat to the Balden Taylor. Read the News at the Golden Ball. Saw a Hare near the Wood & spoke to Nickols in it. A roasted Calves Heart for Din. The Carpenter fixt the two Scrapers in the Kitchen Court etc.

JAMES NEWTON, 1761

24th

Breakfasted at Manchester. Ere we left, the senior churchwarden came to offer us his services, to show us the town, principal manufacturers, etc. We declined his polite offer, pleading haste. I found his opinion about the state of trade more agreeable than I had ventured to expect. He said times were mending gradually but steadily, and that the poor-rates were decreasing, of which none can be so good a judge as the churchwarden. Some months back the people had been in great discontent on account of the power engines, which they conceived diminished the demand for operative labour. There was no politics in their discontent, however, and at present it was diminishing. We again pressed on – and by dint of exertion reached Kendal to sleep; thus getting out of the region of the stern, sullen, unwashed artificers, whom you see lounging sulkily along the streets of the towns of Lancashire, cursing, it would seem by their looks, the stop of trade which gives them leisure, and the laws which prevent them employing their spare time. God's justice is requiting, and will yet further requite those who have blown up this country into a state of unsubstantial opulence, at the expense of the health and morals of the lower classes.

SIR WALTER SCOTT, 1826

25th

Mr –, the curate of Laughton, came to the shop in the forenoon, and he having bought some things of me (and I could wish he had paid for them), dined with me, and also staid in the afternoon till he got in liquor, and being so complaisant as to keep him company, I was quite drunk. How do I detest myself for being so foolish!

THOMAS TURNER, 1763

26th

They [the Jacobite forces of Bonnie Prince Charlie] are at Preston this morning, came in there at ten o'clock, behaved very civilly; everybody is going out of town and sending all their effects away, there is hardly any family left but ours and our kin; they have sent their shops and shut up shop, and all the warehouses in town almost are empty; to-night the bellman is going about to forbid anybody sending provision out of town, for a great many have to-day; Dr Mainwaring says the rebels have done nothing but what a rabble without a head might have done.

They have pulled up Stockport bridge and Barton bridge, and we expect every minute they will begin at Salford bridge (they have begun at Cross street), if they do, some folks say they will set the fire bells of ringing to raise a mob to stop them.

ELIZABETH BYROM, 1745

27th

Howse kill'd the great black Sow. Two letters from Polly & one from the Rev'd Mr Davies of Chilton. Howse repair'd the Hovel in Long Mead. Gave some of my Parishioners good Advice. Gave Tom Chapman a Pint of Ale. Edmond Baker put up the Mounding [in] the Backside. The Pidgeons got out of the Cock Loft.

JAMES NEWTON, 1759

28th

The 28th day of November the Queen removed to the Tower from the Lord North's place, which was the Charterhouse. All the streets unto the Tower of London were new-gravelled. Her Grace rode through Barbican and Cripplegate, by London wall, unto Bishopsgate, and up to Leadenhall and through Gracechurch Street and Fenchurch Street; and afore rode gentlemen and many knights and lords, and after came all the trumpets blowing, and then came all the heralds in array; and my Lord of Pembroke bore the queen's sword; then came her Grace on horseback, apparelled in purple velvet with a scarf about her neck, and the sergeants-at-arms about her Grace; and next after rode Sir Robert Dudley, the master of her horse; and so the guard with halberds. And there was such shooting of guns as never was heard afore; and so to the Tower, with all the nobles. And so her Grace lay in the Tower unto the 5th day of December, that was St Nicholas' Eve. And there was in certain places children with speeches, and (in) other places, singing and playing on regals.

HENRY MACHYN, 1558

29th

Went to rehearsal [in Dublin] and underwent another trial of endurance from the ignorance and utter incompetency of the man to whom Calcraft has consigned the care and direction of his stage (!) and from the gross inefficiency of the actors. It was most wearying and distressing. Endeavoured to act King Lear, but with such actors – Kent, Fool, Gloster, etc. – and with *such a prompter* and with such an audience where is the man with any feeling for his author or for his art that could make any way at all? I believe there was some call, but as no one reported it to me I had not occasion to refuse going on. The audience (of course I mean individuals among them – who knew they could be guilty of such licence with impunity! – so far it is discreditable to the whole body) – uttered their own senseless jests, when Lear is carried off asleep – a situation that *never before* failed to excite the sympathy and applause of an audience, when Cordelia kissed the cheek of her sleeping father, when she lay dead in his arms – *the brutes!* – for is it not an evidence of sheer brutality of mind to be so wanting in decency and taste? I told Calcraft I would not play the play again; I want to get away from this place – I *detest* it. How I am to get through this engagement I do not know. It is one solacing reflection that they crowd to see Mr and Mrs Charles Kean and applaud Forrest. They are well suited.

WILLIAM MACREADY, 1845

30th

Visit Poorhouse, Tom Read, crazy man with small sharp black eyes; sometimes keeps a piece of iron on his head to do his brain good; plays on a fiddle the first and second strings only packthread, 'Ain kind Dearie,' 'Pandun o' Rafferty,' grunting and groaning all the while, and groaning fiercely when he struck a note out of tune. I promise him strings. 'Does your Honour live far away?'

WILLIAM ALLINGHAM, 1907

DECEMBER

1st

On 24th October 1878, died at Upper Heyford, aged 74, Susannah Smith, a gipsy. She was a tall, well built woman, of a dark swarthy complexion, with the gipsy feature well defined. She was never married, the last man with whom she lived being one Hayward of Ardley a thatcher, but a son & a daughter are now living at Upper Heyford. For many years the old woman had been a house-dweller & in receipt of parochial relief, but a cancer of the Tongue, which literally starved her to death, carried her to her last home, not I think without good hope for the land beyond the grave, as she I believe always attended a place of worship, and was not, of my own knowledge, destitute of knowledge of religion. Poor old 'Sookey' was very fond of my little dog, & she has told me about her 'travelling' life; how warm she laid (*sic*) in her camp, & what pleasant times she spent on Cottisford Heath in the palmy days of old when no policeman disturbed their repose, nor hindered them in their wanderings: How her daughter was born by the hedge-side on a cock of hay in Radris Bottom' on the old Roman 'Akeman Street' in Kirtlington parish. Her daughter (Sophia Draper, a widow) & her son Ernest Merry (whose father was a house dweller, a miller) now living at U. Heyford have lost much of the gipsy feature, but it still lingers in their children. I have noticed that Gipsies seldom camp under trees, (& I not unfrequently see in my travels now where their camps have been made) the cause of which I was informed is that the trees in wet & moist weather drip so much that it is drier in the open air, a heavy shower with a cessation being preferable to a continual dripping. . . . A new reading-room at Chesteron, built solely at Lord Jersey's expense, was opened on Oct. 28, 1878, at evening. I went into it on the afternoon of that day, & met Lady Jersey & the Vicar of Chesterton just going into it as I was coming out. Whether it will be as attractive as the 'Red Cow' public house at the other end of the village remains to be seen. The farm labourers of rural England spend for the most part all their spare money at the alehouse, & live upon the poor rates in old age.

GEORGE JAMES DEW, 1878

2nd

After the Company was all gone and we thought everything were agreeable and happy in my House, we were of a sudden alarmed by a great Noise in the kitchen, and on my immediately going out there found my Servant Man Will: Coleman beating about the Maids in a terrible manner and appeared quite frantic and mad. I seized him by the Collar and as soon as he was loose, he ran out into the Yard and jumped into the Pond there in a moment but he was soon taken up by Ben, which frightened us so much that we were obliged to sit up all night. We got him to bed however about 1 o'clock and after some time he was somewhat quiet – but it frightened us so much that Nancy and self did not go to bed till 6. in the morning. Ben and Jack did not go to bed at all. The reason of his being so, was on Lizzy's Account, as he wants to marry her and she will not, and he is very jealous. Am afraid however that it proceeds from a family complaint, his Father having been crazy some time. It is therefore now high time for him to leave me which I shall endeavour to do the first opportunity. It made me very ill almost instantly and made my niece very unhappy as well as ill also.

JAMES WOODFORDE, 1783

3rd

Preached at Walbrook. Called upon Mr Blydestine, who has failed lately by great losses at sea and in the West Indes where we have crowded the marketts so full, to procure a false credit, that our woollen goods sell cheaper at Jamaica than they cost us at home. He says that if the truth was known it was as bad with many Merchants who look high and live at a great rate which he has never done, baring the expense of a Coach which was his wife's fault. In all other respects he had behaved well. Been industrious and saving. But times were never so bad. Money in few hands who make others pay for it. I comforted him as well as I could. My wife a little better with her fever gone off.

THOMAS WILSON, 1750

4th

The Quene's Majestie [Elizabeth I] called for me at my dore circa 3½ a meridie as she passed by, and I met her at Estshene gate, where she graciously, putting down her mask, did say with mery chere, "I thank thee, Dee; there was never promisse made but it was broken or kept." I understode her Majesty to mean of the hundred angels [gold coins of the period] she promised to have sent me this day, as she yesternight told Mr Richard Candish.

JOHN DEE, 1590

5th

On the road we met T. [the poet Alfred Tennyson] himself, most friendly, who turned back with us and left H. in charge of his Sister; then he came out again and finished his walk in my company.

T. – 'I'm an old fellow and must exercise. One may do without it in youth, but not in age.'

W.A. – 'Carlyle used to praise London for affording night walks in winter.'

T. – 'I can't walk in London by night. The lights dazzle me.'

We spoke of William Morris (from whom I had just had a long letter).

T. said 'He has gone crazy.' I said I agreed with many of Morris's notions. Labour does not get its fair share.

T. – 'There's brain labour as well as hand labour.'

W.A. – 'And there are many who get money without any labour. The question, how to hinder money from accumulating into lumps, is a puzzling one.'

T. – 'You must let a man leave money to his children. I was once in a coffee-shop in the Westminster Road at 4 o'clock in the morning. A man was raging "Why has So-and-So a hundred pounds, and I haven't a shilling?' I said to him, "If your father had left you £100 you wouldn't give it away to somebody else."

He hadn't a word to answer. I knew he hadn't.'

WILLIAM ALLINGHAM, 1884

6th

I know now — I love her with passion. Health and ambition and sanity are returning. Projects in view: –

(1) To make her happy and myself worthy.

(2) To get married.

(3) To prepare and publish a volume of this Journal.

(4) To write two essays for *Cornhill* which shall surely induce the Editor to publish and not write me merely long complimentary and encouraging letters as heretofore.

Wired to A –, 'The brave little pennon has been hauled down.'

W. N. P. BARBELLION, 1914

7th

Called on old Sally Killing after Church. She asked me the usual and indeed invariable question whether I remembered her old thatched cottage, near the road, by the lilac bush, and the old house in Westfield. I asked her how she passed her time. 'Aw ther,' she said, 'I do rock and sway myself about.'

FRANCIS KILVERT, 1873

8th

This Bedle related further of ye manner of taking of rabbats from All Saints till ye Ladie Day upon ye night in a warren with a haine or nett. About Oxford there are ten warrens or thereabouts drie ground a warren in compasse may be about 40 acres & such a one will yeild per annum 700 li. Some particular men are bound in bond of 30 or 40 li to find soe many couple of rabbits all ye yeare long every weeke. as at New Coll*edge*. There are warrens at Fifeild, Cumnor, Cullom, Blechingdon, Ricot –

THOMAS CROSFIELD, 1633

9th

The 9th day of December did preach at Paul's Cross Doctor Borne, bishop of Bath, and prayed for the pope of Rome, Julius the third, and for all the souls of purgatory.

The same day in the afternoon was a bear-baiting on the Bankside, and there the great blind bear broke loose, and in running away he caught a serving man by the calf of the leg, and bit a great piece away, and after by the hokyll [ankle, or heel] bone, so that within three days afterwards he died.

HENRY MACHYN, 1554

10th

Still a foggy unpleasant morning, I did not stir out. George has been very busy in cutting wood and placing it out of the rain he works a good deal with fair words. Phebe, tho a good servant, is continually scolding him, tis a pitty. This day ended as it usually does in cleaning and scouring. George and Phebe have been very busy in putting up the bacon up our Brew House Chimney to smoak and hope it will be well done, for this is the first in our town house as it must be done with wood fire and we burn coal except in the Brewhouse. Smoaking bacon is not the practice in this county but my wife is a Berkshire woman.

WILLIAM HOLLAND, 1808

11th

The bells are ringing, for they expect the Duke [of Cumberland, commander of the forces sent in pursuit of Bonnie Prince Charlie's rebel army] every minute; now the bellman is going for everybody to provide for the army. Dr Mainwaring is come home, he looks mighty gruff, he is gone straight through the town to meet the Duke. Now the bellman is going again to tell folks they must not illuminate for the Duke will not be here to-night, and desired the folks to go to their own homes, for all the country is come in to see. Miss Vigor and me went up to my aunt Brearcliffe's, found Mr Greaves and my uncle Houghton there, and saw 200 horse dragoons come in, they are all that are come to-day.

ELIZABETH BYROM, 1745

12th

Came down about ten; read reviews, wrote to Mrs Siddons, and then went to the ice; came home only in time to dress and go to my mother's to dinner. About half-past seven went to Dr Johnson's, where I stayed chiefly in the outer room till past eleven. Strahan there during the whole time, and latterly Mr Cruikshanks and the

apothecary. I only went in twice, for a few minutes each time. The first time, I hinted only what they had been before urging, viz. that he would be prevailed upon to take some sustenance, and desisted only upon his exclaiming, 'It is all very childish; let us hear no more of it.' The second time I came in, in consequence of a consultation with Mr Cruikshanks and the apothecary, and addressed him formally. After premising that I considered what I was going to say a a matter of duty, I said that I hoped he would not suspect me of the weakness of importuning him to take nourishment for the purpose of prolonging his life or a few hours or days. I then stated what the reason was, that it was to secure that which I was persuaded he was most anxious about, viz. that he might preserve his faculties entire to the last moment. Before I had quite stated my meaning, he interrupted me by saying that he refused no sustenance but inebriating sustenance, and proceeded to give instances where, in compliance with the wishes of his physicians, he had taken even a small quantity of wine. I readily assented to any objections he might have to nourishment of that kind, and observing that milk was the only nourishment I intended, flattered myself that I had succeed in my endeavours, when he recurred to his general refusal, and begged that there might be an end of it. I then said that I hoped he would forgive my earnestness – or something to that effect; when he replied eagerly, 'that from me nothing would be necessary by way of apology;' adding with great fervour, in words which I shall (I hope) never forget – 'God bless you, my dear Windham, through Jesus Christ;' and concluding with a wish that we might meet in some humble portion of that happiness which God might finally vouchsafe to repentant sinners. These were the last words I ever heard him speak. I hurried out of the room with tears in my eyes and more affected than I had been on any former occasion.

WILLIAM WINDHAM, 1784

13th

—At night. Lady Kerry, Mrs Pratt, Mrs Cadogan, and I, in one coach; Lady Kerry's son and his governor, and two gentlemen, in another; maids and misses, and little master, (Lord Shelburn's children,) in a third, all hackneys, set out at ten o'clock this morning from Lord Shelburn's house in Piccadilly to the Tower, and saw all the sights, lions, etc. then to Bedlam; then dined at the chophouse behind the Exchange; then to Gresham College, (but the keeper was not at home,) and concluded the night at the puppet-show, whence we came home safe at eight, and I left them. The ladies were all in mobs; how do you call it? undressed; and it was the rainiest day that ever dripped; and I'm weary, and 'tis now past eleven.

JONATHAN SWIFT, 1710

14th

My face rather swelled more than Yesterday tho' not very painful. It is generally worse in the morning than at any other time of the Day. I am afraid it is some gouty matter lurking about me as my teeth are pretty easy tho' my gums are rather painful and swelled. I applied flannel last night, but it did not seem to be one bit the better in the Morning. In every other respect (thank God) tolerable well. Mild open Weather with some Sun Shine. At 2. o'clock this

Afternoon I walked to Church and buried Harrison's last child an Infant Girl, by name Virtue Harley Harrison not quite one Year old, 10 Months only. Dinner to day fryed Beef and Potatoes and Hare rosted.

JAMES WOODFORDE, 1792

15th

A remark of Captain Selby about the widespread fame of Barclay and Perkins led to a conversation between him and Mr Houghton about the great breweries and brewers and their combinations, then about the bakers, then the farmers, and the raising the price of corn in scarcities, and the wealth acquired by corn speculations. This led to a conversation about the old and the new poor laws, the reduction of the rates, and the ruin they were causing. Mamma made a remark about the advantage of small allotments to labourers, upon which Captain Selby said that there was not a greater curse to the country than the enclosing open commons, which were such a blessing to the poor people, who can thereby support a cow, a donkey, etc. Mr Houghton opposed this and asserted that these lands, when brought into cultivation, are a source of much greater profit to the community in general. Captain Selby grew very warm, and with his amusing vehemence of manner contended that if would be an incalculable loss to the poor man if he could have no place to walk on but the highway, etc.; in the midst of which eloquence Louisa and I marched out to the deck, and were soon followed by mamma.

EMILY SHORE (AGED 18), 1838

16th

I had appointed to be at Sheerness on *Wednesday,* December 16th. Accordingly, I took horse between five and six, and came thither between five and six in the evening. At half an hour after six, I began reading prayers (the Governor of the fort having given me the use of the chapel), and afterwards preached.

Such a town as many of these live in is scarce to be found again in England. In the dock adjoining to the fort there are six old men-of-war. These are divided into small tenements, forty, fifty, or sixty in a ship, with little chimneys and windows; and each of these contains a family. In one of them, where we called, a man and his wife, and six little children lived. And yet all the ship was sweet and tolerably clean; sweeter than most sailing ships I have been in.

JOHN WESLEY, 1767

17th

Richard Porter caught a marten in a trap. Mr Ward spent the night at Dr Hollowhead's and when he was taking off his leggings a strange dog came up behind and bit his shin, and they feared the dog was mad, because next day in the fields it bit a man two or three times, and since then they have heard nothing about it. Thomas Pole bought a lantern, to be hung by the kitchen door. Father returned the guns to my brothers.

THOMAS ISHAM (AGED 16), 1672

18th

Edward Horseley a Painter in York is now painting ye lodging chamber above ye new parlour, in colours sutable to those hangings I have bought to hang it withall. Ye hangings I bought of Peter Pope in Bednall Greene, as also those that are in ye withdrawing Roome to ye new Parlour, wherein ye 9 Muses are. Those in ye Lodgin chamber are calfe skins silver'd, & wrought upon with a large flower in blew worstett: they come short of ye ground having ye breath of a pannell of wainscott below them & a frieze & cornish above them. The chimney peice is paint'd answerable in blew and sylver. There is above ye door that goes into ye inner chamber a head carv'd in wood like a Roman head, which I caused to be made for him that keeps ye chambers and hath charge of the Wardrope, as a remembrance of him that hath so long & faithfully serv'd. This man Francis Oddy was servant to my father many years & since hath served me: my father at his death (who dy'd at Numounton at my Newphew George Marwood's house ye 17 of December 1634) did recommend this man Francis Oddy unto me having had good experience of his fidelity and diligence, and even such I find him hitherto. He serves me in ye way of an upholsterer when there is need to furnish ye Lodgin rooms and dress them up: he serves me for a Caterer to bye all mannor of provisions for ye house, and to keep ye wine cellar. He is of a very low stature, his head little,

& his hair cut short, his face lean and full of wrinkles, his complection such that it shows he hath endur'd all wethers: his disposition not sutable with the rest of his fellow servants which doth either by diligence breed envy, or else thro' plain dealing stir up variance: and having a working head is in continual debate.

SIR HENRY SLINGSBY, 1638

19th

The sick woman at Cross Foot, Mary Price, cowering before a roaring fire. She said, 'Six weeks ago I was in bed at night and suddenly a young one came on my left arm, like a little angel. It was not one of my own. It was dressed in white clothes long and it had a cap like the dear little children when they are put into their coffins'. She told the story in such a strange weird way that I felt uncomfortable. It was not a dream, she said, she was broad awake.

FRANCIS KILVERT, 1870

20th

Lay down on the sofa and read part of Brutus. Acted the character *well* – with energy, dignity, and freshness. I was anxious to do so, and I felt my own superiority. Mr Vandenhoff again resorted to his dirty tricks of endeavouring to impede my effects, and take the applause from them, but I left him to the enjoyment of his unavailing efforts, and made my character stand conspicuously foremost in his despite. At the end of the play Mr Kemble lingered in a ridiculous manner about the scenes, so that I was forced to pass by him. I heard some noise afterwards and sent to see if the audience were not applauding on the occasion of Mr Kemble "going forward." The prompter came to say that the audience were calling for me, Mr Kemble having gone on; I merely observed that I should not go. I cannot believe that the sense of the audience (if sense were indeed among them) could be in favour of paying a compliment to the worst among the leading actors of the play, and for such a miserable performance as is the Mark Antony of Mr C. Kemble, and that at the expense of those who stood before him. If they did it was very insulting, whether through ignorance or prejudice.

WILLIAM MACREADY, 1836

21st

Went into Holborn, and there saw the woman that is to be seen with a beard. She is a little plain woman, a Dane: her name, Ursula Dyan; about forty years old; her voice like a little girl's; with a beard as much as any man I ever saw, black almost, and grizzly; it began to grow at about seven years old, and was shaved not above seven months ago, and is now so big as any man's almost that ever I saw; I say, bushy and thick. It was a strange sight to me, I confess, and what pleased me mightily.

SAMUEL PEPYS, 1668

22nd

I wrote six of my close pages yesterday which is about twenty-four pages in print. What is more I think it comes off twangingly. The story is so very interesting in itself that there is no fear of the book answering. Superficial it must be but I do not disown the charge. Better a superficial book which brings well and strikingly together

the known and acknowledged facts than a dull boring narrative pausing to see further into a mill stone at every moment than the nature of the Mill stone admits. Nothing is so tiresome as walking through some beautiful scene with a minute philosopher, a botanist or pebble gatherer who is eternally calling your attention from the grand features of the natural scenery to look at grasses and chucky stones. Yet in their way they give useful information and so does the minute historian – Gad, I think that will look well in the preface.

SIR WALTER SCOTT, 1825

23rd

Yesterday morning I was dreaming I was with George Simcox and was considering how to get away in time to ring the bells here which as porter I had to ring (I was made porter on the 12th of the month, I think, and had the office for a little more than two months). I knew that I was dreaming and made this odd dilemma in my dream: either I am not really with Simcox and then it does not matter what I do, or if I am, waking will carry me off without my needing to do anything – and with this I was satisfied.

Another day in the evening after Litanies as Father Rector was giving the points for meditation I shut my eyes, being very tired, and without ceasing to hear him began to dream. The dream-images seemed to rise and overlie those which belonged to what he was saying and I saw one of the Apostles – he was talking about the Apostles – as if pressed against by a piece of wood about half a yard long and a few inches across, like a long box with two of the long sides cut off. Even then I could not understand what the piece of wood did encumbering the apostle.

GERARD MANLEY HOPKINS, 1869

24th

Something ought to be done by the authorities to wipe out the scandal of the homeless people who are forced to sleep out on these wintry nights. I walked home along the Embankment this morning at two o'clock with Byron Curtis, editor of the *Standard*. Every bench from Blackfriars to Westminster Bridge was filled with shivering people, all huddled up – men, women, and children. The Salvation Army people were out giving away hot broth, but even this was merely a temporary palliative against the bitter night. At Charing Cross we encountered a man with his wife and two tiny children. They had come to town from Reading to look for work. The man had lost his few shillings, and they were stranded. We took them to Charing Cross Station, got them a hot meal, and beds for the night. This unemployment question is really a great problem. I talked with Mr Chamberlain about it the other day, and he repeated his known sentiments about our Free Trade policy being to blame for loss of work. If foreign goods were taxed the British workman would have a chance.

R. D. BLUMENFELD, 1901

25th

With my boy walked, it being a most brave, cold, and dry frosty morning, and had a pleasant walk to White Hall, where I intended to have received the Communion with the family, but I came a little too late. So I walked up into the house, and spent my time looking over pictures, particularly the ships in King Henry the VIIIth's voyage to Boulogne; marking the great difference between their build then and now. By and by down to the chapel again, where Bishop Morley preached upon the song of the Angels, 'Glory to God on high, on earth peace, and good will towards men.' Methought he made but a poor sermon, but long, and, reprehending the mistaken jollity of the Court for the true joy that shall and ought to be on these days, he particularized concerning their excess in plays and gaming, saying that he whose office it is to keep the gamesters in order and within bounds, serves but for a second rather in a duel, meaning the groom-porter. Upon which it was worth observing how far they are come from taking the reprehensions of a bishop seriously, that they all laugh in the chapel when he reflected on their ill actions and courses. He did much press us to joy in these public days of joy, and to hospitality; but one that stood by whispered in my ear that the Bishop do not spend one groat to the poor himself. The sermon done, a good anthem followed with viols, and the King came down to receive the Sacrament. But I stayed not, but calling my boy from my Lord's lodgings, and giving Sarah some good advice, by my Lord's order, to be sober and look after the house, I walked home again with great pleasure, and there dined by my wife's bed-side with great content, having a mess of brave plum-porridge and a roasted pullet for dinner, and I sent for a mince pie abroad, my wife not being well to make any herself yet.

SAMUEL PEPYS, 1662

26th

To Penjerrick to dine with my people as usual on roast beef & plum pudding. Settled accounts which were satisfactory, & had the further gratification of seeing Mary Ann at the Cottage & dining with her new Ma. Got home in time to join the Christmas revels taking place at our house. We had 28 at tea of 6 years old & upwards, from little Minny up to Sterling. The evening went off most brilliantly, & the fund of enjoyment so easily given to so many little hearts, was not the least enjoyable part of it. First the venerable

effigies of Father Christmas with scarlet coat & cocked hat, stuck all over with presents for the guests, by his side the old year, a most dismal & haggard old beldame in a night cap & spectacles, then 1843, a promising baby fast asleep in a cradle. Then we had a 'galvanic shock', which was played on Juliet Sterling & myself, blinding us & dressing up our hands & arms into the exact imitation of baby's by the aid of a little paint & flannel, to the no small consternation & surprise of the patient on removing the bandage. Then with the aid of a good mask, nightcap, kneebreeches, pillow, & coat & waistcoat of my father's, I was enabled to make a very passable elderly Friend & bestow some wholesome advice on the children & on Sterling who was vastly entertained. We then had lots of tableaux vivants, which were very good, then supper, then fireworks, then everything else, & we separated in high good humour with ourselves & our company.

BARCLAY FOX, 1842

27th

Went to Church. Walked with the Trants to see the Skaters in the Park. I wonder, setting religious feeling aside, that *gentlemen* can like to make such a public display.

CLARISSA TRANT, 1829

28th

The year is nearly over. Snow has fallen, and everything is white. It is very cold. I have changed the position of my desk into a corner. Perhaps I shall be able to write far more easily here. Yes, this is a good place for the desk, because I cannot see out of the stupid window. I am quite private. The lamp stands on one corner and in the corner. Its rays fall on the yellow and green Indian curtain and on the strip of red embroidery. The forlorn wind scarcely breathes. I love to close my eyes a moment and think of the land outside, white under the mingled snow and moonlight – white trees, white fields – the heaps of stones by the roadside white – snow in the furrows. Mon Dieu! How quiet and how patient! If he were to come I could not even hear his footsteps.

KATHERINE MANSFIELD, 1914.

29th

This day, by long arrangement, I expected to receive a visit from my father. He had engaged himself to me for three days, and was to reside at Mrs Delany's.

I acquainted the Queen with my hopes, which she heard with the most pleased expression of approbation. She told them to the King, who inquired, with an air of real satisfaction in my happiness, when he would come?

At three o'clock our dearest Padre arrived – well, gay, and sweet – and we spent near two hours wholly alone, and truly happy.

At dinner the party was enlarged by the presence of Mrs Delany and Mr Smelt; to these were added the lovely and lively Miss P—, the gentle Mlle Montmoulin, and the friendly Miss Planta.

My dear father was the principal object to all, and he seemed to enjoy himself, and to be enjoyed throughout.

We returned to my own apartment to our coffee, and the two governess ladies retired; and then came the King for Mrs Delany; and not for that soley, though ostensibly, for his behaviour to my father proved his desire to see and converse with him.

He began immediately upon musical matters, and entered into a discourse upon them with the most animated wish of both hearing and communicating his sentiments; and my dear father was perfectly ready to meet his advances. No one, at all used to the Court etiquettes, could have seen him without smiling; he was so totally unacquainted with the forms usually observed in the Royal presence, and so regardless or thoughtless of acquiring them, that he moved, spoke, acted, and debated, precisely with the same ease and freedom that he would have used to any other gentleman whom he had accidentally met.

A certain flutter of spirits, which always accompanies these interviews, even with those who are least awed by them, put my dear father off the guard which is the customary assistant upon these occasions, of watching what is done by those already initiated in these royal ceremonies: highly gratified by the openness and good humour of the King, he was all energy and spirit, and pursued every topic that was started, till he had satisfied himself upon it, and started every topic that occurred to him, whether the King was ready for another or not.

While the rest, retreating towards the wainscot, formed a distant and respectful circle, in which the King alone moves, this dear father came forward into it himself, and, wholly bent upon pursuing

whatever theme was begun, followed the King when he moved away, and came forward to meet his steps when he moved back; and while the rest waited his immediate address ere they ventured to speak a word, he began and finished, sustained or dropped, renewed or declined, every theme that he pleased, without consulting anything but his feelings and understanding.

This vivacity and this nature evidently pleased the King, whose good sense instantly distinguishes what is unconscious from what is disrespectful; and his stay in the room, which I believe was an hour, and the perfect good humour with which he recieved as well as returned the sprightly and informal sallies of my father, were proofs the most convincing of his approbation.

FANNY BURNEY, 1786

30th

Visiting the Queen I faithfully related what pass'd with the Duke of Marlborough, how affectionately he Spoke of her, which melted her, that he said that he long'd to have his Wife quiet, which nothing could do but the Queens goodness, and her Patience, as said above, that it as Duty and Submission to the Queen that made him serve now. At this time it was more difficult, because the War was in a worse posture, and he would have more difficultys, for he did 20 things before, which he could not, Yea durst not do now, but depending on the Queens Favour he would not lay down. I said to the Queen he needed to have his mind easy by Smiles, from her self. The Duchess told me that if the Queen smil'd or said any thing pleasant he thinks nothing amiss. Her Majesty said she was sorry to see him so broken. That there was no thought of putting him out.

SIR DAVID HAMILTON, 1710

31st

Thersie was at Church twice to-day. A few days ago she was teaching Florence and asking her who died for us on the Cross. 'Lord Chesterfield', replied Florence promptly, having heard a good deal lately about his death in connection with the Prince of Wales and Londesborough Lodge.

Look at the first page of this book, "It began with a lass and it will end with a lass'. It began with a lass and it *has* ended with a lass.

I read to Thersie my last song, 'Loud roars the wind'. Then I was going to bed but Dora came down on tiptoe in a loose wrapper with her hair falling on her shoulders, soon followed by Thersie in the same state. We sat round the fire talking of domestic matters in whispers, not to disturb my Mother who was immediately overhead sleeping the sleep of the just.

At 5 minutes to midnight the bells of Chippenham Church pealed out loud and clear in the frosty air. We opened a shutter and stood round the window listening. It was a glorious moonlit night.

And here is the end of another year. How much to be thankful for. How much to be mourned over. God pardon the past and give grace for the future, and make the new year better than the old.

FRANCIS KILVERT, 1871

The Diarists

William Allingham (1824–1889)
Until the age of fifty-six William Allingham worked as a customs officer, but this did not prevent him establishing himself among leading Victorian poets and men of letters. Although his verse is less read today, Tennyson, Carlyle, Thackeray and Browning counted him a friend and his diary records many close details of the time he spent in their company.

Elias Ashmole (1617–1692)
Elias Ashmole supported the Royalist cause during the Civil War, made a study of science and astrology, qualified as a solicitor and amassed a private collection of antiquities and curiosities which he presented to the University of Oxford. Oxford's Ashmolean Museum, the oldest in the world, is named after him.

W. N. P. Barbellion (1889–1919)
This was the pen-name of Bruce Frederick Cummings, the son of a Devon journalist who kept a diary from the age of thirteen. When he was sixteen Cummings won a post at the Natural History Museum in London, which enabled him to pursue the interest in science he had had since childhood. Even in his teens, however, he suffered from disseminated sclerosis from which he died six weeks before his thirtieth birthday.

ARNOLD BENNETT (1867–1931)
The novelist Arnold Bennett was born in the Staffordshire Potteries which formed the backcloth for many of his well-known novels. After studying law, he took up journalism and worked on the staff of *Woman* for four years. His first novel, *A Man from the North*, was published in 1898 and a succession of successful works followed until he died. Arnold Bennett lived in France for ten years and married a Frenchwoman. He began his journal in 1896 and missed few entries over the next thirty years.

A. C. BENSON (1862–1925)
Arthur Christopher Benson is probably best remembered today as the author of 'Land of Hope and Glory'. He was a scholar, the son of the headmaster of Wellington College who later became Archbishop of Canterbury. A. C. Benson was a housemaster at Eton College before moving to Magdalene College, Cambridge, where he was first made a Fellow and from 1915 Master of the College. He published biographies, several books of verse and three popular collections of essays.

DEARMAN BIRCHALL (1828–1897)
A cloth manufacturer in Leeds, Dearman Birchall moved to Gloucestershire in 1869, settling at Bowden Hall, near Gloucester, where he recorded the day-to-day details of his life as a Victorian squire.

THOMAS BLAIKIE (1750–1838)
Born in Edinburgh, Blaikie moved to France as a young man to develop the enthusiasm for the English style of gardening among the French aristocracy. While there, he kept an eyewitness account of the French Revolution.

R. D. BLUMENFELD (1864–1948)
The son of German Jewish parents, R. D. Blumenfeld was born in Wisconsin. He began his career as a journalist in England in the 1890s, rising to become editor of both the *Daily Mail* and the *Daily Express*. He had a significant influence in the development of popular journalism.

SIR WILLIAM BRERETON (1604–1661)
During the Civil War Sir William Brereton was the principal commander of Parliamentary forces in the West Midlands and North-West of England. He captured Nantwich and Wrexham, and laid siege to Chester.

FANNY BURNEY (1752–1840)
A novelist and diarist, Fanny Burney began her writing career at the age of ten and started keeping her diary when she was fifteen. Her first novel, *Evelina: or, A Young Lady's Entrance into the World*, was published anonymously and caused a sensation. The author was soon identified and Fanny Burney became a favourite of Dr Johnson among other literary luminaries. Between 1786 and 1791 she was Second Keeper of the Robes to George III's wife, Queen Charlotte. Two years after resigning her post at court she married General Alexandre D'Arblay and together they spent several years on the Continent, including a stay in Brussels at the time of the Battle of Waterloo in 1815.

LADY CHARLOTTE BURY (1775–1861)
Although she was the author of a number of novels, Lady Bury is chiefly remembered for the *Diary illustrative of the Times of George IV*, an anonymous work that she is supposed to have compiled during her time as a lady-in-waiting to Caroline, Princess of Wales.

JOHN BYNG (1743–1813)
For the whole of his later life the 5th Viscount Torrington was known as Colonel John Byng. It was under this name that he compiled the day-to-day accounts of his summer holidays, spent in a succession of riding tours, which were eventually published as *Rides Round Britain*.

ELIZABETH BYROM (1722–1801)
Elizabeth Byrom was the daughter of John Byrom, the poet and inventor of a new system of shorthand. Her father inherited family estates when Elizabeth was eighteen.

JANE WELSH CARLYLE (1801–1866)
Jane Baillie Welsh was the daughter of a Scottish doctor. In 1821 she met Thomas Carlyle, the great nineteenth century Scottish historian and essayist, whom she married five years later. Famous for her letters, she also kept a diary intermittently.

THOMAS CARTWRIGHT (1634–1689)
Thomas Cartwright was an Anglican clergyman who later became Bishop of Chester.

ANNE CHALMERS (b. 1813)
Anne Chalmers was the daughter of the Scottish minister and philanthropist, Dr Thomas Chalmers. In 1830 she made a visit to England and recorded her impressions in the diary she kept during her stay. Six years later she married Dr William Hanna.

CHARLES COMPTON (1828–1884)
Charles Compton was an artist and civil servant living in London during the heyday of Queen Victoria's reign.

WILLIAM CORY (1823–1892)
Author of the 'Eton Boating Song', Cory was educated at Eton and was an assistant master there for twenty-six years. He was an accomplished classical scholar, writing verses in Latin and Greek, and published a collection of lyrics anonymously in 1858. His best-known poem is 'Heraclitus'.

NOEL COWARD (1899–1973)
Actor, playwright and composer, Noël Coward made his first stage appearance in 1911 and from the early 1920s established himself as one of the most popular and successful performers and writers for stage and screen on both sides of the Atlantic. Knighted in 1970, the closing years of his life saw successful revivals of several of his plays written nearly half-a-century earlier.

THOMAS CROSFIELD (1602–1663)
Thomas Crosfield was a Fellow of Queen's College, Oxford, who recorded the day-to-day life of the university and the world at large during the turbulent years of the mid-seventeenth century, which saw the Civil War, the execution of Charles I and the restoration of Charles II.

ROLAND DAVIES (1649–1721)
Roland Davies was the Dean of Ross whose extensive travels throughout Ireland were carefully recorded in his diary.

DR JOHN DEE (1527–1608)
Dee was a mathematician, geographer and alchemist in an age when the distinction between science and magic was frequently blurred. As astrologer to Mary I, he was imprisoned on suspicion of compassing her death by magic. Her step-sister, Elizabeth I, showed him greater favour and made Dee warden of Manchester College in 1595. For much of his life Dr Dee applied his extensive knowledge of geography and navigation to the search for a Northwest Passage to the Far East. His publications included works on logic, astronomy, alchemy and navigation.

ABRAHAM DE LA PRYMME (1671–1704)
A cleric who served as a curate in Hull and later took the living of Thorne, Abraham de la Prymme was educated at Cambridge. Three years before his death he was made a Fellow of the Royal Society.

SOPHIE V. DE LA ROCHE (1730–1807)
Sophie V. de la Roche was a German visitor to Hanoverian England. The diary she kept during her stay was published under the title *Sophie in London, 1786.*

GEORGE JAMES DEW (1846–1928)
A relieving officer in Oxfordshire, George James Dew's diary provides a closely observed record of nineteenth and early twentieth century rural life.

WILLIAM DYOTT (1761–1846)
General William Dyott served in Canada, the West Indies and Egypt as well as travelling extensively throughout Europe. He acted as aide-de-camp to George III and was a friend of the future William IV.

EDWARD VI (1537–1553)
Edward VI succeeded his father, Henry VIII, as King of England in 1547. The following year he began keeping a diary which he maintained until he was fourteen. During his reign government of the country was first entrusted to his uncle the Duke of Somerset and, following his execution in 1552, the Duke of Northumberland. It was the latter who persuaded the dying king to name the duke's own daughter-in-law, Lady Jane Grey, as his successor in preference to his Catholic half-sister, Mary Tudor (later Mary I).

GEORGE ELIOT (1819–1880)
George Eliot was the famous pen-name adopted by the novelist born Mary Ann, or Marian, Evans. After a spell as assistant editor of the *Westminster Review* and translator of German religious and philosophical works, she was nearly forty before her genius for writing fiction was realized with the publication of *Adam Bede* in 1859. In the works that followed she confirmed her position among the major English novelists of the nineteenth century.

JOHN EVELYN (1620–1706)
One of the great diarists in the English language, John Evelyn kept his diary from 1624 to 1706 and filled it with fascinating details of public and private events. It stands alongside the diary kept by Samuel Pepys as one of the most vivid accounts of the seventeenth century.

CAROLINE FOX (1819–1871)
Caroline Fox was born into a wealthy Quaker family living in the Cornish port of Falmouth, a situation that enabled her to mix with many of the leading literary figures of her day when they travelled into the West Country. She began writing her diary when she was sixteen.

(ROBERT) BARCLAY FOX (1817–1855)
The elder brother of Caroline Fox, Barclay Fox began his journal in 1832 at the age of fourteen. He married in 1844 and continued intermittent diary entries until the year before his death.

BETSY FREMANTLE (1779–1857)
Betsy Fremantle was the sister of Harriet Wynne (extracts from whose diary are also included in this anthology). She married Vice-Admiral Sir Thomas Fremantle and as a naval commander's wife during the Napoleonic Wars recorded in her diary accounts of many of the historic actions fought by Nelson, among others. She kept her diary from the age of ten until the year she died.

CHARLES GREVILLE (1794–1865)
Following various official appointments at court and in government, Charles Greville was made Clerk to the Privy Council in 1821, a position that gave him access to all the major political issues and personalities of his day. These were recorded in the journals he kept spanning the period 1820 to 1860, which amount to one of the most informative records of the period.

SIR DAVID HAMILTON (1663–1721)
Sir David Hamilton was the physician to Queen Anne and recorded his time at court in his diary from 1709 to 1714, the year of his royal patient's death.

THOMAS HARDY (1840–1828)
The Dorset-born novelist and poet trained as an architect before writing became his principal occupation. His first great novel, *Far From the Madding Crowd* was published in 1874 and for twenty years Hardy concentrated his energies in a succession of celebrated novels before turning to poetry.

COLONEL PETER HAWKER (1786–1853)
Colonel Peter Hawker served in the Peninsular War until he was wounded and forced to retire from the army in 1813. As a keen sportsman and wild-fowler, he kept a diary full of wildlife and sporting observations.

BENJAMIN ROBERT HAYDON (1786–1846)
Haydon was a painter of historical subjects whose life was plagued by debt and depression that eventually led to him shooting himself in his studio.

THOMAS HEARNE (1678–1735)
Born into a poor Berkshire family, Thomas Hearne was able eventually to win a place at St Edmund Hall, Oxford. After graduating he became second keeper in the university's Bodleian Library, where he worked for four years until he was forced to resign because of his Jacobite sympathies. He published forty-one antiquarian works as well as keeping a diary that spanned the final thirty years of his life.

OLIVER HEYWOOD (1630–1702)
Oliver Heywood was a Presbyterian minister in Yorkshire during the religious turbulence of the second half of the seventeenth century.

LADY MARGARET HOBY (1571–1633)
Lady Margaret Hoby was lady of the manor of Hackness, near Scarborough, in north Yorkshire.

WILLIAM HOLLAND (1746–1819)
William Holland served as rector of the parishes of Over Stowey in Somerset and subsequently Monkton Farleigh, near Bath.

GERARD MANLEY HOPKINS (1844–1889)
One of the most innovative English poets, Gerard Manley Hopkins was profoundly effected as a young man by the religious ferment that surrounded the Oxford Movement. As a result of this he converted to Roman Catholicism in 1866. He was ordained a priest in 1877, taught for two years and then became professor of Greek at University College, Dublin. None of his poems were published during his lifetime, but his use of 'sprung rhythm' caught the poetic spirit of the times when they first appeared in print nearly twenty years after his death.

I

THOMAS ISHAM (1657–1681)
Thomas Isham lived at Lamport Hall in Northamptonshire. For two years of his life, when he was sixteen and seventeen, he kept a diary in Latin which was later translated.

J

RALPH JOSSELIN (1617–1683)
After several years as a teacher Ralph Josselin was ordained in 1640 and the following year moved to the Essex parish of Earls Colne, where he spent the rest of his life and where he also served as schoolmaster for eight years.

RICHARD KAY (1716–1751)
Richard Kay was a doctor with a medical practice in Baldingstone, near Bury in Lancashire.

(ROBERT) FRANCIS KILVERT (1840–1879)
Until 1937 Francis Kilvert was largely unknown outside his family. However, the publication of three volumes of his diary, which first appeared in 1938, transformed this otherwise obscure country priest into one of the most widely read and enjoyed diarists of the nineteenth century. Kilvert died at a tragically early age, only a month after his wedding, in spite of which the picture he paints of his life and ministry in the Welsh Marches is one of the most evocative and accessible descriptions of Victorian country life.

JOHN KNIGHT (b. 1900)
The manuscript of John Knight's diary gives no clues about his very comfortable family background or circumstances outside those that can be gleaned from the text itself. He evidently lived in London but was accustomed to holidaying in the West Country and the Cotswolds. The diary entries quoted here show considerable maturity for a boy of twelve.

LADY KNIGHTLY OF FAWSLEY (1842–1914)
One of the early campaigners for 'Votes for Women', Lady Knightly of Fawsley applied her reforming zeal to social and political causes throughout her life.

M

HENRY MACHYN (c. 1498–c. 1563)
Henry Machyn was a devout Roman Catholic who lived in London during the reigns of Henry VIII and his three children: Edward VI, Mary I and Elizabeth I. His diary concentrates for the most part on public events and provides historians with a valuable first-hand account of life in the capital during Tudor and early Elizabethan times.

WILLIAM MACREADY (1793–1873)
Macready was the leading English actor of his day, famous for his productions of Shakespeare's plays at Covent Garden, Drury Lane and later on tours through the provinces as well as to Paris and the USA. He quit the stage in 1851 and his *Reminiscences and Diaries* were published two years after his death.

KATHERINE MANSFIELD (1888–1923)
This was the pen-name of the New Zealand writer of short stories, Kathleen Mansfield Beauchamp. Educated in London, she married in 1909, but left her husband after only a few days. Two years later she met the critic John Middleton Murray with whom she spent the rest of her life (they were married in 1918). Her use of atmosphere rather than incident to structure and mould her short stories has led to comparisons with Chekhov.

BENJAMIN NEWTON (1761–1830)
The Reverend Benjamin Newton served in parishes in the Welsh borders, in Wiltshire, Somerset and Yorkshire. He was also a magistrate in the North Riding of Yorkshire.

JAMES NEWTON (1714–1786)
James Newton was rector of Nuneham Courtenay, a village a few miles to the south-east of Oxford.

JOHN WARD (O'NEIL) (fl. 1865)
John Ward (O'Neil) was a nineteenth century weaver whose diary records the hardships faced by Lancashire cotton workers in the middle of the last century.

SAMUEL PEPYS (1633–1703)
Between 1 January 1660 and 31 May 1669, when his failing sight forced him to abandon it, Samuel Pepys wrote what has become the most famous diary in the English language. Pepys was a Londoner, born and educated in the capital before going to Magdalene College, Cambridge, where he bequeathed his books, manuscripts and collections after his death. Thanks to family connections, Pepys rose through the ranks of the civil service. In 1660 he was appointed Clerk of the Acts to the Navy. Twelve years later he became Secretary of the Admiralty, and undertook many significant and far-reaching reforms. Pepys served as MP for Harwich and for two years was President of the Royal Society. His lasting memorial is the diary kept in a form of cipher that was first translated in 1825. In this Pepys records his impressions of life at court, major historical and political events as well as candid details of his home and private life.

(HELEN) BEATRIX POTTER (1866–1943)
Born in Kensington, Beatrix Potter was educated at home by governesses who fostered her love of drawing and animals. As a child she had many pets who inspired the characters in the much-loved stories she wrote and illustrated herself. *Peter Rabbit*, her first collection of stories, was published in 1900. In 1906 she bought Hill Top Farm, at Sawrey near Windermere, which provided the background for further stories. Seven years later she married William Heelis and at the age of forty-seven entered into thirty happy years of married life.

THOMAS RAIKES (1777–1848)
After an early career in his father's business, Thomas Raikes became a socialite and counted Beau Brummell among his friends. He travelled widely on the continent, where financial troubles forced him to live for eight years. His diary, begun in 1831, covered this period abroad and all but the final year of his life following his return to London in 1841.

ELIZABETH RAPER (d. 1778)
Elizabeth Raper spent all her life living at Twyford House in Hertfordshire. There she acquired a reputation as an accomplished housekeeper and cook, a forerunner of Isabella Beeton. Indeed her diary takes the form of a journal-cum-recipe book.

HENRY CRABB ROBINSON (1775–1867)
As a young man Henry Crabb Robinson studied for five years in Germany where he met many leading writers and intellectuals, among them Goethe and Schiller. He covered the Peninsular War as a war correspondent for *The Times*, the first journalist to act specifically in this capacity. As a man of letters in later life, he was friends with most of the principal literary figures of the time and was a founder of London University and the Athenaeum Club.

DR JOHN RUTTY (1698–1774)
John Rutty was born in Wiltshire but moved to Dublin after his medical training. The son of Quaker parents, he charted the course of his austere spiritual life in the diary he kept for twenty years until the time of his death. In an age when excess in food and drink was the norm, Rutty took an unfashionable interest in healthy eating and wrote a number of informative works on health and diet.

DUDLEY RYDER (1691–1756)
Dudley Ryder was a lawyer who rose in later life to the position of Attorney-General and Chief Justice in the Court of King's Bench.

S

SIR WALTER SCOTT (1771–1832)
Following an early career in his father's legal practice, Scott established his literary credentials through translations of German ballads and ballad compositions of his own. His first novel, *The Lay of the Last Minstrel*, made him famous and despite business set-backs in later life he became a towering national figure with a far-reaching influence on authors right across Europe.

ROBERT SHARP (1773–1843)
Robert Sharp lived in the Yorkshire village of South Cave near Hull, where he acted as schoolmaster, village constable, shopkeeper and tax inspector.

EMILY SHORE (1819–1839)
The daughter of a Suffolk clergyman, Emily Shore showed a precocious literary talent in her short life. As well as her journal, she wrote poetry, fiction and essays on historical and scientific subjects.

LOUIS SIMOND (1767–1831)
Louis Simond was an American travel writer whose visit to England, recorded in the journal of his stay, vividly portrays life in the Regency period.

JOHN SKINNER (1772–c. 1839)
After completing his education at Cambridge, John Skinner was ordained priest in 1799 and the following year became rector of the Somerset parish of Camerton, south-west of Bath.

SIR HENRY SLINGSBY (1601–1658)
Sir Henry Slingsby served as MP for Knaresborough and during the Civil War fought for King Charles against the forces of Parliament. He was executed after being implicated in a Royalist plot in Hull.

'JOHN SOWERBY' (fl. 1938)
John Sowerby was the pen-name adopted by the anonymous mental patient and keen cyclist who recorded his pre-war excursions in his book entitled *I Got on my Bicycle.*

JOHN STEVENS (d. 1726)
Captain .John Stevens was a Jacobite soldier who fought in Ireland on behalf of King James II in his vain bid to regain the throne at the end of the seventeenth century.

JONATHAN SWIFT (1667–1745)
Anglo-Irish poet, satirist and clergyman, Jonathan Swift wrote one of his most enigmatic works, the *Journal to Stella*, between 1710 and 1714. The 'Stella' to whom this was addressed was Esther Johnson, niece to Sir William Temple for whom Swift had worked as a secretary in his youth. Swift was also Stella's tutor and she played an important role in his life thereafter. Following Sir William's death in 1699, Stella moved with a female companion to live near Swift in Dublin and it is generally believed that they married, although they never lived together.

RICHARD SYMONDS (b. 1617)
Richard Symonds came from Black Notley, near Braintree in Essex. He served in the Royalist army during the Civil War and kept a diary of the marches and campaigns in which he took part.

T

WILLIAM TAYLER (1807–1892)
Born in Grafton, in west Oxfordshire, William Tayler entered domestic service and became a footman. It was while he was in service that he began his journal.

W. J. TEMPLE (1739–1796)
A lawyer until the age of twenty-seven, William Johnstone Temple changed profession when his father was made bankrupt and entered the church, becoming rector of Mamhead, Exeter. For the last thirty years of his life he was vicar of the prosperous living of Gluvias in Cornwall.

HENRY TEONGUE (1621–1690)
Henry Teongue was a respectable parish priest in Alcester in Warwickshire until financial difficulties forced to him boost his income. For four years he served as a naval chaplain while his son saw to the needs of his parishioners. The diary he kept during his time in the navy is a swashbuckling account of life at sea, one in which the Revd Teongue felt entirely at home.

RALPH THORESBY (1658–1725)
Ralph Thoresby was a man of letters with particular interests in antiquities and regional history.

CLARISSA TRANT (1800–1844)
Born into an old Roman Catholic family in Ireland, Clarissa Trant was the daughter of Brigadier-General Sir Nicholas Trant, a hero of the Peninsular War.

THOMAS TURNER (1729–1793)
Thomas Turner was a Georgian schoolmaster turned shopkeeper in East Hoathly in Sussex. He kept his diary for twelve years between 1754 and 1765, a period overshadowed by the Seven Years War.

JOSEPH TURRILL (1841–1925)
Turrill was a market gardener in Garsington, a village a few miles to the east of Oxford. In the closing years of his life, Garsington Manor, the lovely Elizabethan home of Lady Ottoline Morrell, became a popular rendezvous for many of the foremost young artists and writers of the time.

QUEEN VICTORIA (1819–1901)
From the age of thirteen Queen Victoria kept an almost daily diary. She came to the throne in 1837 and three years later married Prince Albert of Saxe-Coburg and Gotha. She bore him nine children and when he died in 1861, his widow went into a period of deep mourning and almost total seclusion from which she only slowly emerged. Queen Victoria was the longest reigning British monarch and her *Leaves from a Journal of our Life in the Highlands, 1848–61*, published in 1868, and its sequel were widely enjoyed by her subjects.

EVELYN WAUGH (1903–1966)
After his education at Lancing College and Oxford, Evelyn Waugh worked for two years as a schoolmaster, an experience that gave him little pleasure but which did supply him with material for his first and hugely successful novel *Decline and Fall*. In addition to a series of humorous satirical novels, Evelyn Waugh was an accomplished travel writer and biographer. He was married twice and served in the Marines and Commandos in the Second World War. In 1930 he converted to Roman Catholicism.

EILEEN WEETON (b. 1776)
After a disastrous marriage Eileen Weeton worked as a governess. Her journal is a noble account of a life marred by tragedy but borne with great resilience and strength of character.

JOHN WESLEY (1703–1791)
With his brother Charles, John Wesley founded the Methodist movement in 1738 and thereafter devoted the rest of his life to travelling and preaching in the open air to huge crowds. During the fifty years in which he followed his mission, Wesley is reckoned to have journeyed 250,000 miles in Great Britain, Ireland and the Continent. In spite of this intense activity he was also a prolific author and hymn-writer. His diary, begun in 1725, most fully covers the last fifty years of his life.

ADAM WHEELER (fl. 1685)
Adam Wheeler was a drummer with the Wiltshire Militia at the time of the rebellion led by Charles II's illegitimate son, James Duke of Monmouth, against his uncle King James II. The rebels' short-lived campaign in the summer of 1685 ended in total defeat at the battle of Sedgemoor, near Bridgwater. Monmouth was executed a fortnight later and his followers received brutal punishment at the 'Bloody

Assize'. Adam Wheeler's diary gives a first-hand account of the course of events in the West Country.

GILBERT WHITE (1720–1793)
Clergyman and naturalist, Gilbert White was born in Selborne, Hampshire and returned there in 1755 to spend the rest of his life in the pursuit of his abiding interest, natural history. As friend and correspondent of other men of science, his letters written over a period of twenty years provided material for *The Natural History and Antiquities of Selborne*, the work published in 1789 which ensured his fame.

HOWARD WILLIAMS (1854–1933)
The son of wealthy middle-class parents, Howard Williams was born in Greenwich and grew up in London. In the summer of 1875 he went with his two brothers and two friends on a rowing tour through the centre of England, beginning in Oxford and ending in London. Howard kept a diary of their holiday which recalls many events similar to those in Jerome K. Jerome's classic tale of the 'river set', *Three Men in a Boat.*

THOMAS WILSON (1703–1784)
Thomas Wilson was the son of the English churchman of the same name who became Bishop of Sodor and Man in 1698 and whose works of Christian instruction became standard Anglican texts.

WILLIAM WINDHAM (1750–1810)
William Windham was a statesman who was first elected to Parliament in 1784. As a supporter of William Pitt, he held a number of important government posts. Windham was a member of the Literary Club and counted William Cobbett and Samuel Johnson among his friends.

F. E. WITTS (1783–1854)
The Revd F. E. Witts was a Cotswold parson who served as rector of Upper Slaughter and afterwards vicar of Stanway, the living where he spent the last forty years of his life.

ANTHONY WOOD (1632–1695)
Anthony Wood was born in Oxford, educated in Oxford and spent the greater part of his life in studying the history and personalities of the university, the city and the county.

JAMES WOODFORDE (1740–1803)
Parson Woodforde, as he is popularly known, began adult life as a Fellow of New College, Oxford, where he had studied as an undergraduate. In 1776 he moved to the Norfolk living of Weston Longeville, which was his home for the rest of his life. Woodforde never married and from 1779 his niece Nancy lived with him as his housekeeper.

VIRGINIA WOOLF (1882–1941)
One of the principal innovators of the modern English novel, Virginia Woolf was born in London and educated at home. Following the death of her father, Sir Leslie Stephen, she moved with her sister and brothers to Bloomsbury where they formed the nucleus of the gathering of artists and writers that became known as the Bloomsbury Group. In spite of her literary success and the esteem in which she was held, Virginia Woolf suffered from increasing bouts of depression, which eventually claimed her life when she drowned herself near her Sussex home.

DOROTHY WORDSWORTH (1771–1855)
Only sister and devoted companion of the poet William Wordsworth, Dorothy Wordsworth's journals show her to be a writer of exquisite prose with a deep appreciation of the natural world. Her journals provided her brother with the inspiration and imagery for several of his poems.

HARRIET WYNNE (b. 1784)
The sister of Betsy Fremantle, mentioned above, Harriet Wynne began keeping her diary while she was at boarding school.

WALTER YONGE (c. 1581–1649)
Walter Yonge was a lawyer by profession, who became sheriff of Devonshire and was elected MP for Honiton. He served as victualler for the navy during the Civil War.

A 'YOUNG LADY' (fl. 1850)
The manuscript of this diary sheds no light on the diarist's identity, other than the fact that she lived somewhere in the Cheltenham area. However, it provides a fascinating personal account of high Victorian life seen through the eyes of the daughter of a member of the gentry.

ACKNOWLEDGEMENTS

We gratefully acknowledge permission to reprint extracts of copyright material in this book from the following authors, publishers and executors:

The Estate of Professor R. L. Brett for *Barclay Fox's Journal* edited by Professor R. L. Brett (Bell & Hyman 1979)

The British Academy for *The Diary of Robert Sharp of South Cave: Life in a Yorkshire Village 1812–1837* edited by Janice E. Crowther and Peter A. Crowther (Records of Social and Economic History, New Series 26, Oxford University Press for The British Academy 1997)

Alan Brodie Representation and the Estate of Noël Coward for *The Noël Coward Diaries* edited by Graham Payn and Sheridan Morley (Weidenfeld & Nicolson 1982)

The Council of the Chetham Society for *The Diary of Richard Kay* (The Chetham Society 1968)

Peter Coombs for *The Diary of a Somerset Rector, 1803–1834* edited by Howard and Peter Coombs (Kingsmead Press 1971)

David & Charles for *Miss Weeton's Journal of a Governess* (David & Charles Reprints 1969)

David Higham Associates for *The Journal of Louis Simond* edited by Christopher Hibbert (Robert Maxwell 1968)

Historic Society of Lancashire and Cheshire for *The Diary of John Ward (O'Neil)* (Transactions of the Historic Society of Lancashire and Cheshire 1953 Vol. 105, 1954)

Oxford University Press for *The Diary of Sir David Hamilton 1709–1714* edited by Philip Roberts (Clarendon Press 1975); *The Journals and Papers of Gerard Manley Hopkins* edited by Humpry House and Graham Storey (Oxford University Press 1959); *Dorothy Wordsworth; The Grasmere Journal* edited by Ernest de Selincourt (Oxford University Press 1941); *The Wynne Diaries* edited by Annie Fremantle (Oxford University Press 1935–40); *The Diary of Thomas Crosfield* edited by F. S. Boas (Oxford University Press 1935)

The Peters Fraser and Dunlop Group Limited on behalf of the Estate of Evelyn Waugh for *The Diaries of Evelyn Waugh, 1911–1965* edited by Michael Davie (Weidenfeld & Nicolson 1976)

Random House UK Limited and the Estate of William Plomer for *The Diary of Francis Kilvert* edited by William Plomer (Jonathan Cape 1938–1939); the Executors of the Virginia Woolf Estate for *The Diary of Virginia Woolf* edited by Anne Olivier Bell (Hogarth Press 1977)

The Society for the Promotion of Christian Knowledge (SPCK) for *The Diaries of Thomas Wilson D.D.* edited by C. L. S. Linnell (SPCK 1964)

Sutton Publishing for *The Diary of an Oxfordshire Market Gardener; Joseph Turrill 1841–1925* edited by E. Dawson and S. R. Royal (Sutton Publishing 1993); *The Diary of a Victorian Squire; Extracts from the Diaries and Letters of Dearman and Emily Birchall* edited by David Vercy (Sutton Publishing 1979); *The Diary of a Cotswold Parson: Reverend F. E. Witts, 1783–1854* edited by David Verey (Sutton Publishing 1979); *The Deserted Village: The Diary of the Reverend James Newton of Nuneham Courtenday 1736–86* edited by Gavin Hannah (Sutton Publishing 1992); *Paupers & Pig Killers: The Diary of William Holland, A Somerset Parson 1799–1818* edited by Jack Ayres (Sutton Publishing 1984); *The Diary of a Rowing Tour: From Oxford to London in 1875* Howard Williams (Sutton Publishing 1982)

Frederick Warne & Co. for *The Journal of Beatrix Potter 1881–1897* (Frederick Warne & Co. 1966)

A. P. Watt Ltd on behalf of Rosemary Beresford, B. W. Beresford, J. C. Beresford and Ruth Longman for *The Diary of the Reverend James Woodforde* edited by John Beresford (Oxford University Press 1926–27); on behalf of Mme V. M. Eldin for *The Journals of Arnold Bennett* edited by Frank Swinnerton (Penguin Books 1954)